# IB Economics Paper 2

# 20 Full Exam Style Questions with Answers.

# Data Response Paper 2 (New 2020 Syllabus)

# Higher & Standard Level

<u>First examination in 2022.</u>

# by Dipak Khimji & Barbara Macario

ISBN:
ISBN-13:

# –1 ACKNOWLEDGMENT

This specimen, all in one, question and answer book, for the (**paper 2**) data response paper is dedicated to all the students that we have served over the last 30 years and to our families and friends who have continuously supported in the writing of this book A big thank you goes out to Samarth & Soumya Agarwal for their invaluable help in sorting out the graphics. Bansari Ben Naik helped me in the layout for which we are grateful for. Emmanuel Power has kindly donated his artwork.

In addition, Mani Amini (house), Chrystina Angeline (factory) and the Swiss Confederation (bus) are thanked for letting us use their symbols to make the diagrams prettier. Delve Fonts are thanked for allowing the use of their very-readable font family *Overpass* in the diagrams.

# 0 AIMS

The chief aim of this book is to help students to prepare fully with the requirements of paper 2 of the new IB economics syllabus for both higher and standard level through specimen paper type exam questions. This book is meant to be taken as a proactive tool to help consolidate detailed knowledge of the new IB economics course and prepare students for class tests as well as the final IB exam. Students should be able to get a fair degree of practice, self-confidence and guidance from their teacher.

For the economics teacher, this book of data response specimen papers, along with detailed answers book provides a way of ensuring students have adequate knowledge, analysis, evaluation skills and practice to approach IB paper 2 questions. The 20 specimen questions can be used in class, at home and as revision material for exams. The questions can act as a record of student progress in class and at home. Questions for higher students only are marked by 'h'. Standard level only questions carry a 's' beside the question. All the other non-marked questions are part of the core syllabus for both levels.

CONTENTS

| 17 | **MYANMAR** | 182 |
|----|-------------|-----|
| 18 | **VIETNAM** | 192 |
| 19 | **UNITED KINGDOM** | 204 |
| 20 | **CHINA 2** | 218 |
| | **NOTE:** *'s'* denotes standard level questions only<br><br>*'h'* denotes higher level questions only | |

## 1.　CHINA

*Study the texts and data below and answer the questions that follow.*

### Text 1- Overview of China

Today China is the world's second largest economy. Since embarking on economic reforms in 1978, the **_nominal GDP_** has risen from $214bn to $9.2trn today. Modernisation has expanded the manufacturing sector to 45% of GDP while the tertiary sector has grown to 44% of the economy and the primary sector today accounts for only 11% of GDP. To combat the 2008 global economic recession, China introduced a $585bn stimulus package of massive investment projects. These stimulus programs, while promoting economic growth have also created macroeconomic imbalances. Consumer spending continues to be low at 50% of GDP and household savings high compared to OECD countries, the current account surplus has diminished and Chinese banks, fully stretched, in their loan capacity financing more and more risky projects.

In the last few decades, China's real economic growth rate has consistently above 6.5% annually. This has lifted hundreds of millions of China's citizens out of poverty as well as creating mounting environmental problems and rising inequalities. The incoming premier Xi Jinping has introduced measures aimed at achieving a more balanced economic model even at the expense of rapid economic growth.

China's new approach to economic growth and development is to make strategic investments abroad. An example of this is the large-scale infrastructure project, One Belt One Road (OBOR). OBOR is an attempt to create a road of economic activity from China to Europe, aimed at benefiting Chinese companies wanting to expand abroad. Like many other projects such as building skyscrapers and cities that end up uninhabited and unused, turning into ghost cities, OBOR highlights the fact that the majority of the Chinese economy is state owned and planned focused on job creation above all. Critics of OBOR claim that many more free market based projects are necessary in order for China to grow sustainably and efficiently.

## Text 2- Sales of cigarettes fall in China: WHO

The World Health Organization (WHO) commented that last year's hike in tobacco taxes has reduced overall volume sales by 3.3% and 9.5% for the cheapest brands in China. The country has 300 million smokers and another 740 million people exposed to the effects of second-hand smoke. While the average price of cigarettes rose by 10%, the price of the cheapest brands rose by 20%.

Smoking is particularly prevalent among young men, two-thirds of whom start smoking before the age of twenty. Half of them die due to smoking related diseases. While government tax revenue directly from the new measure rose by 11$bn there has been a strong push back from the state's own monopoly tobacco companies which account for nearly 8% of total tax revenue for China's government.

## Text 3- China loosens the Yuan

From 1995 to 2005, China maintained a ***fixed exchange rate*** against the US dollar at 8.28 Yuan. However 2005 onwards, the authorities switched towards a more managed float. In recent years, the currency has operated more and more under a floating regime.

## Table 1- Economic data for China

|  | 2015 | 2016 | 2017 | 2018 |
|---|---|---|---|---|
| Exchange rate (CNY/USD) | 6.15 | 6.25 | 6.28 | 6.95 |
| Current account balance (USD bn) | 148 | 236 | 304 | 370 |

Data Response-Paper 2

## Table 2- Development data for China

|  | 1996 | 2006 | 2016 |
|---|---|---|---|
| Human Development Index | 0.55 | 0.66 | 0.73 |
| Gini coefficient | 0.37 | 0.44 | 0.55 |
| Life expectancy at birth (years) | 70.42 | 74.29 | 76.25 |
| Adult literacy rate (% ages 15 and over) | 84 | 91 | 96 |

## QUESTIONS

(a)  (i) Define the term *nominal GDP* indicated in bold (Text 1 - paragraph 1).  [2 marks]

(ii) Define the term *fixed exchange rate* indicated in bold (Text 3 - paragraph 1).  [2 marks]

(b)s  (i) Using information in text 1 calculate China's real GDP last year.  [3 marks]

(b)h  (i) Calculate the effect of a $ 585bn injection on the GDP of China.  [3 marks]

(b)  (ii) Use a demand and supply diagram to show the change in China's exchange rate against the US$ from 2017 to 2018.  [Table 1]  [2 marks]

7

**(c)s**	Use table 1 to explain the correlation between China's exchange rate and the trade account balance.	[4 marks]

**(c)h**	Explain and apply the Marshall Lerner Theorem to the figure in Table 1.	[4 marks]

**(d)**	(i) Using an AD/AS diagram explain the possible effects of the One Belt One Road Project on China's Economy, as it approaches full employment. (Text 1 - paragraph 3)	[4 marks]

**(e)s**	Calculate the PED for cheaper brands of cigarettes.	[4 marks]

**(e)h**	Calculate the PED for cheaper cigarettes and cigarettes overall and comment on their values.	[4 marks]

**(f)**	Using a market failure diagram, explain why a tax on cigarettes may be necessary but insufficient to reduce the overall numbers of smokers.	[4 marks]

**(g)**	Using information from the texts / tables and your knowledge of economics, discuss the possible outcomes in economic development resulting from the 'One belt, one road' (OBOR) project.	[15 marks]

**ANSWERS:**                    **1. CHINA**

---

**QUESTIONS**

**(a)**     **(i) Define the term _nominal GDP_ indicated in bold (Text 1 - paragraph 1).**          **[2 marks]**

*This is the value of all final goods and services produced in an economy in a given period of time. This value has **not** been adjusted to consider the effect of inflation.*

            **(ii) Define the term _fixed exchange rate_ indicated in bold (Text 3 - paragraph 1).   [2 marks]**

*This is a <u>set</u> price of changing one currency into another. The price / rate is determined by the country's currency board or authority.*

**(b)s**     **(i) Using information in text 1 calculate China's real GDP last year.**          **[3 marks]**

|  |  |  |
|---|---|---|
| GDP *(last year)* +  6.5 % of GDP*(last year)* | = | $ 9.2 trn |
| 1.065 GDP *(last year)* | = | $ 9.2 trn |
| GDP*(last year)* | = | 9.2/1.065 |
| GDP *(last year)*   = | **$ 8.64 trn** | (2 decimal places) |

**(b)h**    **(i) Calculate the effect of a $ 585Bn injection on the GDP of China.**     **[3 marks]**

The $ 585bn injection will have a multiplier effect. Since on average consumption is 50% of GDP according to the text, mpc = 0.5 (marginal propensity to consumer).  This means the value of the

multiplier, k  =  2 So China's GDP will rise by $ 585  x  2  =  **$ 1170 Bn**

**(b)  (ii) Use a demand and supply diagram to show the change in China's exchange rate against the US$ from 2017 to 2018.   [Table 1]**     **[2 marks]**

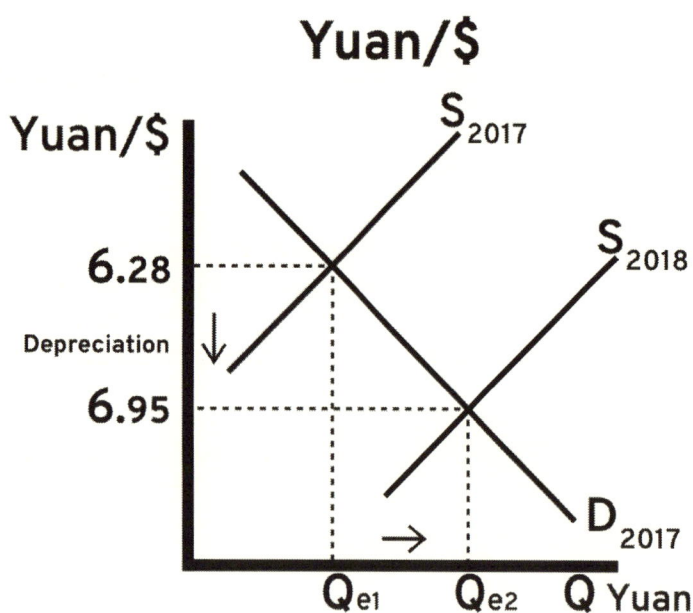

With greater trade, the supply of Yuan on the foreign exchange markets will have probably increased resulting in the depreciation of the Yuan from 6.28 Yuan per US $ to 6.95 Yuan per US$.

**(c)s    Use table 1 to explain the correlation between China's exchange rate and the trade account balance.                                                                            [4 marks]**

The correlation is positive. As the Chinese currency depreciates against the US$, US$ currency holders will find Chinese Produced goods cheaper. This may lead to more exports out of China in value terms and less imports. Overall the trade balance improves for China as table 1 shows.

**(c)h  Explain and apply the Marshall Lerner Theorem to the figure in Table 1.          [4 marks]**

The Marshall Lerner Theorem applied here implies that if China's PED + PED $_M$ > 1 then the depreciation of the Yuan will improve the Balance of Trade (Value of exports of goods – Value of imports of goods) Since China exports and imports thousands of goods, we use a weight index of exports and imports.

**(d)        (i) Using an AD/AS diagram explain the possible effects of the One Belt One Road Project on China's economy as it approaches full employment. (Text 1 - paragraph 3)          [4 marks]**

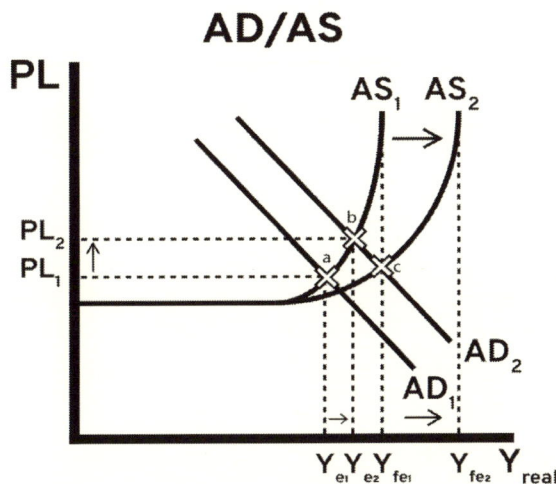

If China's economy is already near full employment the OBOR project will require more factors of production (FOPs). Skilled and unskilled labour from China may be in short supply. Some sectors already at full employment attract workers from other sectors or firms. Wages tend to accelerate upwards causing firms to pass on the higher costs to consumers through higher prices. There is a likelihood of inflation PL$_1$ rises to PL$_2$ as real output struggles to rise from Ye$_1$ to Ye$_2$.

However in the longer run the OBOR project can create a lot more capacity and efficiency in the supply Export and import chain, AS$_1$ rises to AS$_2$ and as the capacity and efficiency rises there is pressure for the price level to fall, Overall we may more from equilibrium a to *b* to *c*.

11

**(e)s   Calculate the PED for cheaper brands of cigarettes.**                    **[4 marks]**

   Define PED.        PED = = (- 9.5 % )/(+ 20 %)   **For cheap cigarettes PED = - 0.48**

**(e)h   Calculate the PED for cheaper cigarettes and cigarettes overall and comment on their values.**
                                                                          **[4 marks]**

   Define PED.   From above cheap cigarettes **PED = - 0.48**

   For cigarettes overall PED = (- 3.3 % )/(+ 10 %)   **PED = - 0.33**

**(f)   Using a market failure diagram, explain why a tax on cigarettes may be necessary but insufficient to reduce the overall numbers of smokers.**                    **[4 marks]**

## Cigarettes

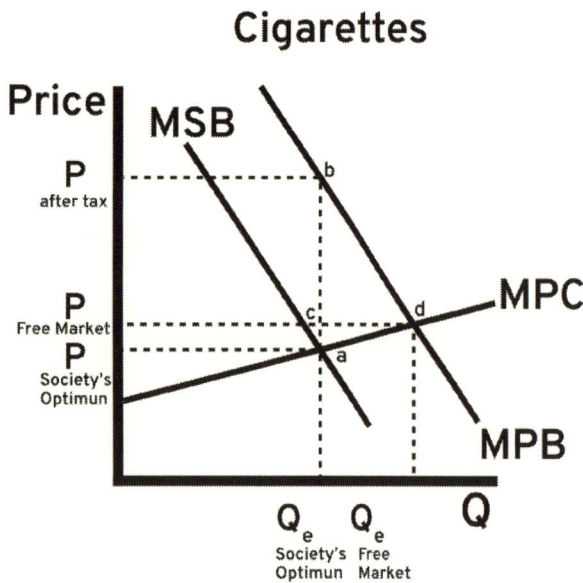

Market failure occurs when smoking MSB does not equal MSC. For cigarettes we have:

- Negative externality of consumption
- PED is significantly lower than PES.

Given the low PED = - 0.33 and a likely very high PES for cigarettes, the size of the tax necessary to restore society's optimum Qe (soc opt) needs to be very high (a to b) and most of it passed on to the smoker (b to c). This is probably more than the 10 % average. In addition, as Chinese incomes rise, the cigarette tax will have to rise even more. Clearly additional deterrents will be needed.

**(g)**    **Using information from the texts / tables and your knowledge of economics, discuss the possible outcomes for economic development resulting from the 'One belt, one road' (OBOR) project.**
**[15 marks]**

OBOR project's effect on economic development can be broadly measured through the changes in HDI (income, health, literacy broad indicators)

## Positives from OBOR

- More job creation for the skill and unskilled, especially those who are geographically mobile.
- More use of FOPs leading to more income and a positive multiplier effect.
- Higher incomes for Chinese workers.
- Government will collect more tax revenues, direct and indirect.
- More resource potential for the government to address education and gender inequalities to reverse Gini coefficient values. (Table 2).
- With higher incomes education and the health sector can expand resulting in improvement in life expectancy and literacy rates.

## Dangers of OBOR

- Rural and remote areas abandoned. These areas lack basic amenities.
- Urban areas become overcrowded.
- OBOR gains not equitably shared.
- Chinese banks over leveraged, more vulnerable in a sudden downturn due to higher default rates.
- Higher inflation rates in fixed assets.
- Poor living conditions can result in lower life expectancy.
- China may dominate and act as an imperialist power by proxy
- Faster depletion of the environment.

## 2.    PAKISTAN

*Study the texts and data below and answer the questions that follow.*

### Text 1- Overview of Pakistan

Pakistan along with many other developing countries continuously face the problem of high rates of unemployment caused by structural constraints. Poor or even negative job growth can at times accompany a growing economy. Pakistan has tried cutting taxes but this instrument has not reduced the **_unemployment rate_** or increased government tax receipts through greater work or **_tax evasion disincentives_**.

During the decade 2010s the annual average economic growth was steady at around 4.7%. while the average unemployment rate rose to 6.8% for the corresponding decade significantly up from 5.7% average in the previous decade, according to Pakistan Bureau of Statistics data.  This again pointed towards a long term structural problem in Pakistan. The decade has also seen the labour force grow from 35.1 million to 45.5 million.

Similar to other developing economies, the reasons given for rising long-term unemployment are the growing rural-urban divide and the agriculture-manufacturing divide. The picture is further complicated with the existence of formal, organised industrial sector functioning side by side with the informal sector made up of self-employed craftsmen, retailers, street vendors and mechanics. Pakistan's economic development has moved factors of production from agriculture to the organised urban sector.

The fallout from the global financial crisis has meant central banks across the world including Pakistan have loosened monetary policy to historical levels for more than a decade. The Pakistani government has extended this liberalising the economy and offering subsidies to the organised urban sector.  This sector has been encouraged to expand, globalise and create jobs.  While the formal sector, particularly services has expanded at an accelerating rate the rural commodity producing sector of agriculture and manufacturing has seen growth rates diminish to only 3%.

The liberalisation policy of drastic import tariff reductions has not resulted in job creation through a move from import substitution to export led growth strategy for Pakistan. Free Trade Agreements (FTA) with China has meant more job cuts. FTA, lower tariffs and lower income tax rates together have worsened the income disparities and skills gap.

**Text 2A- Pakistan sugarcane exports up.**

Just in the last year, foreign demand for sugar coming from Pakistan has risen dramatically from 302268 tonnes to 1.359 million tonnes. Foreign currency earnings from sugar exports have risen this year to $474m compared to only $158m in the previous year.

**Text 2B- Pakistan's farmers grow more sugar despite falling global prices.**

Cotton followed by sugarcane is Pakistan's leading cash crop. Sugar prices have been trending downwards while cotton prices have been rising on the global market. Per unit of land, growing sugarcane requires much more water than growing cotton. Despite the growing demand for raw cotton, farmers in Pakistan continue with sugarcane production, reluctant to switch over to growing cotton, making the country among the top ten global sugar producers and net exporters. Costs of production for sugar are higher in Pakistan than its competitors. This perverse behaviour goes against free market discipline, since Pakistan's government introduced a price fixing agreement nearly a decade ago costing nearly $18m annually. Cotton production is under no such agreement and subsequently cotton is often subject to 30% to 50% price fluctuations. The Competition Commission of Pakistan (CCP) is now formulating a report for the Pakistani government recommending an overhaul of the current government sugarcane support in favour of a fully liberalised market.

**Text 3- Remittances from Pakistani workers abroad near the $20b mark**

Remittances are peer-to-peer funds sent by expatriate workers often to their families in their country of origin. Pakistani expatriates have steadily increased their remittances steadily from $13.2 billion in 2012 to nearly $20 billion in 2018. Officials from Pakistan's central bank said that remittances are more consistent than FDI and act as a neutralizing force to keep current account deficit low and the exchange rate stable. While contributions from Saudi Arabia and other Gulf countries fell by 8.7% chiefly due to falling oil prices, the shortfall was more than compensated by a 43% increase in remittances coming from the economic recovery in the Eurozone.

## Table 1- Economic data for Pakistan

|  | 2009 | 2010 | 2011 | 2012 | 2013 | 2014 | 2015 | 2016 | 2017 |
|---|---|---|---|---|---|---|---|---|---|
| Rate of consumer inflation | 13.65 | 13.88 | 11.92 | 9.69 | 7.69 | 7.19 | 2.53 | 3.75 | 4.9 |
| Annual rate of interest | 14.4 | 12.0 | 9.0 | 10.0 | 6.50 | 5.75 | 5.75 | 6.0 | 6.5 |
| Annual growth rate | 4.9 | 0.6 | 2.58 | 3.7 | 4.1 | 4.1 | 4.6 | 5.4 | 5.8 |

## Table 2- Development data for selected countries

Account ownership at a financial institution including mobile-money-service providers.

Female (% of population ages 15+)

|  | Sri Lanka | Malaysia | India | Bangladesh | Cambodia | Pakistan |
|---|---|---|---|---|---|---|
| 2011 | 67.24 | 63.10 | 26.49 | 26.01 | 3.71 | 2.95 |
| 2017 | 73.44 | 82.48 | 76.64 | 35.84 | 21.53 | 7.03 |

## QUESTIONS

(a)   (i)  Define the term *unemployment rate* indicated in bold. (Text 1 – paragraph 2) [2 marks]

(ii) Define the term *tax evasion disincentives* indicated in bold. (Text 1 – paragraph 3)
[2 marks]

(b)s   (i)  Using information from Text 1, paragraph 2, calculate the number of workers employed.
[3 marks]

(b)h   (i) Using text 2 paragraph 1 calculate the average price of sugar per tonne in Pakistan and the price  elasticity of demand for Pakistan's sugar exports.                               [3 marks]

(b)      (ii) Use a labour market diagram to illustrate the employment rising rate of unemployment with a rising labour force in Pakistan.                                                              [2 marks]

(c)      Using an AD / AS diagram and information from text 1. Explain how monetary policy can stimulate productivity and economic activity.                                                         [4 marks]

(d)      Using a tariff diagram explain how Pakistan's free trade agreement with China can result in job cuts in Pakistan.  (Text 1 - paragraph 5)                                                          [4 marks]

(e)      Using an exchange rate diagram explain how rising remittances from the Eurozone help to stabilize the Pakistan Rupee.                                                                         [4 marks]

(f)      Using Table 1 and text 1 - paragraph 4 Pakistan's comment on the relationship between growth rate and its rate of consumer inflation and interest rates.                                     [4 marks]

(g)      Using the information in the texts / tables and your knowledge of economics, evaluate the extent to which significant remittances into Pakistan help in improving economic growth and achieving sustainable development goods (SDGs).                                                        [15 marks]

17

**ANSWERS:**             **2. PAKISTAN**

**(a)**     **(i)  Define the term _unemployment rate_ indicated in bold. (Text 1 – paragraph 2)   [2 marks]**

Unemployment Rate  = (Number Unemployed)/(Labour Force) × 100/1

Anyone willing, able and actively looking for work at the current wage but cannot find a job is considered unemployed.

**(ii) Define the term _tax evasion disincentives_ indicated in bold. (Text 1 – paragraph 3) 2 marks]**

These are measures such as fines, lower tax rates, greater degree of scrutiny which help to reduce the desire to not pay taxes.  Tax evasion is illegal whereas tax avoidance is legal.

**(b)s**     **(i)  Using information from Text 1, paragraph 2, calculate the number of workers employed.**
**[3 marks]**

| | | |
|---|---|---|
| Labour Force | = | employed  +  unemployed |
| 45.5m | = | employed  + 6.8 % of Labour Force |
| 45.5m - 6.5 % of  45.5m | = | employed |
| 45.5m  -  2.9575m | = | **42.54m  =  employed** |

**(b)h**     **(i) Using text 2 paragraph 1 calculate the average price of sugar per tonne in Pakistan and the price  elasticity of demand for Pakistan's sugar exports.                      [3 marks]**

Price of sugar last year  =  (Value of Sales)/Quantity    =  ($ 158000000)/302268

Last year price  =  $ 522.71  per ton

Price of Sugar this year  =  ($ 474000000)/1359000

This year's Price  =  $ 348.79  per ton

18

PED = ((1359000 − 302268)/302268)/((348.79 - 522.71)/522.71)

= 3.496/(- 0.332) = **10.53 = PED**

Sugar exports are very price sensitive for Pakistan. If global prices rise by 1%, Pakistani sugar exporters are very keen to increase their exports by 10.53%.

**(ii)** **Use a labour market diagram to illustrate the employment rising rate of unemployment with a rising labour force in Pakistan.** **[2 marks]**

**One possible interpretation**

## Pakistan Labour Market

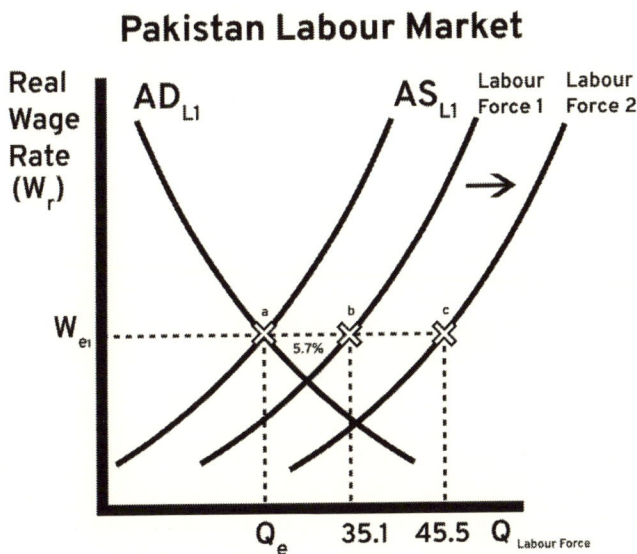

Assuming a labour market in equilibrium unemployment rate in the previous decade would be 5.7 % (a to b). In the subsequent decade (2010s) the labour force grew from 35.1 m to 45.5m and unemployment rate rose to 6.8 % (a to c)

19

**(c)    Using an AD / AS diagram and information from text 1. Explain how monetary policy can stimulate productivity and economic activity.                                                    [4 marks]**

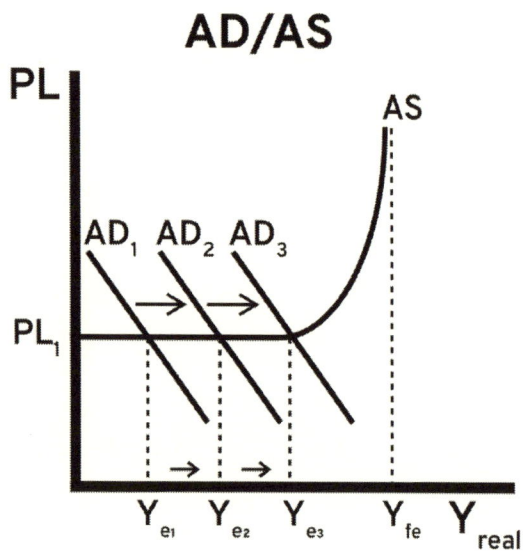

## AD/AS

PL

AS

AD$_1$  AD$_2$  AD$_3$

PL$_1$

Y$_{e1}$  Y$_{e2}$  Y$_{e3}$      Y$_{fe}$  Y$_{real}$

Loosening monetary policy entails dropping interest rates (i %) and increasing the availability of credit in Pakistan's economy.  The fall in  *i %* may encourage:

- Rise in consumer spending, (C)
- Rise in borrowing for investment projects which tend to be of higher productivity. (I)
- Rise in government borrowing and spending (G)
- Weakening of Pakistani Rupee, thereby increasing export demand. (X- M) rises.

AD = [ C + I + G + (X - M) ]  increases.

AD1 rises to AD2 due to an injection and this has a multiplier effect to AD3. Overall equilibrium level of output rises from Ye1 to Ye2 to Ye3. (We are assuming no inflation).

**(d)** **Using a tariff diagram explain how Pakistan's free trade agreement with China can result in job cuts in Pakistan. (Text 1 - paragraph 5)** **[4 marks]**

## Tariff Diagram

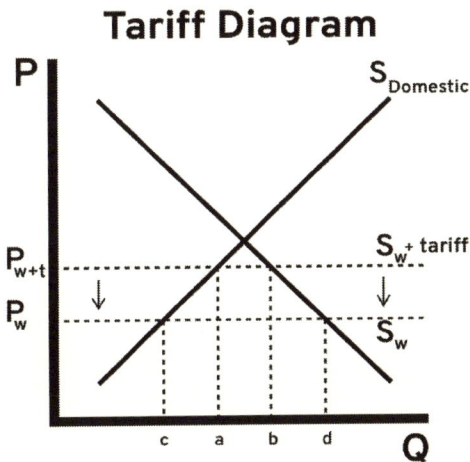

Free trade agreement will mean a significant fall in tariffs and other barriers. Prices in Pakistan will fall from Pw+t to Pw. The level of imports may rise from ab to cd. This may result in inefficient Pakistani firms not being able to compete with the might of China. If these firms in Pakistan shutdown then jobs losses may occur in the manufacturing sector.

**(e)** **Using an exchange rate diagram explain how rising remittances from the Eurozone help to stabilize the Pakistan Rupee.** **[4 marks]**

## Pakistani Rupee

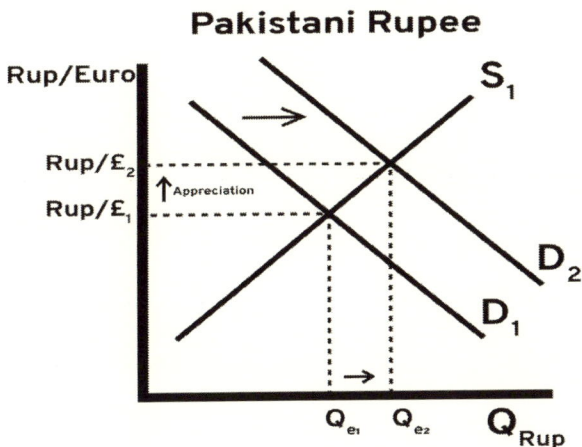

A remittance from Euro land means more Euros are supplied and in turn more Rupees are bought. D1 rises to D2 for rupees. The Pakistani Rupee appreciates against the Euro and more Rupees are traded Qe1 to Qe2.

**(f)** **Using Table 1 and text 1 - paragraph 4 Pakistan's comment on the relationship between growth rate and its rate of consumer inflation and interest rates.** **[4 marks]**

The global financial crisis slowed down global growth and demand for Pakistani's exports. AD subsequently fell along with demand pull inflation. (Text 1 - paragraph 4)

As global interest rates fell, Pakistani's Central Bank felt obliged to follow suit to prevent appreciation of its currency and losing price competitiveness on the global commodity market such as cotton, sugar, global currency wars, can be a precursor to trade wars. Interest rates were lowered over a 5 year 2009 - 2015 from 14.4 % to historically low of 5.75 % as consumer inflation continued to fall.

The stimulative effect of falling interest rates has run its course after 2015 as structural inflation and economic growth are both rising. This may be due to the rural to urban move in resources and higher asset prices.

**(g)** **Using the information in the texts / tables and your knowledge of economics, evaluate the extent to which significant remittances into Pakistan help in improving economic growth and achieving sustainable development goods (SDGs).** **[15 marks]**

- Define SDGs Point out empowerment of women is particularly crucial for Pakistan.
- Table 2 shows clearly that Pakistan is really behind others in Asia.
- Remittances can encourage women to open bank accounts, particularly mobile banking. Money can be used to spend on education, healthcare and food to improve the wellbeing of families. (could use a poverty cycle diagram).
- Pakistani financial institutions can use the Euros to boost their reserves. This value currency can help Pakistani businesses buy capital goods from the Eurozone to boost their productive capacity and productivity.
- Remittances are much more stable than other forms of FDIs. Other FDIs are dependent on risks, rates of return, and the case at which foreign businesses can repatriate their gains. The instability of the Pakistani rupee and social / political problems make FDIs into Pakistan less likely.
- FDI acts as an injection into Pakistan's circular flow of Income. (Could use a diagram to show this)

22

## 3.    CUBA

*Study the texts and data below and answer the questions that follow.*

### Text 1- Overview of Cuba

The Cuban economy is moving at a snail's pace in transforming itself from a planned economy to a more free market economy. This slowness has been partially a result of problems associated with a slow growing economy, falling prices of Cuba's most important exports, sugar and nickel, as well as loss of subsidized oil from Venezuela. Cuba has lost its guaranteed market to the former Soviet Union after its collapse in the 1990s. It then had to seek purchases of everyday food on the more expensive global markets using its rapidly depreciating peso currency.

Today after nearly 30 years and some minor reforms introduced by the late leader Fidel Castro, Cuba finds itself in an almost deflationary mode. Economic growth rate is barely 1% down from 4% in the last few years, wages and prices in the private retail and the state sector are extremely far apart, such that many trained professionals in the government have left to become taxi drivers for tourists and renting rooms in their homes on Airbnb. President Obama's visit in 2016 was a shot in the arm for the Cuban economy promoting tourism further to account for 10% of Cuba's GDP and a promise of new foreign investment. The subsequent Trump administration reinstated the debilitating sanctions with US foreign investment falling. This combined with Venezuela's inability to supply Cuba with oil in return for trained Cuban medical personnel at well below global market rates has resulted in overvalued exchange rate which has forced the Cuban government to ration out the currency to cover the bare essentials. Oil imports are down to 60,000 barrels per day down from 115,000 two years ago.

The Cuban government is now reluctantly introducing radical reforms in order to help it find new sources of income. Already the number of self-employed has grown 400% to greater than 500,000. This is in spite of the government not forthcoming in approving permits and licenses but quick to introduce new taxes and regulation. Foreign joint ventures continue to remain subdued. Meanwhile, electricity and fuel consumption has been cut by 30% and government workers asked to shorten their day or work from home. A glimmer of hope is coming from remittances that helps provide private funds for ***investment*** directed towards small family businesses.

**Text 2- Tourists and locals fight for food in Cuba**

With a population of 11 million, the annual 3.5 million tourists on the small island raises the issue of sustainability. While one would expect greater prosperity from the inflow of tourist dollars, the nation's slow transition towards capitalism is causing massive economic hardship for the majority of Cubans. The United States embargo has caused high prices and empty supermarkets. Staples such as onions, pineapples, limes, green peppers and garlic as well as beer and soda are all been redirected towards the visitors. The division between the private and public sector has never been more pronounced. The Cuban Government's policy response is to set price caps on agriculture produce and crack down on middle-men practicing ***price gouging***. President Raul Castro told reporters, ``We cannot sit with our hands crossed before the unscrupulous manner of middlemen who only think of earning more``.

Cubans are able to shop in both state owned and controlled markets, and private sector markets. Cheap food and low quality rice, beans, sweet potatoes, bananas and watermelons can be found in the state owned and run markets. Quality fruit and vegetables can be found beautifully stacked and plentiful in the commercial private markets. Here mostly buyers from restaurants are seen bargaining over the prices of rarities like avocados, ginger, kiwi fruits and seedless grapes. These goods are simply beyond the reach of Government workers, the majority of whom earn around $30 a month.

Government nurse, Leticia Alvarez Canada, 41, complains that with prices so high and wages so low, "we have to be magicians, "she said. 'There's just no equilibrium between the prices and the salaries". Leticia has left her nursing job to start a food cart selling snacks where she earns eight times more. University of Havana economist, Juan Alejandro Triana says, "We have to feed 14 million and not 11 million people, the government has failed to properly invest in the agriculture sector". Trucks and tractors break down often, rotting the produce in transit, bureaucracy makes it difficult to efficiently allocate agriculture land use. Farmers are forced to grow food organically forgoing the high yield from chemical fertilizers".

While many restaurant owners have resorted to providing seeds to grow specialty produce like coriander, cherry tomatoes, zucchini and arugula and sourcing directly from farmers to ensure consistent supply, new government regulations have been brought in and the number of new restaurants opening heavily restricted in Havana. Laura Fernandez, manager of El Cocinero, a high-priced restaurant, says, ``but it's not the fault of the private sector. The markets here are in disorder chaotic".

**Text 3- Cuba boosts Internet access and IT for economic development**

Communications Minister Maimir Mesa said on Tuesday, 'Cuban government is committed to speeding up internet access to 10 million Cubans from the current 4.5 million. Both 3G and 4G technology infrastructure will allow the internet via mobile phones and result in our country's development, productivity and employment'. The government has acknowledged that the current $1 connection charge given standard salaries of $30 a month for most Cuban government workers is still a problem, but Cubans are willing to make this sacrifice to be informed, interact with their loved ones and friends, and research content related to their professional and individual needs. At present only 28000 homes are internet connected.

**Table 1- Economic data for Cuba**

GDP growth (annual %)

| Year | 2009 | 2010 | 2011 | 2012 | 2014 | 2015 | 2016 | 2017 | 2018 | 2019 |
|---|---|---|---|---|---|---|---|---|---|---|
| Cuba | 4.11 | 1.45 | 2.39 | 2.80 | 3.01 | 2.74 | 1.04 | 4.43 | 3.01 | 1.11 |
| Haiti | 0.84 | 3.08 | 5.49 | 5.52 | 2.88 | 4.23 | 2.810 | 1.21 | 1.45 | 1.17 |
| Jamaica | -0.81 | -4.33 | -1.46 | 1.73 | -0.62 | 0.491 | 0.68 | 0.89 | 1.37 | 0.48 |

Inflation, GDP deflator (annual %)

| Cuba | -0.34 | 0.63 | 1.20 | 4.32 | 2.91 | 2.65 | 3.46 | 3.43 | 4.32 | 5.44 |
|---|---|---|---|---|---|---|---|---|---|---|
| Haiti | 12.89 | 3.70 | 5.45 | 7.51 | 5.28 | 6.59 | 4.50 | 6.87 | 11.96 | 13.36 |
| Jamaica | 13.54 | 11.64 | 9.81 | 5.76 | 6.57 | 8.39 | 7.01 | 6.61 | 4.59 | 6.95 |

Exports of goods and services as a % of GDP

| Cuba | 20.56 | 17.45 | 22.57 | 25.10 | 25.51 | 24.10 | 22.08 | 17.14 | 15.23 | 12.54 |
|---|---|---|---|---|---|---|---|---|---|---|
| Haiti | 12.72 | 15.71 | 15.34 | 17.44 | 16.90 | 18.25 | 18.51 | 20.00 | 20.72 | 18.83 |
| Jamaica | 41.94 | 34.47 | 31.33 | 30.37 | 30.19 | 30.60 | 31.25 | 29.91 | 31.36 | 31.54 |

Imports of goods and services as a % of GDP

| Cuba | 24.34 | 15.45 | 17.72 | 21.85 | 20.35 | 20.22 | 17.19 | 14.45 | 11.62 | 9.55 |
|---|---|---|---|---|---|---|---|---|---|---|
| Haiti | 43.58 | 42.57 | 64.74 | 58.97 | 53.16 | 52.29 | 52.73 | 50.54 | 52.62 | 56.48 |
| Jamaica | 71.63 | 52.40 | 49.58 | 53.47 | 51.87 | 52.76 | 53.49 | 46.20 | 44.93 | 45.5 |

**Table 2**

| 2018 | Life Expectancy | Literacy Rate % |
|---|---|---|
| Cuba | 79 | 99.75 |
| Haiti | 63.6 | 61 |
| Jamaica | 76 | 88.1 |

Cuba 2018                                    **Gender development data for Cuba**

| Life expectancy at birth | | Mean years of schooling | | GNI per capita US$ | | HDI values | | Labour force participation rate % | |
|---|---|---|---|---|---|---|---|---|---|
| Female | Male | Female | Male | Female | Male | Female | Male | Female | Male |
| 81.6 | 77.6 | 11.5 | 12.0 | 5013 | 9874 | 0.75 | 0.792 | 42.6 | 58.6 |

## QUESTIONS

(a)(i) Define the term in bold *investment*. (Text 1 - paragraph 3)                    [2 marks]

   (ii) Define the term in bold *price gouging*. (Text 2 - paragraph 1)                [2 marks]

(b) (i) Draw a demand/supply diagram to explain the effects on a price cap on staples such as onions. (Text 2- paragraph 1).                                        [3 marks]

   (ii) Using an AD / AS diagram explain how a US embargo can lead to inflation and a fall in the standard of living for public sector workers. (Text 2 - paragraph 3).        [2 marks]

(c)   Using a production possibility curve. Explain how the speed of internet access can help improve economic growth, economic development and economic productivity of Cuba.  (Text 3)   [4 marks]

(d)   Using table 1, explain which one of the three countries, Cuba, Haiti and Indonesia is a more open economy.                                            [4 marks]

(e)   Explain the trade- off between efficiency and equality in the agriculture sector in Cuba.  (Text 2)
[4 marks]

(f)      Using table 1 calculate which country has the highest nominal growth rate in 2019.   [4 marks]

(g)      Using the texts / tables and your knowledge of economics, evaluate the proposition that only a greater degree of privatisation, liberalization and deregulation policies can increase economic development for Cuba.
[15 marks]

**ANSWERS:**                              **3. CUBA**

(a) (i)  **Define the term in bold _investment_. (Text 1 - paragraph 3).**                    **[2 marks]**

This is the rise in the capital stock of Cuba. Investment goods go to make consumer goods and services.

(ii) **Define the term in bold _price gouging_. (Text 2 - paragraph 1).**                    **[2 marks]**

Price gouging is an unethical practice where a seller buys a life and death product in a low fixed price market, as in Cuba's case, then resells the product at an unreasonable / unethically high price to capitalize on extreme shortages and peoples' misery.

**(b) (i)  Draw a demand/supply diagram to explain the effects on a price cap on staples such as onions. (Text 2- paragraph 1).**                    **[3 marks]**

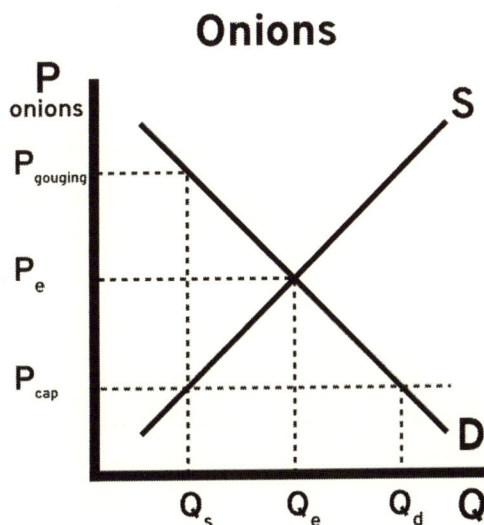

**Onions**

Cuban Government set a price ceiling (Price cap) below equilibrium price (Pe) since low income households cannot afford $P_e$.  At $P_{cap}$, $Q_D > Q_S$. a shortage occurs. Some sellers who are able to buy onions at $P_{cap}$, will then profit from reselling onions at a higher price, P gouging.

**(ii) Using an AD / AS explain how an US embargo can lead to inflation and a fall in the standard of living of workers in the public sectors. (Text 2 - paragraph 3)** **[2 marks]**

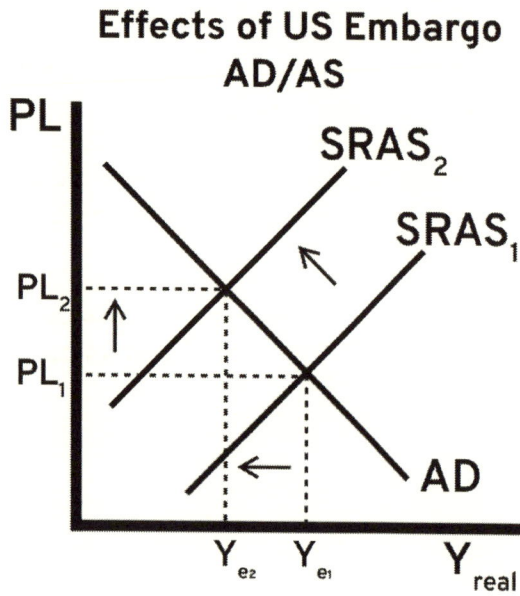

### Effects of US Embargo AD/AS

US embargo means essential consumer and investment goods cannot come into Cuba. This results in higher costs of production and subsequently prices. $PL_1$ rises to $PL_2$. Output falls from $Y_{e1}$ to $Y_{e2}$. Public sector workers may not be able to get a pay rise to compensate for the high prices. This means their real wages fall leading to lower standards of living.

**(c)** **Using a production possibility curve. Explain how the speed of internet access can help the economic growth, the economic development and economic productivity in Cuba. (Text 3)  [4 marks]**

## Effect of High Speed Internet PPF

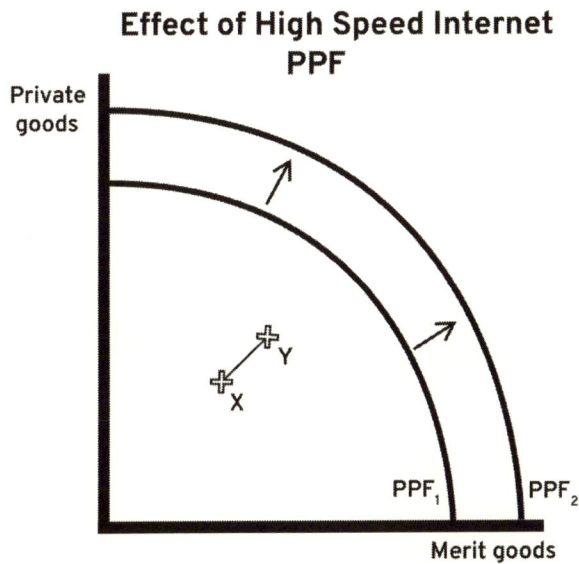

High speed internet enables Cuba to increase its potential ($PPC_1$ to $PPC_2$) to produce as faster movement of information enables greater economic activity and productivity resources are released to be used in producing more merit goods (basic health care, basic education).

Actual economic growth will result in X moving to Y where more merit and private goods / services are produced.

**(d)** **Using table 1, explain which one of the three countries, Cuba, Haiti and Indonesia is a more open economy.**  **[4 marks]**

We can measure the openness of an economy through the size of its foreign sector as a % of GDP. (Export Imports as a % of GDP)

- ☐ Cuba feels the effect of the US embargo. Imports have shrunk proportionately and this deprives Cuba of resources which can be used directly and indirectly to increase export and collect foreign currency. (Foreign sector shrunk from 44.90 % to 22.09 % of GDP)
- ☐ Jamaica has also seen the importance of its foreign sector fall from 113.5 % to 77.04 %. This may well be due to restructuring of its economy where it is becoming less reliant on imports and aiming for greater self-sufficiency.

31

☐ For Haiti foreign sector has grown from 56.30 % of GDP in 2009 to 75.31 % GDP in 2019. This is chiefly because it is still highly dependent in Foreign Aid and US domination as a result of its slow recovery from natural disasters.

Haiti is the most open economy.

**(e)** **Explain the trade- off between efficiency and equality in the agriculture sector in Cuba. (Text 2)** **[4 marks]**

Cuba is faced with a dilemma, given the US embargo and the new higher oil prices. In the agriculture sector given the growing demands from the tourist sector for food prices and profit margins are rising. According to free market principles more resources, FOPs, are reallocated towards serving the relatively wealthy tourists. However, they cannot offer higher prices given their low incomes. This creates the issue of basic inequality.

Free market principles of allocating FOPs towards where they are valued the most (efficient) comes in direct conflict with most Cubans whose incomes fail to compete with tourist dollars. This is the rationale behind government intervention in agriculture.

**(f)** **Using table 1 calculate which country has the highest nominal growth rate in 2019. [4 marks]**

Nominal Growth Rate = Growth Rate Real + inflation

For 2019 Cuba Nominal Growth Rate = 1.11 + 5.44 = 6.55 %

Haiti Nominal Growth Rate = 1.17 + 13.36 = 14.53 %

Jamaica Nominal Growth Rate = 0.48 + 6.95 = 7.43 %

**Haiti at 14.53 %, has the highest nominal growth rate chiefly due to high inflation.**

**(g)** **Using the texts / tables and your knowledge of economics, evaluate the proposition that only greater degree of privatisation, liberalization and deregulation policies can increase economic development for Cuba.** **[15 marks]**

- Define Privatisation : Selling of public sector assets to private sector partially or fully. It can also include outsourcing of government services to the private sector.
- Define Liberalisation : This is the lowering of the trade barriers and floating the currency.
- Define Deregulation : This is allowing the forces of free markets to function with more efficiency in that the barriers to entry in any field are lowered and land or FOPs use according where they are valued the most or bring the highest profit margins for a given level of risk.
- Cuba following the above will attract more private sector investment. Prices will change to equate demand with supply in the agriculture sector. The expansion of the tourist sector will create new jobs and higher productivity and wages. Public sector services can be moved into the private sector. Efficiency of the public sector can also rise through greater use of the internet and with few workers there is less burden on the taxpayer. Greater expansion of the private sector can lead to higher yields and overall supply. The pie can become bigger.
- **The Cuban government can use behavioural economics to promote the creation of small private businesses, eg making form filling online very simple and cheap to register a new business. (higher only)**
- Cuba transitioning to a free market and allowing foreign ownership of assets may well persuade the US to remove trade embargo and attract foreign investment.
- However, it is likely that inequalities will rise. Government sector may well be deprived of resources and many health and education programmes may be shut down. Workers may find that their terms and conditions do not improve but worsen. Job insecurities rise and worker's unions lose bargaining power. Removal or lowering of social safety nets may well mean many citizens are stuck in poverty and unable to move up the social ladder. A consumer debt culture may form. Energy use per capita as well as environmental degradation may rise in the guest of economic growth. Foreign multinationals may well wield great economic and political power in Cuba. They are more likely to use Cuba as part of their corporate strategy and their interests are unlikely to be aligned with the interests of the majority of Cuban citizens.
- Removing trade barriers may well mean the Cuban currency will depreciate and the terms of trade will worsen.

## 4.    <u>TURKEY</u>

*Study the texts and data below and answer the questions that follow.*

### Text 1- Turkey's President Erdogan, struggles with the effects of rising inflation.

The Turkish economy is in a self-perpetuating circle with higher inflation leading to a ***depreciating currency*** and this consequently increases prices. Since 2015, Turkey's external balances have been deteriorating with the current account deficit reaching 5.6% of GDP.  In June 2018, the rate of inflation reached 15.4%, while the exchange rate touched 4.89 to the US dollar. The central bank in Turkey is expected to raise interest rates further at next week's meeting. However, this is at odds with both Turkey's prime minister and President Erdogan. Both believe higher interest rates are unlikely to tame inflation significantly.

President Erdogan's fiscal stimulus program, including a government credit guarantee scheme and new employment incentives, has raised domestic demand and created 1.6 million net new jobs in 2017. However, the unemployment rate is still hovering near 10% in 2018. Investment picked up at the end of 2017 with the proportion of GDP spent on machinery and transportation equipment is back to its long term average of 13%, one of the tops among OECD countries.  The fiscal stimulus was withdrawn in the third quarter of 2018 and corporation tax rate raised from 20% to 22%.

### Text 2- Turkish Lira weakens further

The Turkish lira is depreciating fast against the US$ and the Euro. Turkish President Erdogan is urging citizens to borrow and restructure their loans in the currency they are paid. This warning is however too late for Turkish energy producers. They have borrowed extensively in low interest currency like the US$ and Euro to import specialised equipment to improve the nation's efficiency in power generation and distribution over the last 15 years. Zumrut Imamoglu, the chief economist of Turkish industry and business association Tusiad says, "While costs are increasing because of the currency shock, companies can't adjust their prices accordingly due to state regulation and price ceilings, which in turn, causes financial problems."

## Text 3- Turkey's eye watering prices of onions

The food markets of Istanbul, one of Turkey's major cities, have seen the price of onions rise from 1.3 Liras per kilo to 6.5 Turkish Liras in the past month. Similarly potatoes prices have also risen from 1.5 Liras per kilo to 6 Liras per month. Milk and meat products have also seen sharp increases.

In the past few decades, the government has tamed food inflation by reducing the import **_tariff_** by 30% on these basic foods and encouraging imports. This has helped to reduce prices in the short run while reducing local production in the long run. However, this time round, the rise in imports has not pushed down domestic prices. Government critics say, "The high demand from Turkey is driving up prices also in the countries from which we import. Soon we will not be able to buy cheap meat from them either."

Saribal, an engineer from the agriculture ministry, pointed out in his report that while agriculture output prices have risen by 300% in the past 15 years, the corresponding increase in input prices is 500%. More and more farmers are selling out and moving to the cities or living in villages and dependent on welfare. During this time, Turkey has seen its population rise by 14.4 million, the population employed in this sector fall from 35% to 19% and the amount of land allocated to farming fall by 10%. Workers in Turkish farming sector now only earn a fifth of the GDP per capita. Turkish farmers have had to look for shepherds from Azerbaijan after failing to attract local workers.

## Table 1- Economic data for Turkey

|  | 2013 | 2014 | 2015 | 2016 | 2017 | 2018 |
|---|---|---|---|---|---|---|
| GDP per capita (USD) | 12386 | 12026 | 10 898 | 10 805 | 10 536 | 10 386 |
| GDP (USD bn) | 950 | 934 | 858 | 862 | 851 | 848 |
| Economic Growth (GDP, annual in %) | 8.5 | 5.2 | 6.1 | 3.2 | 7.4 | 4.6 |
| Inflation Rate (CPI, %) | 7.5 | 8.9 | 7.7 | 7.8 | 11.1 | 12.3 |
| Inflation (PPI, %) | 7.0 | 6.4 | 5.7 | 9.9 | 15.5 | 16.1 |

| Policy Interest Rate (%) | 4.50 | 8.25 | 7.50 | 8.00 | 8.00 | 8.00 |
| --- | --- | --- | --- | --- | --- | --- |
| Exchange Rate (vs USD) | 2.15 | 2.33 | 2.92 | 3.53 | 3.79 | 4.89 |
| Current Account Balance (USD bn) | −63.6 | −43.6 | −32.1 | −33.1 | −47.4 | −60.2 |
| Trade Balance (USD bn) | −79.9 | −63.6 | −48.1 | −40.9 | −58.9 | −79.3 |

**Table 2- Foreign Direct Investment into Turkey (million US dollars)**

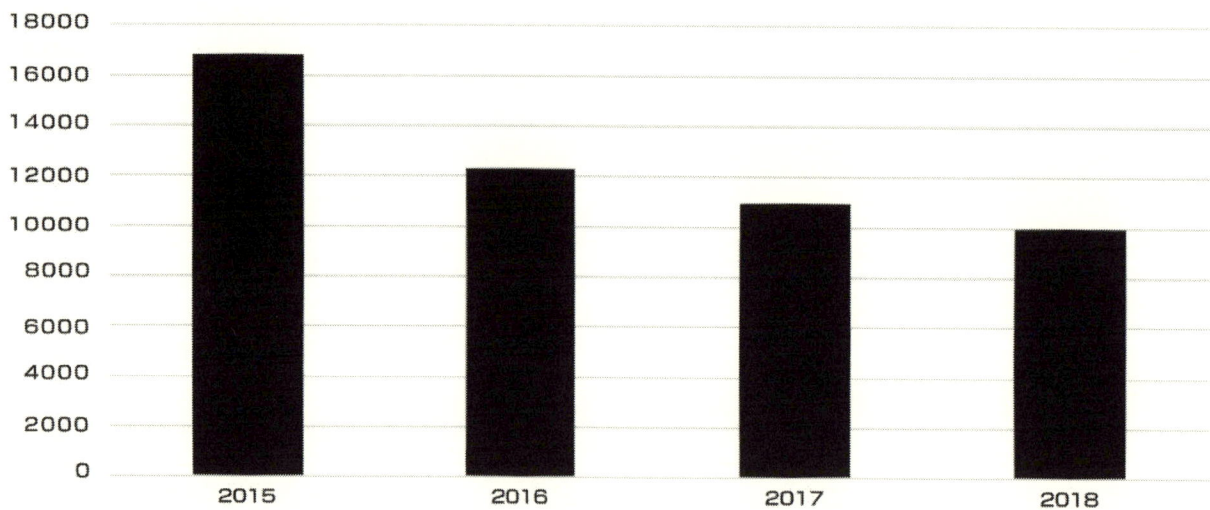

## QUESTIONS

(a)  (i) Define the term *depreciating currency* indicated in bold. (Text 1 - paragraph 1)   [2 marks]

(ii) Define the term *tariff* indicated in bold. (Text 3 - paragraph 2)   [2 marks]

(b)      (i) Draw a demand and supply diagram to show how the exchange rate between the Turkish Lira and the US$ has changed since 2013.                                    [3 marks]

(ii) Using information in table 1 calculate the population of Turkey in 2018.        [2 marks]

(c)      Using a demand and supply diagram and information in Text 3 - paragraph 3, explain why the agriculture sector is contracting terms of local workers and land use.        [4 marks]

(d)s      Explain using a labour market diagram how even with an increase of 1.6 demand for workers, the  unemployment rate can remain at 10 %. (Text 3 - paragraph 2)        [4 marks]

(d)h      Using a J - curve diagram explain to what extent does the data support the Marshall Lerner Theorem  from 2016 to 2018 for Turkey, Table 1.        [4 marks]

(e)      Using Table 1, explain why the CPI, PPI and the policy interest rate are positively correlated.        [4 marks]

(f)      Use a tariff diagram to explain how a fall in tariffs can lead to lower inflation. (Text 3 - paragraph 2)        [4 marks]

(g)      Using the information in the texts and table, evaluate the impact on the Turkish economy of a significant fall in foreign direct investment from 2015 to 2018.        [15 marks]

## ANSWERS:          4. TURKEY

**(a)**     **(i) Define the term _depreciating currency_ indicated in bold. (Text 1 - paragraph 1)**    **[2 marks]**

Depreciating currency is when one currency, Turkish Lira, falls in price against another currency, US dollar is operating under a freely floating exchange rate regime where the forces of demand and supply determine the price of the currency.

        **(ii) Define the term _tariff_ indicated in bold. (Text 3 - paragraph 2)**         **[2 marks]**

Tariff: This is a tax imposed on the value or volume of any goods coming into the country from abroad. This tax may be ad valorem (% tax) or specific tax, (fixed amount per unit).

**(b)**     **(i) Draw a demand and supply diagram to show how the exchange rate between the Turkish Lira and the US\$ has changed since 2013.**         **[3 marks]**

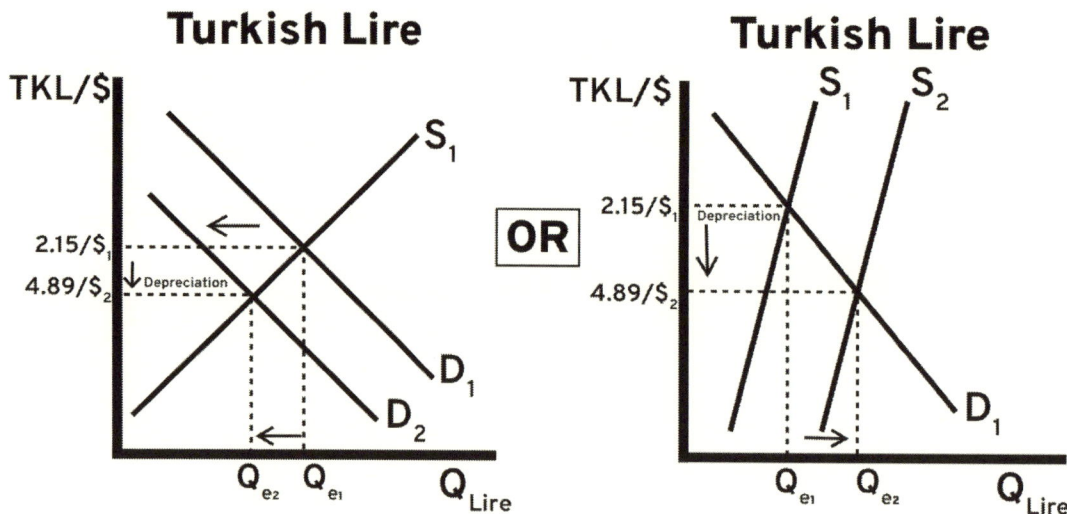

In \$ terms the GDP has fallen or more Liras are traded due to inflation.

**(ii) Using information in table 1 calculate the population of Turkey in 2018.** **[2 marks]**

Population of Turkey for 2018 = GDP 2018 ÷ GDP per Capita 2018

$$= (848 \text{ bn})/10386$$

$$= \underline{81648372} = \text{population } (81.65\text{m approx.})$$

**(c)** **Using a demand and supply diagram and information in Text 3 - paragraph 3, explain why the agriculture sector is contracting terms of local workers and land use.** **[4 marks]**

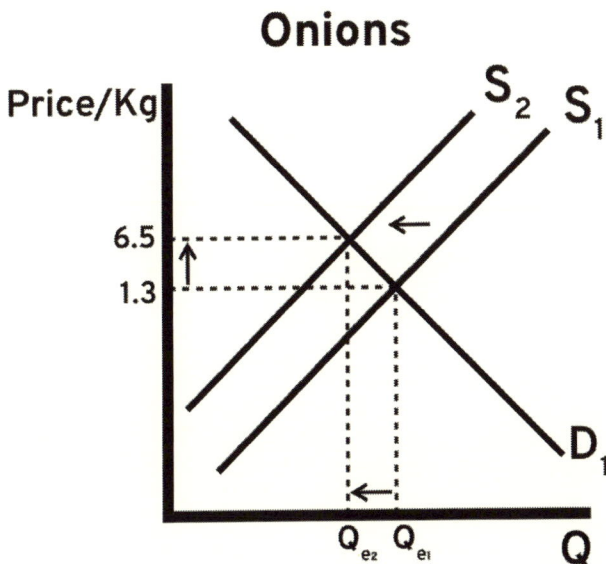

**Onions**

Higher costs of production mean S1 falls to S2. Prices rise dramatically when PES and PED for onions is low.

The drastic rise in onion prices, as well as the prices of other agriculture produce is a symptom. The underlying causes are long decline in profitability and subsequently incomes of Turkish farmers. Incomes of workers in the agriculture sector have not risen as fast as incomes in the secondary and tertiary sectors. This is a global story. Under free markets land use would change, away from traditional low yield farming and move towards higher productivity methods (mechanisation). Another alternative is lower costs through the introduction of low wage workers from Azerbaijan. Turkish workers in the agriculture sector will subsequently move to more urbanised areas which offer higher real wages.

**(d)s     Explain using a labour market diagram how even with an increase of 1.6 demand for workers, the unemployment rate can remain at 10 %. (Text 3 - paragraph 2)                    [4 marks]**

Unemployment Rate  =  (Number unemployment)/(Labour Force)   ×   1000/1  =  10 %

### Turkey
### Labour Market

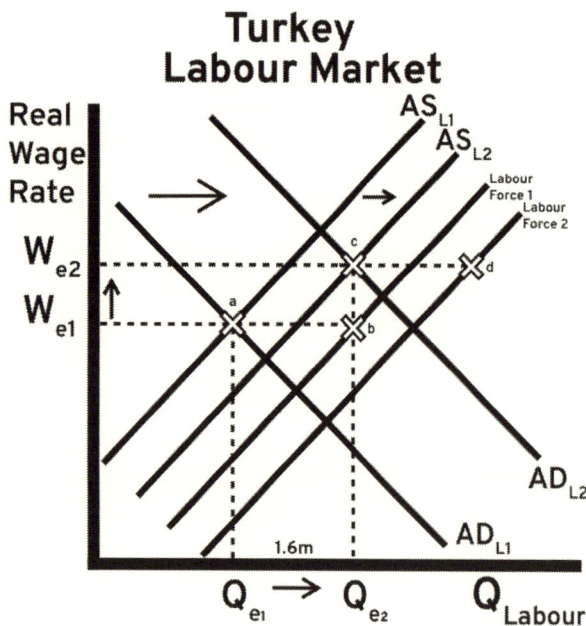

For unemployment Rate to remain at 10% when demand for labour ADL1 has risen to ADL2 (1.6 million = a to b), both supply of labour needs to rise ADL1 to ADL2 as the text shows and the overall size of the labour force also needs to rise as the text points towards the rise in population f 14.4 m (Text 3 - paragraph 3). (a to b) = (c to d) as unemployment rate of 10 %.

**(d)h** **Using a J - curve diagram explain to what extent does the data support the Marshall Lerner Theorem from 2016 to 2018 for Turkey, Table 1.** **[4 marks]**

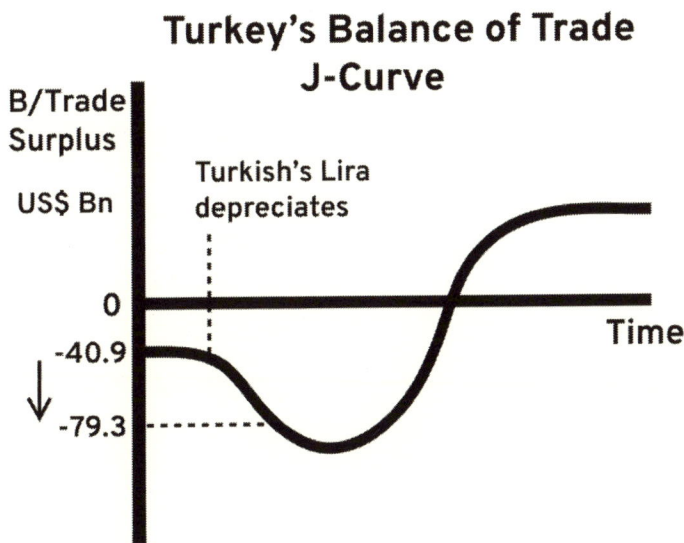

**Turkey's Balance of Trade J-Curve**

J - curve can be defined as a situation where Turkish's balance of trade initially worsens after a depreciation in the Turkish currency before the balance of trade improves beyond the initial level.

From 2016 to 2018 Turkish Lira fell against the US $ from 3.52 per $ to 4.89 TKL per $. This made exports cheaper and imports more expensive. However since the overall balance of trade has worsened from - 40.9 Bn US$ to - 79.3 Bn US$, this means according to the Marshall Lerner Theorem that

PEDxpts + PEDmpts < 1.

Alternatively if PEDxpts + PEDmpts > 1 for Turkey then the above diagram supports the view that the J - Curve is in operation and it is only a matter of time before a correction occurs and B / Trade deficit turns around and improves.

41

**(e)      Using Table 1, explain why the CPI, PPI and the policy interest rate are positively correlated.**
**[4 marks]**

Positive correlation means that the variables move in the same direction, all up or all down. For Turkey, however, the correlation is not one to one.

A rise in PPI implies that costs of production (FOPs) are rising as these are the components of the basket of goods / services for producers. After a time log some producers are forced to pass on these higher costs to consumers or else go bankrupt. Higher prices for consumers get registered as higher valuation of the consumers' basket of goods and services support this.

Higher rates of inflation mean lenders will not lend credit to borrowers unless they are compensated with at least the same level of real interest rates as before.

$$i\% \text{ real} = i\%\text{nominal} - \text{inflation }\%$$

So, if inflation rises, so will the nominal interest rate. Now the table seems to contradict this since 2017 (CPI  i % = negative). This can be called 'financial repression'.

**(f)    Use a tariff diagram to explain how a fall in tariffs can lead to lower inflation.**
**(Text 3 - paragraph 2)**                                                    **[4 marks]**

## Tariff Diagram
## Basic Food

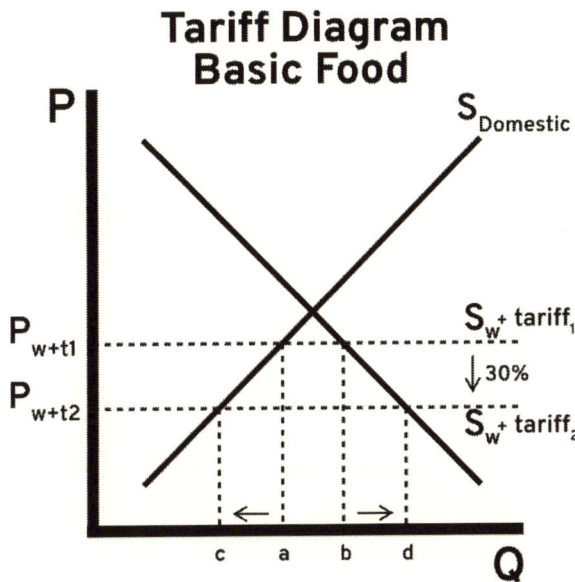

A fall of 30 % in tariff rates on basic food means prices of imports will fall and CPI will be subdued and inflation rate will fall. Imports rise at lower price (a, b) to (c, d)

Population rising in Turkey will buy up all the additional cheap imports without Reading to falls in domestic prices or domestic producers becoming uncompetitive. However in the long run domestic producers must not lose competitiveness in terms of costs when compared to imports.

**(g)** **Using the information in the texts and table, evaluate the impact on the Turkish economy of a significant fall in foreign direct investment from 2015 to 2018.** **[15 marks]**

Define FDI :– This is the inflow of money from a company from one country to another. It can be in terms of setting up new separation, or a joint venture or buying partial or full ownership of a domestic company.

For Turkey FDI values have been falling according to Table 2, from approx 16 % US $ in 2015 to around 10 BN US $ in 2018. This would mean a net fall in injections in the circular flow of income.

With a growing population and slowing FDI, the effect will be felt in changes in the macroeconomic indicators.

- The demand for Turkish Lira has fallen and the currency depreciated from 2.92 to 4.89 Liras to the US $.
- With interest rates steadied at 8 %, domestic companies may pick up the slack and expand to serve the expanding population of 14.4 m.
- Draw an AD / AS diagram to show a negative multiplier effect caused by slowing FDI. Real output and job creation may be adversely affected.
- The Turkish Lira may need to depreciate further in order to correct the growing current account deficit including the worsening of the trading balance. This may or may not attract new FDI to compensate on capital account. (current account deficit 32.1 Bn to 60.2 Bn)
- Rates of technological transfer can slow down and slow down productivity growth in Turkey especially in agriculture.
- Slowdown in FDI can slow down capital deepening and productivity and real wages.
- Slowdown in FDI means less new competition and perhaps higher prices.

## 5.    ITALY

*Study the texts and data below and answer the questions that follow.*

### Text 1- Overview of the Italian Economy.

The post WWII years saw Italy transform itself from chiefly an agrarian economy to one of the most industrialized countries in the world. Small and medium sized family owned manufacturing companies led the way to steady stable growth. Manufacturing and export of high quality and highly specialised products accounted for more than 60% of employment. Oil and other raw materials were Italy's chief imports. The oil crises of the 1970s resulted in ***stagflation***. The recovery plan centered round both a tight monetary policy and fiscal policy aimed at reducing inflation and public sector debts. Economic growth was driven through privatisation, liberalization and deregulation.

After more than 10 years after the 2007-2008 financial crisis Italy is still struggling with economic growth and unemployment. Its GDP today is still 7% lower than the 2007 level. Since joining the single currency, the Euro, in 2002 the standards of living for Italians have barely risen. Fulfilling the conditions of being in the Eurozone has meant that each of the four governments since the 2007 crisis has tried to introduce ***austerity*** measures in one form or another. In the past, Italy would resort to currency devaluation of the Lira to restore its competitiveness. Debtors would gain from falls in the real value of debt they owe. Strong labour unions would ensure that wages rise to compensate for higher levels of inflation. Today, the situation is reversed. Creditors gain from low levels of inflation. Labour unions are significantly weaker and consequently wages are stagnant. The Government finds its debts harder to service and fewer instruments available to kick start the economy, reduce unemployment, especially youth unemployment, and inequality. The last two decades has seen investment, both physical and human, tepid. In addition, the family owned small businesses have not innovated sufficiently nor introduced informational technology extensively. This has meant Italy's productivity growth has slowed down to levels below its global competitors. A lack of job opportunities beyond part-time low paid work has resulted in net migration. The economic wealth divide between the industrialised north and the agrarian south has widened significantly over the years.

## Text 2- Either change or die.

'Either change or die' read one of the banners in the recent Italian elections. Successive governments in Italy have been trying to get the country out of its malaise of slow economic growth, high unemployment, stagnant standards of living, rising numbers of families living at the margins of poverty, worrying level of public sector debt and a banking system stuffed with bad loans. One of the major areas ripe for reform is taxation. The new government is faced with addressing the current situation of 48% income and social security tax paid out of average wages, among the highest in the OECD, 22% value-added tax on most goods and services and corporate taxes, capital gains taxes, gift taxes are all ultimately passed on to individuals and workers through lower wages. A start-up company can sometimes end up with a total tax bill amounting to 120% of its income. This may partially explain why businesses may try and hide incomes to put them into a lower tax bracket. Italy's shadow economy is estimated to be about 21% of its $2.72trn GDP in contrast to Germany's 12% of its GDP. The shadow economy deprives the Italian government of $175 billion in lost tax revenues.

The incoming government intends to introduce a 15% flat tax and a 20% corporation tax. This will help finance a program of universal basic income of $910 a month for unemployed Italians over 18 and for those currently earning incomes below the poverty line. Many commentators from the outgoing government point out that this will cost the government an estimated $30bn. However, experience from Eastern European countries and Russia shows that Italy could end up collecting more taxes even when it has a long history of poor implementation.

## Text 3- Portofino, here we come!

Portofino along with nearby towns of Rapallo and Santa Margherita are favourite hotspots on the Italian Riviera. Last week the Mayors introduced new laws at the request of the local residents aimed at curbing anti-social behaviour coming from tourists. The towns' population triples during the holiday periods. Unruly tourists will be fined up to four hundred dollars if caught wandering around the harbour shirtless at any time, sitting on doorsteps of houses or public buildings eating, playing loud music past midnight, occupying benches or porticoes. Cities such as Florence have already introduced similar laws to discipline tourists. Florence City Mayor, Mario Nardella, said 'The historic center of Florence is a World Heritage site, an open-air museum and not a picnic spot'.

**TABLE 1- Italian national income accounts**

| Values in billions of Euros | 2016 | 2017 |
|---|---|---|
| Consumption Spending | 1022 | 1048 |
| Investment Spending | 288 | 300 |
| Government Spending | 316 | 319 |
| Exports | 501 | 537 |
| Imports | 446 | 484 |
| Gross Domestic Product | 1679.5 | 1695.4 |
| Unemployment Rate | 13% | 11% |

**TABLE 2- Selective Development Indicators for Italy and Germany**

| | | 2013 | 2014 | 2015 | 2016 | 2017 |
|---|---|---|---|---|---|---|
| GDP per capita (Euros) | Germany | 42914 | 43560 | 43937 | 44431 | 45229 |
| | Italy | 34219 | 33945 | 34302 | 34655 | 35220 |
| Rate of overcrowding as a % of population | Germany | 6.7 | 6.6 | 7.0 | 7.2 | 7.6 |
| | Italy | 27.1 | 27.2 | 27.2 | 27.8 | 27.9 |

## QUESTIONS

(a)    (i) Define the term *stagflation* indicated in bold. (Text 1 - paragraph 1)        [2 marks]

(ii) Define the term *austerity* indicated in bold. (Text 2 - paragraph 2)        [2 marks]

(b)s    (i) Calculate total tax paid by a worker standard earning 40000 Euros per year and spending 10,000 Euros on goods / services. (Text 2 - paragraph 1)        [3 marks]

**(b)h** **(i)** Calculate the total value of economic activity formal and shadow for Italy. (Text 2- paragraph 1)                                                                [3 marks]

**(b)** **(ii)** Draw a Laffer Curve to show how a flat tax rate above or below 15% can decrease the tax revenues collected. (Text 2 - paragraph 2)                                [2 marks]

**(c)** Using an AD / AS diagram, explain how a tight monetary and fiscal policy can help in reducing inflation. (Text 1 - paragraph 1)                                     [4 marks]

**(d)** Using a market failure diagram explain how rules and fines can be used to curb 'anti-social' behaviour coming from terrorists' in Portofino and other terrorist destinations. (Text 3)      [4marks]

**(e)** Using Table 1, calculate and explain in which year the Italian economy is closer to equilibrium.                                                                         [4marks]

**(f)** Using Table 1 and an AD / AS diagram work out the approximate value of the injections and explain the effects of a 20 billion Euro stimulus on the GDP of Italy.        [4 marks]

**(g)** Using information from the text / data and your knowledge of economics, discuss the value of data in Table 2 to policy makers in improving the welfare of citizens in the two countries.    [15 marks]

**ANSWERS:**                          **5. ITALY**

**(a)      (i)  Define the term _stagflation_ indicated in bold. (Text 1 - paragraph 1)          [2 marks]**

Stagflation is a situation where an economy like Italy, is experiencing a recession continued with inflation. Very slow economic growth as well as rising prices was caused by a very sudden rise in imported oil costs.

**(ii) Define the term _austerity_ indicated in bold. (Text 2 - paragraph 2)          [2 marks]**

Austerity is a government policy which is designed to cut public sector expenditure and services during an economic slowdown. Government budget deficits are drastically reduced.

**(b)s      (i) Calculate total tax paid by a worker standard earning 40000 Euros per year and spending 10,000 Euros  on goods / services. (Text 2 - paragraph 1)          [3 marks]**

Worker's income (Y)  =  40000 $_E$

Income and social security tax = 46 % of  40000  =  19200 Euro

Y disposable    = 20800  Euros

Indirect tax     = 22 % of 20800  =  4576 Euros

Total tax paid  =  19200 + 4576 = **23776  Euros**

**(b)h    (i)  Calculate the total value of economic activity both formal and shadow for Italy.
(Text 2-  paragraph 1)**                                                                    **[3 marks]**

Total value of economic activity          =  Formal  +  Shadow

                                          = 2.072  trn $ +  21 % of  2.072 trn $

                                          = 2.072 trn $  +  435.12 Bn $

                                          = **2.50712 trn $**

**(ii) Draw a Laffer Curve to show how a flat tax rate above or below 15% can decrease the tax
revenues collected. (Text 2 - paragraph 2)**                                           **[2 marks]**

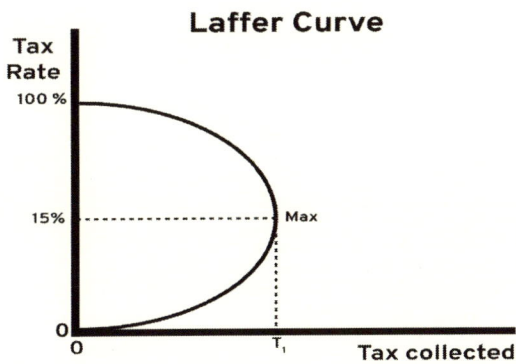

According to the question a 15 % tax rate has to be the optimal tax rate in order to maximise the tax revenue, $T_1$ for the Italian government.

**(c)    Using an AD / AS diagram, explain how a tight monetary and fiscal policy can help in reducing inflation.  (Text 1 - paragraph 1)**                                                    **[4 marks]**

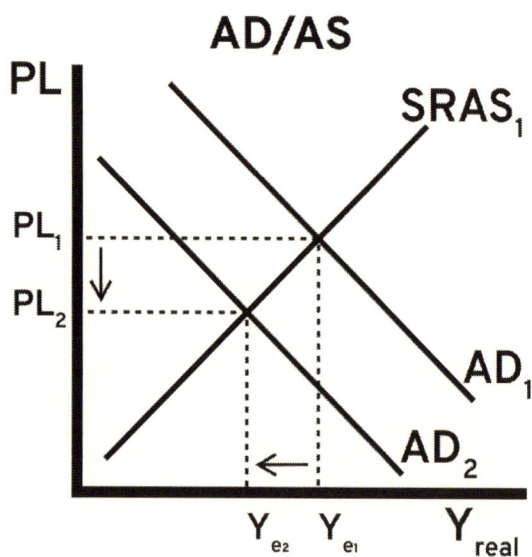

A tight monetary policy of increasing  i %  and restricting credit will discourage consumption and investment.  A contractionary fiscal policy of reducing government spending and / or raising taxes will reduce AD even more.  AD$_1$ will fall to AD$_2$. Resources may well become idle and underutilized. This will result in demand deflation leading to a fall in the price level, PL$_1$ falls to PL$_2$.

**(d)     Use a market failure diagram, explain how rules and fines can be used to curb 'anti- social' behaviour coming from terrorists' in Portofino and other terrorist destinations. (Text 3)     [4marks]**

### Market Failure
### Due to Antisocial Behaviour

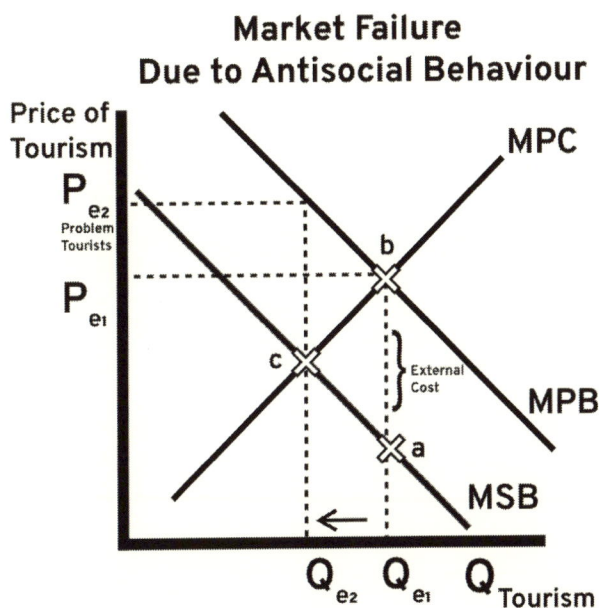

At the current of tourists $Qe_1$ the nuisance value of antisocial behaviour is (*a* to *b*), the external cost on the rest of society. Society's optimum level of tourism is $Qe_2$. Rules and fines deter problematic tourists to stay away from Portofino and other places. The price that unruly tourists must pay will rise to P2 through fires. The area *abc* represents the costs of correcting antisocial behaviour, which the original equilibrium ignored.

**(e)** Using Table 1, calculate and explain in which year the Italian economy is closer to equilibrium.

[4marks]

Equilibrium occurs when      AD = AS = Y

In 2016      AD = C + I + G + X - M

AD = 1022 + 288 + 316 + 501 - 446 = 1681  but Y = 1679.5

AD > Y = 1.5

In 2017      AD = 1720      Y = 1695.4

AD > Y = 24.6

**In 2016 the economy is closer to equilibrium.**

**(f)** Using Table 1 and an AD / AS diagram work out the approximate value of the injections and explain the effects of a 20 billion Euro stimulus on the GDP of Italy.          [4 marks]

Investment multiplier value $k$ = (change in Income )/(change in Investment)

= (1695.4 - 1679.5)/12 = 15.9/12 = 1.325

Investment 2016 = 288

Investment 2017 = 300

Investment multiplier $k$ = 1.325

Effect of a 20 Bn Euro stimulus through investment will raise GDP by $k$ × Injection = 1.325 × 20 = 26.5 Bn

**Italy's GDP will rise by 26.5 Bn Euro**

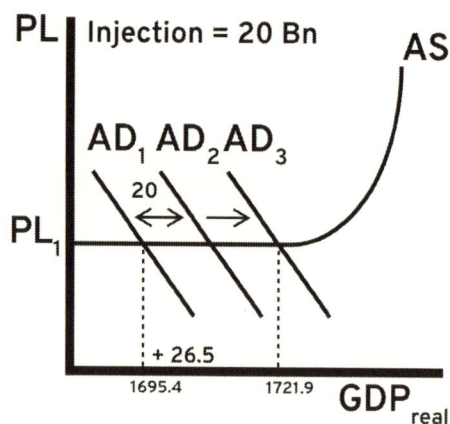

**(g)     Using information from the text / data and your knowledge of economics, discuss the value of data in Table 2 to policy makers in improving the welfare of citizens in the two countries.   [15 marks]**

The positive correlation between GDP per capita and the rate of overcrowding is partially due to urbanisation and apartment living.

- Italy is experiencing at least three times greater incidence of overcrowding than Germany. More than  a quarter of the Italian population is living in overcrowded conditions.
- Policy makers in Italy have to firstly accept the validity of the date and acknowledge that they have a problem today and it is likely to get worse in the future given the current trends.
- Overcrowding creates negative external costs in terms of health, congestion, noise and pollution. The presence of an additional individual creates greater risk of illnesses longer journey times, higher decibels etc on the rest of the city's residents.
- Policy makers in Italy may need to look at best practices in Germany and elsewhere to address the overcrowding issue. Upgrading of infrastructure, introducing beans, restrictions, tax on use, education on cities, community service programs, health and hygiene regulations are some of possible policies. Policy makers can also encourage companies to relocate outside the cities by building better quality infrastructure, schools, roads, fiber optics, and health clinics.

There are many drawbacks. Voters may not be interested. Taxpayers may not be willing to contribute or local and state governments may already be in heavy debt. Time lays may be long. Dissipations during the change may be unacceptable. Cities like Rome have tough digging regulations to protect its history. Companies may relocate to other countries altogether.

# 6.    New Zealand

*Study the texts and data below and answer the questions that follow.*

## Text 1- Overview of New Zealand

Growth in New Zealand is slowing down just a little while unemployment has risen only slightly and inflation is still timid in the first two quarters of 2019. This was the summary delivered to the Finance Minister, Grant Robertson, to the parliament.  The opposition party speaker, Amy Adams, says the ruling government is ignoring other important data such as the ANZ business confidence data which says firms' optimism on New Zealand's economy is at its lowest since the 2008 Financial Crisis. Adams criticised the vagueness of Minister Robertson's phrases such as 'the New Zealand economy is in transition'.

Finance Minister, Robertson, explained, 'what I meant was that New Zealand is in a period of transition where economic growth was chiefly driven by population growth and ***housing market speculation***'. The minister talked up the government's role in promoting new investment in infrastructure such as installing Ultra-Fast Broadband (UFB) throughout the country to help put New Zealand on the path of sustainable growth. Government's economists claim that UFB will attract new foreign businesses to New Zealand while raising ***productivity*** in the long run. These claims at the moment remain un-realised.

## Text 2- New Zealanders are becoming tenants on their own land.

The Economist in 2017 reported New Zealand had the most unaffordable house prices in the world. Auckland house prices have risen 75% in the last four years alone.  However the gradual rise in interest rates in the United States has cooled the New Zealand housing market down in recent months. On top of this a new law banning new foreign buyers from purchasing property comes into effect next month. This however, does not affect the current foreign buyers who have already scooped up 470,000 hectares, an increase of 600% in the last year alone. This amounts to 3.2% of farmland.

The fast rise in house prices has flowed into the rental market. Many professionals find themselves unable to save for the deposit needed for a loan as an increasing proportion of their income is taken up by rising rents. Already the number of strike action days over wages has risen significantly as public sector workers are unable to live in three major cities, Auckland, Wellington and Napier.

University of Auckland professor, Tim Hazeldine, points out that the housing crisis is now a macro-economic issue for New Zealand and in a sense it reflects the desirability of our country as a global destination. The new ban will have a knock on effect of cooling down prices in rundown neighbourhoods, giving young people a chance to get on to the property ladder and spending their weekends slowly renovating their homes. However, Joe Carolan, the chair of Auckland housing committee, says scapegoating immigrants is not the solution. The government needs to build 100000 units of social housing in Auckland alone and more in other cities. The way to tackle empty properties is to penalise speculations by bringing back the land value tax, which if sufficiently high will only attract those willing to live in the house or rent to tenants at a fair value. The tax will reflect the value of the land use.

### Text 3- Stolen avocados on sale on Facebook, New Zealand.

The North Island of New Zealand has experienced dozens of raids at night by thieves on avocado orchards. The stolen avocados have then shown up on sale on Facebook and other social media sites. This behaviour is driven by the rise in global and local demand for the fruit which local growers are unable to satisfy. The industry body, New Zealand Avocado, reported an additional rise in local demand of 96,000 on top of the expanding global demand for New Zealand avocados which grew retail sales this year by $64m to $198m. The number of trays produced rose by nearly 80% this year compared to 4.2 m trays of 20 avocados each in 2018. Prices in 2019 are now highest on record up by around 37% higher than last year's high of $3.69 each. While New Zealand avocado growers are benefitting in the short run, growers of mandarins, kiwifruit and broccoli have seen prices for their produce fall by 35% to 40%.

### Table 1- Economic data for New Zealand

NEW ZEALAND LABOR FORCE PARTICIPATION RATE

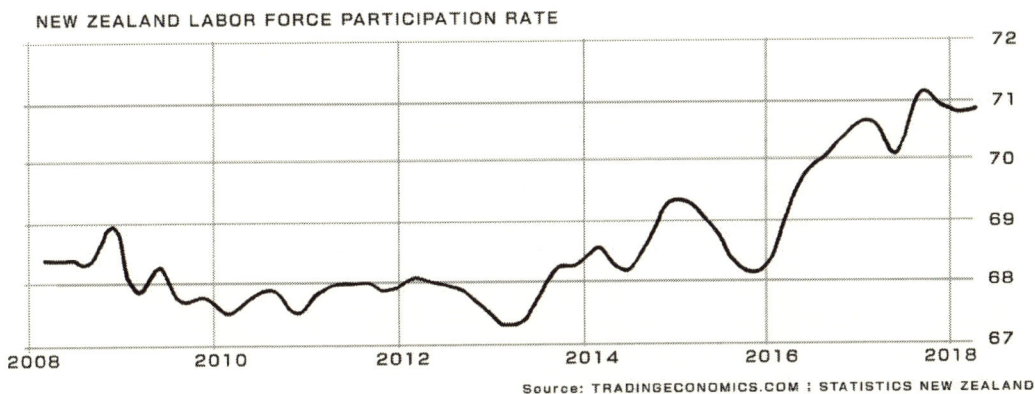

Source: TRADINGECONOMICS.COM : STATISTICS NEW ZEALAND

Data Response-Paper 2

## Table 2- Development data for New Zealand, Australia & Sweden

| | 2011 | | 2016 | |
|---|---|---|---|---|
| Country | GNI – HDI ranking | HDI ranking | GNI – HDI ranking | HDI ranking |
| New Zealand | 30 | 5 | 20 | 13 |
| Australia | 16 | 2 | 19 | 3 |
| Sweden | 4 | 10 | 3 | 15 |

## QUESTIONS

(a)    (i) Define the term *productivity* indicated in bold. (Text 1 - paragraph 2)    [2 marks]

        (ii) Define the term *shadow economy* indicated in bold. (Text 2 - paragraph 1)    [2 marks]

(b)s    (i) Calculate the price elasticity of demand for Avocados. (Text 3)    [3 marks]

(b)h    (i) Using a demand and supply diagram show the changes in output demand, price and revenue for avocados in New Zealand.  (Text 3)    [3 marks]

        (ii) Explain what is the business confidence index and why is it considered a leading indicator. (Text 1 - paragraph1)    [2 marks]

(c) Using an AD / As diagram, explain the Investment between difference driven and investment driven model of economic growth. (Text 1 - paragraph 2)                    [4 marks]

(d)      Using a demand and supply diagram for housing.  Explain how a progressive land value tax can help stabilise or reduce rents.                    [4 marks]

(e)      Using an appropriate diagram, explain how changes in the labour force participation rates can affect the macro economy of New Zealand. (Table 1)                    [4 marks]

(f)      Using demand and supply diagrams to explain why prices of agriculture output such as avocados are likely to fluctuate much more than the prices of manufactured goods such as cars.                    [4 marks]

(g)      Using the information in the text / data and your knowledge of economics, discuss the possible policies  that New Zealand may have implemented which help to explain the significant fall in GNI - HDI ranking for New Zealand when compared to Australia and Sweden.                    [15 marks]

## ANSWERS: 5. New Zealand

**(a)** **(i) Define the term _productivity_ indicated in bold. (Text 1 - paragraph 2)** **[2 marks]**

_This is the rise in the amount of good / service produced per person. It could also be the average value each worker produces of output.

**(ii) Define the term _shadow economy_ indicated in bold. (Text 2 - paragraph 1)** **[2 marks]**

Housing market speculation is when properties are bought with the sole intention of reselling them at a higher price soon after to realise a capital gain.

**(b)s** **(i) Calculate the price elasticity of demand for Avocados. (Text 3)** **[3 marks]**

Price Elasticity of Demand = (% change in QD avocados)/(% change in P avocados)

$P_1$ = \$ 3.69     $P_2$ = 3.69 + 37 % of 3.69 = \$ 5.0553 per unit

$QD_1$ = 4.2 m trays x 20 per tray =84 m avocados     $QD_2$ = 84 m + 80 % of 84 m = 151.2 m

PED avocados = ((151.2 m - 84m)/(84 m))/((5.0553 - 3.69)/3.69) = 0.8/0.37

***PED = 2.16 Avocados are demand price elastic***

**(b)h     (i) Using a demand and supply diagram show the changes in output demand, price and revenue for avocados in New Zealand.  (Text 3)                                    [3 marks]**

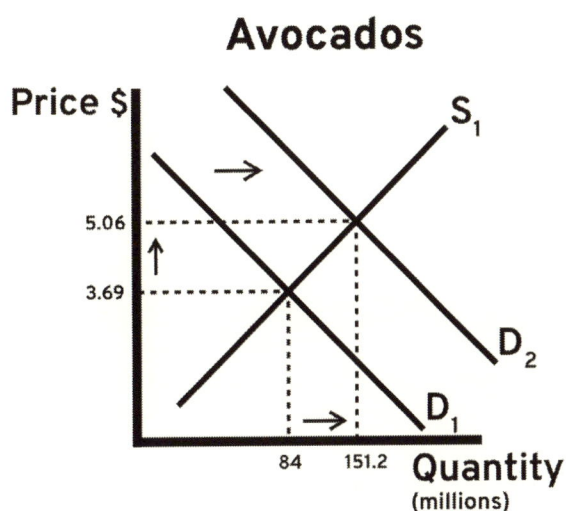

## Avocados

Price $

5.06

3.69

$S_1$

$D_2$

$D_1$

84     151.2     **Quantity**
(millions)

Demand went up and supply partially accommodated the rise to produce at 151.2 m avocados in the short term. The equilibrium price rose from $ 3.69  to  $ 5.06  per avocado.

Initial Total Revenue  = 84 m x  $ 3.69   =  $ 3.9.96 m

New Total Revenue  = 151.2 m  x  $ 5.06 = $765.072 m

**A rise of  $ 455.112 m  in total revenue**

**(ii) Explain what is the business confidence index and why is it considered a leading indicator. (Text 1 - paragraph1)                                                                           [2 marks]**

Business confidence index compares the level of optimism with the level of pessimism about the future of the economy among companies. An index number above the base line of 100 implies business are net optimistic about their book orders and stocks of finished goods. Optimism can be seen in terms of hiring new workers and buying new machinery for expansion.   A number below 100 implies more pessimism than optimism. This indicator is a leading indicator since it tells about future business sentiment. It cannot be used as a fact as lagging indicators.

**(c)** **Using an AD / As diagram, explain the Investment between difference driven and investment driven model of economic growth. (Text 1 - paragraph 2)** **[4 marks]**

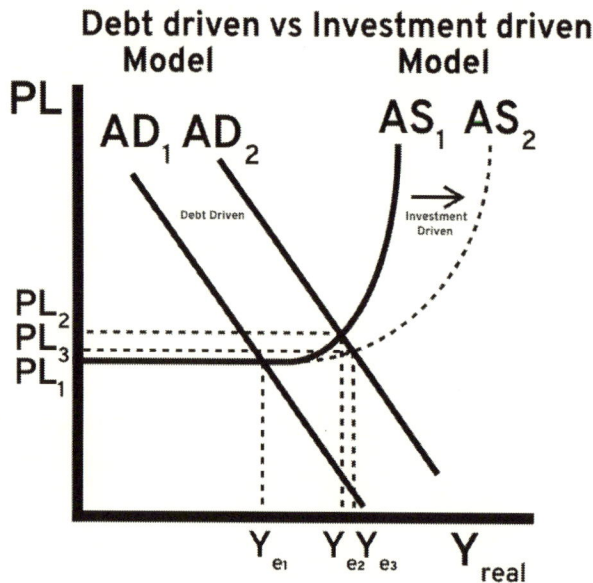

Debt driven vs Investment driven Model

Debt driven model typically involves Central Bank following a loose monetary policy of reducing $i$ % and increasing credit supply. This encourages more consumer spending and spurs on businesses to expand production and make new investments.

A multiplier effect can take place and AD1 rises to AD2 and real output rises from Ye1 to Ye2. If the same sectors of the economy are already at full employment then there may be some inflation $PL_1$ to $PL_2$. New jobs may be created. However, this model has several limitations in that the household debt level may become unsustainable and consumer spending highly dependent on low interest rates which may ultimately hit close to zero. Misallocation of resources most likely occurs.

An investment driven model increases $AS_1$ to $AS_2$ where the capacity to produce rises. Here actual economic growth rises during the construction stage, creating more jobs and when the projects are completed there is more potential growth and less inflation. Danger is over investment as in China and with cheap money, businesses may introduce new machinery to replace man leading to jobless growth. New Zealand has a choice to make in the property market.

**(d)** **Using a demand and supply diagram for housing. Explain how a progressive land value tax can help stabilise or reduce rents.** **[4 marks]**

In diagram (i), the property market will experience a fall in foreign demand due to the ban coming into effect. The progressive land use tax means that higher valued property with pay a higher tax rate which high incomes tend to purchase $S_1$ falls to $S_2$. Foreign buyers will be especially deterred from speculative behaviour $D_1$ falls to $D_2$ and fewer properties left empty. This is especially effective in cities such as Auckland, Napier etc.

More properties will now be available in the rental market, especially with more apartments rather than houses. The supply curve will increase $S_1$ to $S_2$ in diagram (ii) and rents may well stabilize and even fall if more social housing is built.

**(e)** **Using an appropriate diagram, explain how changes in the labour force participation rates can affect the macro economy of New Zealand. (Table 1)** **[4 marks]**

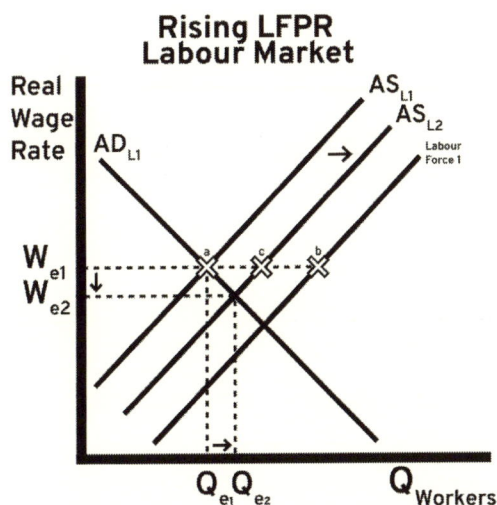

**Rising LFPR Labour Market**

⬚ Labour Force Participation Rate (LFPR) is the part of the working population (10 - 65) currently employed or seeking jobs.

⬚ In New Zealand LFPR has been rising from 67.5 % to 71 % of the labour force. Equilibrium unemployment falls from (ab) to (ac). of wage rate remain at $We_1$.

⬚ If the real wage rates fall (as New Zealand history shows) then more workers are employed $Qe_1$ to $Qe_2$.

⬚ Higher LFPR and jobs can raise the real GDP for New Zealand. However wage rates can remain stagnant as employers have a greater pool of labour to choose from

**(f)** **Using demand and supply diagrams to explain why prices of agriculture output such as avocados are likely to fluctuate much more than the prices of manufactured goods such as cars.**

**[4 marks]**

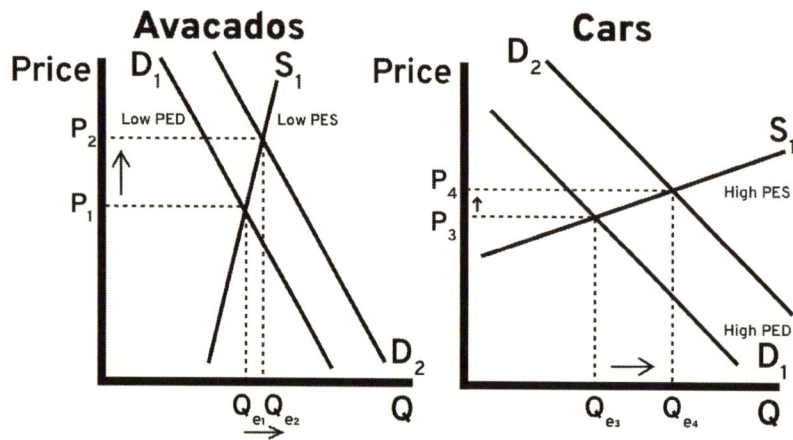

- Define PED, PES
- PED for avocados tends to be lower than cars as avocados take up a very small % of income relative to cars.
- PES for avocados is also much lower than cars as the planting, growing, harvesting cycle is much longer than it is for producing additional cars.
- Global agriculture functions in a more competitive market (lots more buyers and sellers of avocados than cars) with less pricing power for any new farmer than any single car producer.
- This means small rises in demand for avocados $D_1$ to $D_2$ or cars $D_3$ to $D_4$ leads to only small changes in output $Qe_1$ too $Qe_2$ in avocados. But much larger rises in output $Qe_3$ to $Qe_4$. Prices of avocados are going to rise by much higher percentages $Pe_1$ to $Pe_2$ than for cars $Pe_2$ to $Pe_4$.

**(g)** **Using the information in the text / data and your knowledge of economics, discuss the possible policies that New Zealand may have implemented which help to explain the significant fall in GNI - HDI ranking for New Zealand when compared to Australia and Sweden.** **[15 marks]**

- Define GNI and HDI
- Over global data we see generally speak up higher HDI and higher GNI.
- Explain the meaning of GNI - HDI
- New Zealand is much lower in GNI ranking than its HDI ranking. This implies that New Zealand is moving towards a higher human development group. At value 30 (GNI - HDI) they have lower inequality and a lower percent of population which is poor and near poor.
- However from 2011 to 2016 the positive differences in values have fallen significantly from 30 to 20. This means there is more inequality and a higher percentage of poor or near poor families, Australia has improved whereas Sweden more or less the same.
- During this 2011 to 2016 the New Zealand government had focused and favoured Neo-Liberalist policies of greater reliance on free market principles. Allowing liberalisation means New Zealand's housing market is now vulnerable to global demand and foreign exchange rates than reflecting local conditions. Owners of assets gain at the expense of the young asset less class.
- LFPR have risen but real wages are stagnant, social housing policies have been neglected in favour of speculative profit and non- wealth creating outcomes as shown in Text 2 and Table 1.
- Table 2 Implies New Zealand income, education and health indicators have worsened more in comparison to the others. The young have been left to their own devices to cope with the housing crisis.

A reverse of policies may be underway given the democratic structure of New Zealand and the appointment of a new government.

# 7.    Switzerland

*Study the texts and data below and answer the questions that follow.*

## Text 1- Overview of Swiss Economy

Over the years, Switzerland has consistently achieved nearly all of its macroeconomic objectives bar one, economic growth. Even with very low rates of unemployment, inflation as measured by the consumer price index (CPI), has been very tame registering in the range of -1.3% to 0.8 in the last 5 years. The ***current account*** balance has been positive in all its components for many years, even though the country's currency has appreciated against all major currencies.  The current account balance is roughly 10% of GDP.  It is in the ***asset market*** and the labour market where distortions have emerged.

 According to the latest assessment from the Organisation for Economic Co-operation and Development (OECD), the Swiss economy is addicted to low-interest rates causing a doubling of house prices since the 2008 financial crisis. This means an annual asset price inflation of 7% in housing. This is distortionary in an economy, where economic growth has been roughly 1%. Wage growth has been even lower on average.

Switzerland should wean itself off cheap mortgages and improve labour productivity to stay "best in class", OECD chief economist Catherine Mann told reporters as the report was unveiled in Bern on Tuesday.

The OECD advises Switzerland to open its labour market and allow free cross-border movement of labour. This move will raise productivity and lower labour costs for firms to help them remain globally competitive.

The property market problem has been flagged several times in recent years by the OECD. However the Swiss National Bank maintained its very loose stance, since 2008, to keep the Swiss Franc from appreciating. The trade-off for the policy has been household mortgage debt has risen to 120% of GDP, the second highest in the OECD countries.

**Text 2- Switzerland's richest food producer, Nestle receives $95m dollars in export subsidies.**

The Swiss parliament recently voted to continue with the 1974 Chocolate law to compensate food exporters such as Nestle are urged to buy more expensive domestically produced milk and cereals rather than cheaper foreign imports. A compensation of $95m is well within the WTO agreed limit of $155m. Although this parliamentary decision is a victory for the powerful food and farming lobbying groups, it is unlikely to be sustainable in the long-run when the WTO rules change to promote free trade in the next round of talks.

**Text 3-Cocoa farming and chocolate profits.**

Small farms in West Africa supply 70% of the world's cocoa. Over the last four decades, their share of profits from chocolate has diminished from 16% to just 3%. One of the chief reasons for this fall is that the farmers have not organized themselves into a single bargaining force whereas the buyers of cocoa are much more to act as a cohesive force like a cartel.

**Text 4 -Whenever, wherever and however.**

Swiss company Nestle has expanded its modes of selling one of its most profit making products, Nespresso coffee capsules. With patents expiring over its Nespresso capsule and machine system and new players entering the market which has seen a slowdown in growth, Nestle is now selling its products through supermarkets and other third party sellers instead of the original method which limited capsule sales to only Nestle's own boutiques, online website and telephone orders.  The company still retains control over the pricing strategy implemented by the new third party sellers.

## Table 1- Nominal and real wage growth in Switzerland

| Year | Annual nominal growth rate in wages | CPI |
|---|---|---|
| 2011 | 0.8 | 0.7 |
| 2012 | 1.0 | 0.2 |
| 2013 | 0.8 | -0.7 |
| 2014 | 0.7 | -0.2 |
| 2015 | 0.8 | 0.0 |
| 2017 | 0.7 | -0.4 |
| 2018 | 0.4 | 0.5 |
| 2019 | 0.3 | 0.3 |

**Table 2- Development data for Switzerland**

## The World's Worst Electronic Waste Offenders
The biggest per-capita e-waste generators in 2014 (lbs per capita)

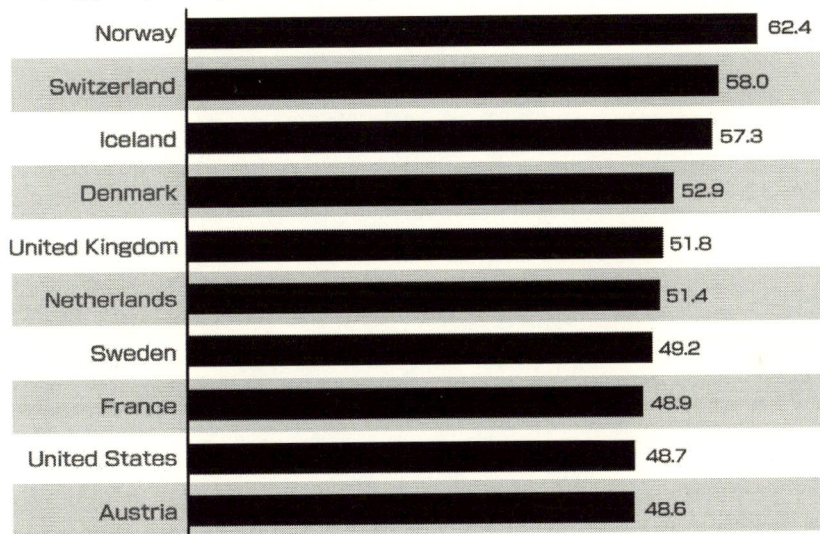

| Country | lbs per capita |
|---|---|
| Norway | 62.4 |
| Switzerland | 58.0 |
| Iceland | 57.3 |
| Denmark | 52.9 |
| United Kingdom | 51.8 |
| Netherlands | 51.4 |
| Sweden | 49.2 |
| France | 48.9 |
| United States | 48.7 |
| Austria | 48.6 |

© ① ⊜
@StatistaCharts  Source: UNU

## QUESTIONS

(a)  (i) Define the term _current account_ indicated in bold. (Text 1 - paragraph 1)  **[2 marks]**

(ii) Define the term _asset market_ indicated in bold. (Text 1 - paragraph 1)  **[2 marks]** (b)s     (i)  Draw a demand-supply diagram for the rental market to explain the effects on rents from using house  prices and mortgages. (Text 4 – paragraph 2)                                                    [3 marks]

(b)h     (i) Draw a labour market diagram to explain the possible effect on new wage rate and employment from as rising inflow of cross border workers in Switzerland.  (Text 1 – paragraph 3)                                                    [3 marks]

        (ii) Using information in Table 1, Calculate which year offers the highest rate annual wage growth for workers.                                                    [2 marks]

(c)        Using information in Table 1, explain which groups are likely to benefit from a period of deflation.                                                    [4 marks]

(d)        Using a demand and supply diagram, explain how cocoa farmers can organize themselves to achieve a highest price for their produce. (Text 3)                                                    [4 marks]

(d) h.  With reference Text 4, use a cost and revenue diagram to show the effects on profits of the expiration of patents for Nestle and comment briefly on its new strategy.                                                    [4 marks]

(e)        Using a market failure diagram, explain why electronic waste is an example of a negative externality of consumption.                                                    [4 marks]

(f)     Using an exchange rate diagram, explain how a persistent positive current account balance can lead to an appreciating Swiss Finance against all major currencies. (Text 1 – paragraph 1)

[4 marks]

(g)     Using information in table 2 and your knowledge of economics, evaluate the policies Switzerland can take to reduce Electronic waste and other European countries to achieve sustainable formula.                                                                                     [15 marks]

## ANSWERS:                    5. Switzerland

**(a)    (i)  Define the term _current account_ indicated in bold. (Text 1 - paragraph 1)        [2 marks]**

This is a financial record of transactions between one country and the rest of the world. The components are goods, services, refunds to factors of production and transfers payment such as international aid.

**(ii) Define the term _asset market_ indicated in bold. (Text 1 - paragraph 1)        [2 marks]**

This can be defined as buyers and sellers coming together to negotiate a price for ownership of property both physical and intellectual. Examples are houses factories, stocks, and bonds etc. These assets are normally capable of generating a stream of revenues.

**(b)s    (i)  Draw a demand-supply diagram for the rental market to explain the effects on rents from using house  prices and mortgages. (Text 4 – paragraph 2)        [3 marks]**

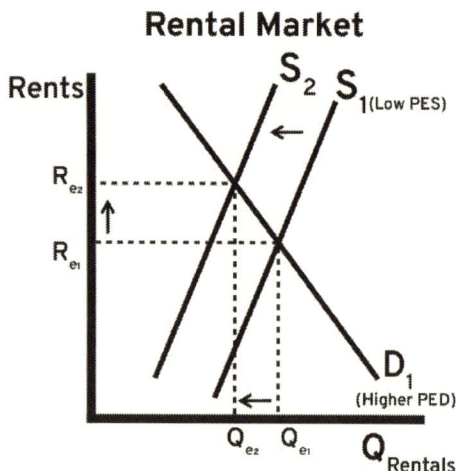

Higher house prices and mortgages (repayments of loans from banks) mean a rise in the cost of production for investors who wish to rent out properties. These higher costs mean profit margins or rates of returns to renting fall. Some landlords may withdraw from the rental market. $S_1$ falls to $S_2$.  A shortage of apartments at the original rental price, $Re_1$ appears.  The market subsequently clears at rent $Re_2$ with fewer rental properties on the market. $Qe_1$ falls to $Qe_2$

**(b)h      (i) Draw a labour market diagram to explain the possible effect on new wage rate and employment from as rising inflow of cross border workers in Switzerland.  (Text 1 – paragraph 3)**

**[3 marks]**

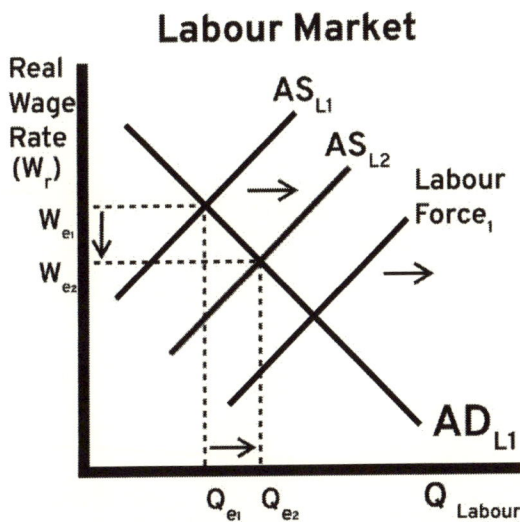

With open borders and higher $We_1$ offered in Switzerland compared to bordering countries of France, Germany, Austria and Italy, the more the potential labour force 1 expands. In addition the overall supply of labour rises $AS_{L1}$ to $AS_{L2}$ looking for full time or part time work. Real wages fall because of surplus workers at wage rate $We_1$. The labour market clears at $We_2$ and $Qe_2$ equilibrium. (Fact: working population of Swiss Cities has expanded faster than real wage rates)

**(b)       (ii) Using information in Table 1, Calculate which year offers the highest rate annual wage growth for workers.**

**[2 marks]**

Real annual wage growth = Nominal growth rate of wages  −  inflation

Year 2013 offers highest Real wage growth  =  0.8 - ( - 0.7 )   = **+ 1.5 % Real wage growth**

73

(c)     Using information in Table 1, explain which groups are likely to benefit from a period of deflation.                                                          [4 marks]

Price deflation is given by negative value for CPI.

Year 2013 = - 0.7,     Year 2014 = - 0.2,     Year 2017 = - 0.4

Consumers benefit from lower prices overall. Pensioners, unemployed and those living on fixed incomes.

(d)     Using a demand and supply diagram, explain how cocoa farmers can organize themselves to achieve a highest price for their produce. (Text 3)                                    [4 marks]

## Cocoa Market

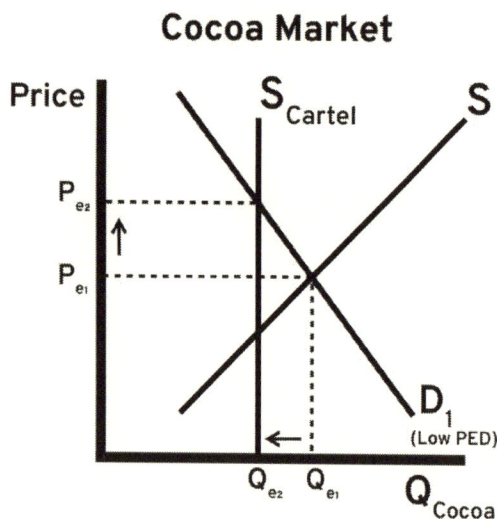

Since Cocoa is a crucial ingredient in making chocolate and the overall price elasticity of demand for cocoa is low, farmers with the help of the government should be able to form a cartel. Here they can collude and act as a single supplier. $S_1$ changes to $S_2$. At the new equilibrium price less is supplied and prices are higher.  This strategy requires farmers agreeing to a set quota and cocoa being less perishable. Free market justifies a cartel especially if buyers of cocoa behave as a monopolist.

**(d) h.  With reference Text 4, use a cost and revenue diagram to show the effects on profits of the expiration of patents for Nestle and comment briefly on its new strategy.**          **[4 marks]**

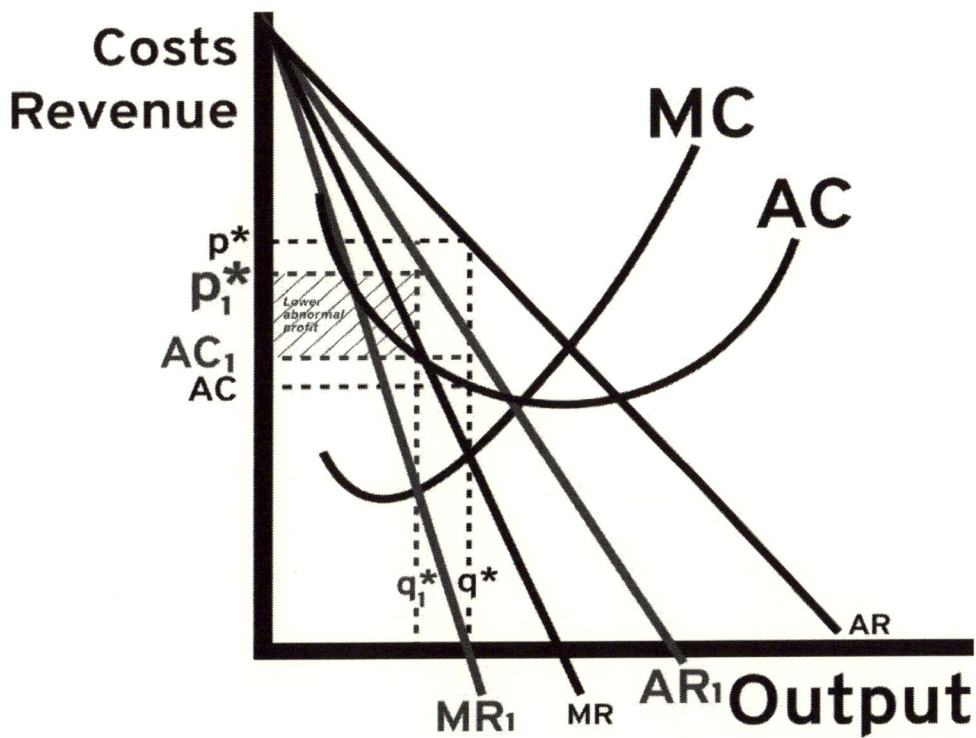

Nestlé will experience a fall in profits as new players means the demand for Nespresso capsules and machines fall.  A change in selling strategy of expanding the number of places where consumers can buy their products is a way of expanding its demand.  (AR and MR) can both shift right and profit margins are prevented from falling.  The strategy seems reasonable and similar to Dell laptops and Apple products.

**(e)** **Using a market failure diagram, explain why electronic waste is an example of a negative externality of consumption.** **[4 marks]**

## Laptop Computers

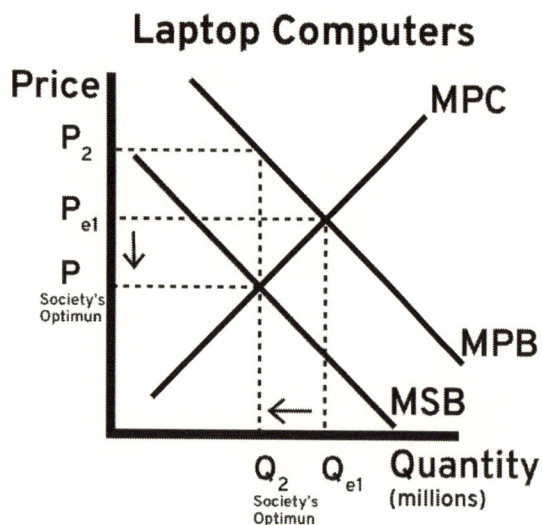

The lack of a repairing culture together with a pricing structure Pe1, means that high labour cost countries like Switzerland develop a throw away culture. Free market here over produces e-waste relative to society's optimum resulting in partial market failure. A recycling tax could be introduced. Price rises to $P_2$. Government could bring in incentives to restore a repairing culture.

Data Response-Paper 2

**(f)    Using an exchange rate diagram, explain how a persistent positive current account balance can lead to an appreciating Swiss Finance against all major currencies. (Text 1 – paragraph 1)**

**[4 marks]**

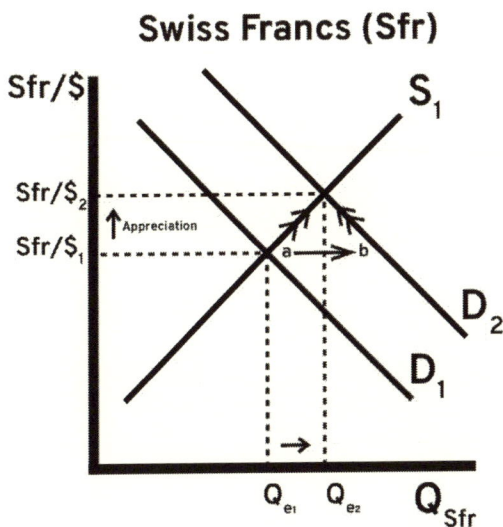

**Swiss Francs (Sfr)**

A persistent current account surplus means that at the current exchange rate $Sfr_1$ / $. The world is buying more from Switzerland than Switzerland is buying from the rest of the world. This means the demand for $Sfr$ is essentially greater than Swiss demand for the $. Overtime $D_1$ rises to $D_2$ and now a new equilibrium is formed with an appreciated $Sfr_2$ against the $.

An appreciating $Sfr$ can create several problems. Firstly the Swiss export sector can become price uncompetitive globally. This can be seen in the tourism sector for example. Skiers to the Alps choose France and Italy instead of Switzerland. Job losses can occur in this sector. Finally Switzerland is forced to improve its productivity just to counteract the appreciating currency. Raising productivity is a slow long term arduous process.

77

**(g)      Using information in table 2 and your knowledge of economics, evaluate the policies Switzerland can take to reduce Electronic waste and other European countries to achieve sustainable growth.                                                                                    [15 marks]**

- ⬚  Define sustainable growth – This is the type of growth whereby future generations have as much access to resources as the current generation.
- ⬚  Table 2 points to European countries as the worst polluters. However this waste is due to consumption in Europe when production of electronics is most likely to be based in Asia including China.
- ⬚  Individual countries can implement policies such as a recycling tax or promote a repairing culture through education and incentives to businesses which focus on repairs. The merits of these initiatives may help reduce e – waste at the margin only. European Governments acting alone may face the worth of voters, hobbyists and arbitrage (consumers buy e- products from neighbouring cheaper countries).  Deciding on the size of e-waste recycling tax may be debatable and not an exact science.
- ⬚  A more collective Europe wide EU approach may be more effective. EU wide, at least maintains a level field for competition. Lobbyists are less powerful when faced with the EU. The EU can influence the polluting products at the design stage. A certain degree of sovereignty loss may have to be accepted by each individual country.

To conclude e-waste creates negative externalities of consumption as it uses up finite resources at an accelerating rate creating problems for future generations. A gamut of policies both within each nation as well as across nations can be effective in reducing waste.

## 8.     United States of America

*Study the texts and data below and answer the questions that follow.*

**Text 1- Overview of United States of America**

Today, more than a decade after the Great Financial Crisis and the subsequent severe recession, the US economy's output of goods and services is growing at an annualised rate of 4.2%. The US GDP per person measured at purchasing power parity stands at 48% above the European Union (EU) average. This growth is expected to continue and outpace the EU further in the coming few years.

The US dollar being the world's reserve currency is strengthening against most other currencies and this is accentuated by the slow rise in US interest rates. Foreign holders of US debt will find it more difficult to service their dollar loans. Producers of ***soft and hard commodities*** will face difficulties in selling their output that are priced in dollars. Many large businesses in emerging economies such as Argentina, Turkey, South Africa, Brazil and India have borrowed in dollars to take advantage of low interest rates may well find rising US rates acting like a tightening noose round the neck. There is a danger of a new currency crisis developing.

On the labour front, the US job growth has been strong, near full employment, while wage growth has been unexpectedly weak. The ***Federal Reserve*** has been mystified and is debating on how quickly to tighten the monetary policy as it forecasts inflation to rise above 2%. Productivity measured in terms of per capita or per hour has risen by an average of only 0.5% over the last decade. Policy makers are warning that wage growth in the near future may not rise unless the US introduces policies to reverse the decline in productivity.

The behaviour of the US consumer tells another story. Retail sales rising at 6.4% annually, US consumer comfort index and sales of new homes have steadily risen every year since 2010. The savings rate in the US continues to trail well behind the EU and other OECD countries, showing no signs of reversing.

2019 saw further rises in the trade gap. The US trade deficit reached $600bn, highest since 2008. The US ran a deficit of $844bn in goods. The deficit in the trading of goods alone with China stood at $390bn while hitting a new high of $75bn with Mexico. The Trump administration sees this as a sign of weakness which needs to be addressed through trade sanctions on China and a renegotiation of the North American Free Trade Association, NAFTA. Other economists simply view this as a sign of a growing US economy where imports fill the gap between consumption and domestic production.

### Text 2 Business Cycle

Economists pay attention to data points which help identify where in the business cycle the economy is currently in. The data comes from gathering and analysing leading, lagging and coincident indicators. For the US, economists consider (1) GDP, (2) consumer price index, (3) personal income, (4) average weekly initial unemployment claims, (5) payroll employment, (6) the ISM index, (7) the average prime rate charged by banks, (8) the Consumer Sentiment Index from the University of Michigan, (9) the duration of unemployment, (10) industrial production, (11) interest charged by banks, (12) building permits. These indicators, economists believe, help policy makers make judgments not only on the current state of the economy but also help to predict the changes expected in the performance of the US economy in the next few quarters.

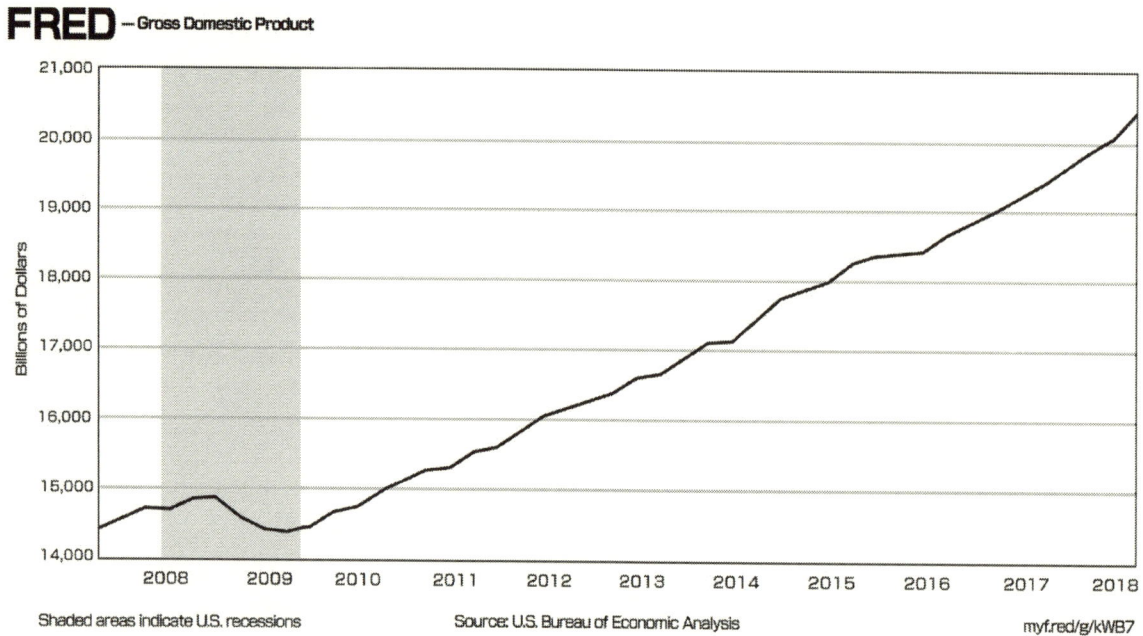

**FRED** — Gross Domestic Product

Shaded areas indicate U.S. recessions    Source: U.S. Bureau of Economic Analysis    myf.red/g/kWB7

The above picture shows the US business cycle above from 2007 to 2018 the last decade or so. The figures are in nominal terms. The expansion in GDP after the second quarter of 2009 seems continuous and unusual.

## Text 3 The Market for buying Lemons

The second-hand or used car market very often suffers from the problem of asymmetrical information. This prevents the second- hand car market, especially the auction market, from working efficiently in allocation. Here is a summary from one customer's experience of buying a used car in an auction.

``*I went to a car auction, and when I arrived everyone was bidding on a pristine-looking Ford Focus. I figured the car looked clean, and people were raising their bids, so it had to be good. Long story short, I won the auction. After completing the paperwork and getting the title and keys I had the car towed home. But when I got in and turned the key, it wouldn't start. I opened the hood to see what I could find, and the problem was instantly clear. There was nothing under the hood – no engine, no transmission, no radiator and no battery. I contacted the auction, who explained that the car was sold as-is.*'

## Table 1A

Figure 1

### As union membership declines, the share of income going to the middle class shrinks

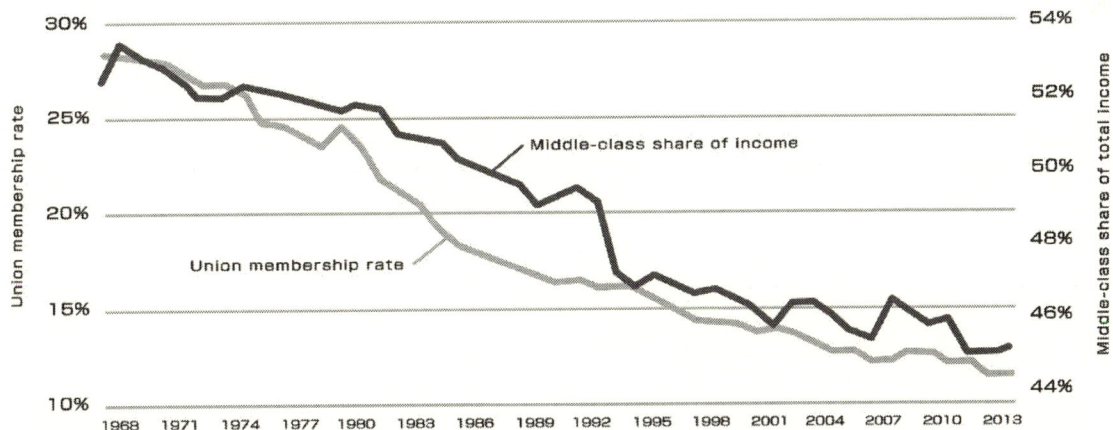

Source: Center for American Progress Action Fund analysis based on union membership rates from updated Barry T. Hirsch, David A. Macpherson, and Wayne G. Vroman. "Estimates of Union Density by State." Monthly Labor Review 124 (7) (2001):51-55, available at http://unionstats.gsu.edu/ MonthlyLaborReviewArticle.htm. Middle-class share of total income is from Bureau of the Census. Table h-2. Share of Aggregate Income Recieved by Each Fifth and Top 5 Percent of Households (2013), availabe at http://www.census.gov/hhes/www/income/data/historical/household.

**Table 1B**

## As Union Representation Fell, the Share of Income Going to the Top 10 Percent Rose, 1917 - 2012

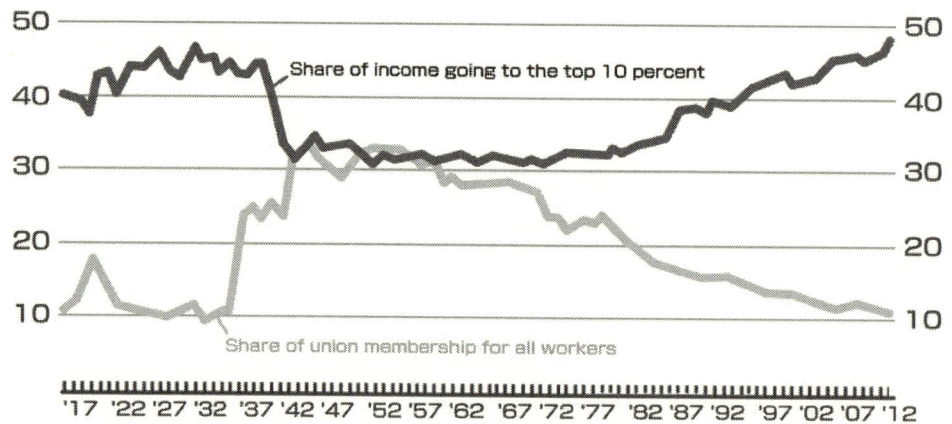

Share of income going to the top 10 percent

Share of union membership for all workers

'17 '22 '27 '32 '37 '42 '47 '52 '57 '62 '67 '72 '77 '82 '87 '92 '97 '02 '07 '12

Source: Colin Gordon's analysis of the Census Bureau, Historical of the United States, and World Incomes Database in Tableau

GradingStates.Org

Table 2:  Better Life Index 2017. (OECD 2017)

| Country | Household net disposable income $ | Quality of support network (% happy) | Feeling safe walking alone at night (%) | Employees working very long hours (%) | Time devoted to leisure (hours per week) | Average Life Satisfaction (0 to 10) |
|---|---|---|---|---|---|---|
| USA | 44 049 | 90 | 74.1 | 11.45 | 14.92 | 6.9 |
| Germany | 33 672 | 92 | 75.9 | 4.6 | 15.55 | 7.0 |

**QUESTIONS**

(a)     (i)  Define the term _soft and hard commodities_ indicated in bold. (Text 1 – paragraph 2)
                                                                                                                        [2 marks]

        (ii) State 2 functions of the _Federal Reserve_. (Text 1 – paragraph 3)          [2 marks]

(b)     (i)  Calculate the level of trade surplus in service in 2019. (Text 1 – paragraph 5)      [3 marks]

        (ii) Using an exchange rate diagram for the Indian Rupee, explain how a rise in the US interest rates affects the value of the Rupee against the US $.                                     [2 marks]

(c)      Using a trade / business cycle diagram and the various leading and losing indicators above describe the likely state of the US economy in the first and second quarter of 2009. (Text 2)   [4 marks]

(d)      Using a demand and supply diagram, explain why asymmetric information leads to allocative inefficiency in the market for cars. (Text 3)                                                        [4 marks]

(e)      Using a Lorenz curve and Gini coefficient explain the changes that have occurred in label of inequalities in income in the US. (Table 1A and 1B)                                          [4 marks]

(f)      Using a labour market diagram, explain what effect do falling trade union memberships have on real wage rates.                                                                          [4  marks]

(g)      Using information from the text / data and your knowledge of economics, evaluation the view that Germans have a higher standard of living than Americans.                              [15 marks]

**ANSWERS:**                    **8. United States of America**

**(a)**      **(i) Define the term _soft and hard commodities_ indicated in bold. (Text 1 – paragraph 2)**
                                                                        **[2 marks]**

Soft commodities are raw materials or output at the first stage of production, such as coffee, corn, cotton and cocoa. They are then refined or produced to be used in the next stage to help make final products. Hard commodities are the same as above but applied to metals such as platinum, palladium iron ore.

**(ii) State 2 functions of the _Federal Reserve_. (Text 1 – paragraph 3)**          **[2 marks]**

The Federal Reserve is the Central Bank of the United States. Its function is to set the monetary policy ( $i$ % , credit conditions) in order to help the US achieve its macroeconomic targets of lower inflation, steady economic growth and low unemployment. Its second function is to exercise oversight over the stability of the banking system and act as a lender of last resort to commercial banks.

**(b)**      **(i) Calculate the level of trade surplus in service in 2019. (Text 1 – paragraph 5)**        **[3 marks]**

According to the passage

$$\text{Balance of Trade in goods and services} = \text{B / Trade in goods} + \text{B / Trade in service}$$

$$-600 \text{ Bn} = -844 \text{ Bn} + \text{B / Trade in service}$$

$$\text{B / Trade in services} = -600 + 844$$

$$= \underline{+ \$ 244 \text{ Bn surplus}}$$

**(ii) Using an exchange rate diagram for the Indian Rupee, explain how a rise in the US interest rates affects the value of the Rupee against the US $.** [2 marks]

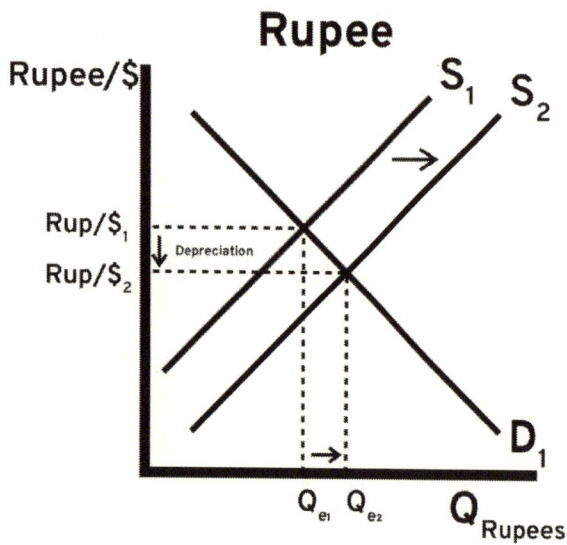

When US interest rates rise, products in India earning in Rupees find their costs of production rising. They subsequently sell more Rupees on the foreign exchange (FX) markets, buy more US $ to repay their debts. The supply of Rupees on FX markets rise and the rupee depreciates against the US $.

(c)     Using a trade / business cycle diagram and the various leading and losing indicators above describe the likely state of the US economy in the first and second quarter of 2009. (Text 2)   [4 marks]

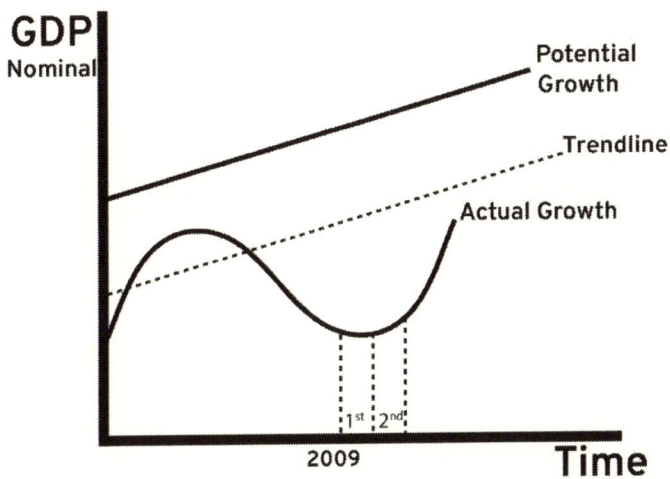

The beginning of 2009 shows the US economy in a recession. The logging indicators CPI, unemployment claims in first quarter are negative or unchanged or even worsening. Leading indicators showing plans and sentiments of business and consumers could be turning positive. Consumer sentiment, Ism index and building permits may show a turnaround indicating that the 2nd quarter of 2009 may show 'green shoots' of recovery. Co-incident indicators show the current state of the US economy. Here GDP, industrial production, personal income are all at depressed levels.

**(d) Using a demand and supply diagram, explain why asymmetric information leads to allocative inefficiency in the market for cars. (Text 3)** [4 marks]

## Used Cars

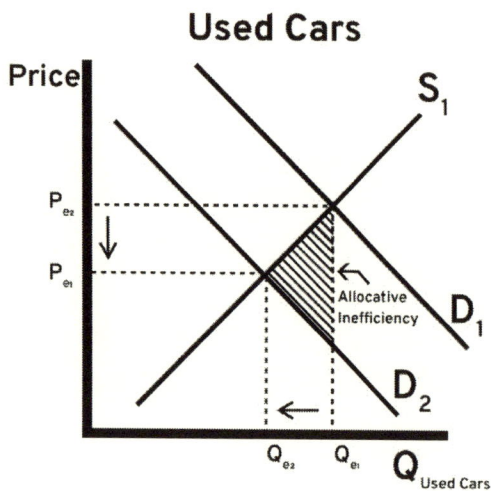

Asymmetrical information in used car market usually means the seller has more information about the car to be sold then the buyer, especially in auction system. If both parties had equal information then according to the text, $D_1$ would be lower at $D_2$. The bought cars would only have fetched a scrap heap price of $Pe_2$ and fewer sold. The shaded area represents the value of allocative inefficiency.

**(e)** **Using a Lorenz curve and Gini coefficient changes that have occurred in label of inequalities in income in the US. (Table 1)** **[4 marks]**

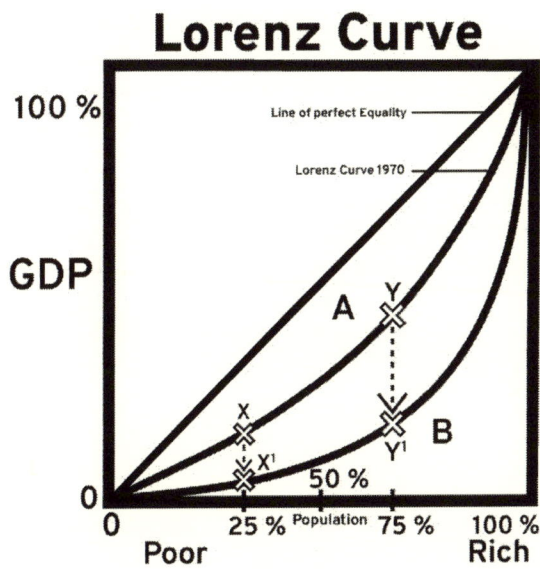

## Lorenz Curve

100 %

Line of perfect Equality

Lorenz Curve 1970

GDP

A  Y

X

X'

Y'  B

50 %

0

0    25 % Population 75 %    100 %
Poor                          Rich

If we assume the US middle class to mean households between the first and third quartiles then Lorenz Curve 1 has moved to Lorenz Curve 2 over time. Point X and Y shift to X ' and Y ' respectively.

Gini Coefficient = (area A)/(area (A+B) )

Perfect equality value = 0

Perfect inequality value = 1

Area A has increased and area B decreased. This will raise the Gini coefficient towards 1.

**(f)** **Using a labour market diagram, explain what effect do falling trade union memberships have on real wage rates.** [4 marks]

## Labour Market US

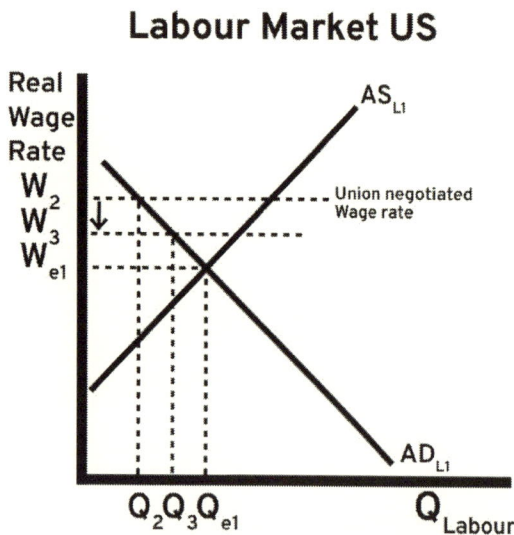

Trade union workers can use their collective bargaining power against employers to help achieve wages higher than $We_1$, $W_2$ may be the negotiated wage rate. At this higher than equilibrium wage rate ($W_1 > We_2$) employers hire fewer workers ($Q_2 < Qe_1$).

Reducing the bargaining power of workers means $W_2$ falls towards $W_3$. Real wage rate falls. Some firms may add additional workers $Q_2$ to $Q_2$. The danger is that over a longer period of time, suppression of wages results in higher levels of inequalities and lower aggregate demand.

**(g)** **Using information from the text / data and your knowledge of economics, evaluation the view that Germans have a higher standard of living than Americans.** [15 marks]

Since Americans earn 30 % more it can be clearly argued that they can buy many more foods and services than the Germans which can be used to raise their standards of living. If the figures are translated into purchasing power parity (PPP) terms, the difference would be even larger in favour of Americans.

- Table 2, Better life Index, points out that the higher incomes earned by US households may be the result of longer working hours. More leisure time has been sacrificed by the Americans. Safety and weaker quality of network support may also be the price of earning more. The quality of life may have been lowered for the Americans.
- The statistics themselves can be questionable :
- Averages are a poor measure of distribution. A median figure may be more telling.
- The figures are in US $. The changes in the exchange rate may cause distortions.
- The stress levels at work, commuting time, the level of public services provided, the debt levels, the level of job security, the length of annual holidays are all factors which here to be considered before an accurate judgment on the comparison of standards of living can be made.

## 9.    Greece

*Study the texts and data below and answer the questions that follow.*

### TEXT 1

### Greece after 3 financial aid bailout packages finally, comes out of intensive care.

Officials from the Troika made up of the ***International Monetary Fund*** (IMF), the European Union (EU) and the European Central Bank (ECB) have been allowed to run Greece's economy for the past eight years in return for providing Greece with emergency financial aid.

As part of the requirement of staying in the Eurozone, Greece had to follow tough budget rules whereby the government had to slash its deficit from 13% of GDP to 5.5% of GDP straightaway in 2010. This move felt even more painful in a rapidly shrinking economy which saw its size diminished by a third from peak to trough. Consequently two further financial rescue plans were required.

One theory was that to attract foreign investment and lenders Greece was required to show fiscal prudence and follow free market based structural adjustment macroeconomic policies. This will help Greece recover and improve its macroeconomic indicators. A policy of expansionary fiscal contraction (EFC) was followed whereby Greece would cut back in order to achieve growth. These cuts would carry on until the big banks of Europe were paid the money owed. Most of the financial package given by the Troika was recycled back out of the country to the large banks while the Greece's citizens were forced to survive under austerity policies.

The alternative view these structural adjustment prescribed policies will lead Greece to an extended period of demand deflation as the economy moves into lower levels of equilibrium, making it ever harder to pay off debts held by EU banks. Here debt write-off is necessary or exiting the Eurozone and returning to the Drachma currency is a precondition to long term stabilisation and growth.

Believers of EFC used the notion of **_crowding out_** to justify the reduction in the size of the public sector through layoffs, wage cuts and serious reductions in pensions, education budgets and health care. Private sector was supposed to make use of the resources released productively and help revive the economy through private sector investment financed by low interest rates and job creation.

Today after more than ten years since the financial crisis Greece is showing some signs of growth. EFC followers everywhere automatically claim that their policies were justified. The Greek economy is still more than 25% smaller in size of output, unemployment; especially among the youth is the highest in Europe even after a significant number of Greeks have left. Greek banks are still insolvent and government cut-backs have left numerous communities without any social care, reliant on food banks and the old struggle on 300 euros per month pensions. The remaining debt has now been restructured to be paid off by 2060 at the earliest.

If the Troika insist on punishing the debtors in Europe for foolishly over borrowing then in all fairness it should be doing the same to European creditors for foolishly over lending to feed their greed.

## Text 2  Paying your debts.

With GDP of only $220bn, government debt in 2018 stands at $396bn while private sector debt is $275bn. To help reduce these debts, the Troika (IMF, EU. ECB) in 2018, forced the government to introduce a privatization program. Last year 14 airports were bought and controlled by the German airport operator, Fraport, for $1.39bn. Then Germany's Deutsche telecom increased its ownership from 40% to 45% for $329m. Italy's Ferrovie dello Stato has bought up Greece's TrainOSE. In 2016 China's Cosco bought a majority stake in one of Europe's largest ports in Piraeus for $312m. The state's water company is being prepared for sale next year. In the past, soon after the privatization of the state's electricity, consumers experienced steep increases in prices and power taxes. Today, Greeks pay the highest prices for electricity in Europe.

## Text 3  Market for taxis in Greece

In 1964 the Greek government first regulated the taxi industry by issuing 6200 taxi licenses. With growing transportation and tourist demand over time the number of new licenses issued grew. However, after 2003 until today no new licenses have been released. This action was intended to support the regulatory framework requested by the taxi drivers union. The imposed shortage of new licenses after 2003 meant the licenses changed hands between taxi drivers for around 200,000 euros each.

The Greek debt crisis has forced the government to deregulate many professions such as lawyers, accountants, civil engineers, pharmacists and so many others including taxi drivers. One method is to allow firms such as Uber and TaxiBeat to introduce their ride hailing apps. TaxiBeat already has 8000 drivers using its apps serving a million rides. An online petition has collected 30,000 signatures in favour of full deregulation which will bring prices down and give more choice through greater competition. The 50,000 strong Greek Union of taxi drivers is unhappy as their head, Thymios Lyberopoulos, said 'innovation needs to adjust to each country's laws. You can't have a group of professional being normally taxed…..and a few others not paying at all for the same job, because there is no specific framework. The government's full deregulation is undermining free market by breaking contracts and violating property rights'

The government is now addressing the concerns of the taxi drivers and the customers by moving away from full deregulation to one which allows more licenses and a ceiling of charges. In addition the ride hailing companies will be required to sign three-year contracts with licensed taxi drivers which essentially turn TaxiBeat into a proper provider instead of an intermediary. The operators will have to pay for licenses and be subject to a different tax system.

## Table 1a, b, c - Economic data on taxes in Greece,

1a.   Value added tax (VAT) receipts as a % of GDP for Greece & EU28 (Eurozone average).

|  | 2010 | 2011 | 2012 | 2013 | 2014 | 2015 | 2016 | 2017 | 2018 |
|---|---|---|---|---|---|---|---|---|---|
| Greece | 7.1 | 7.3 | 7.2 | 7.0 | 7.1 | 7.3 | 8.2 | 8.6 | 8.5 |

| EU28 | 6.8 | 6.9 | 6.9 | 6.9 | 6.9 | 7.0 | 7.0 | 7.0 | 7.0 |
|---|---|---|---|---|---|---|---|---|---|

1b.  Current tax on income/wealth as % of GDP for Greece & EU28 (Eurozone average).

|  | 2010 | 2011 | 2012 | 2013 | 2014 | 2015 | 2016 | 2017 | 2018 |
|---|---|---|---|---|---|---|---|---|---|
| Greece | 8.3 | 9.2 | 10.8 | 10.5 | 9.7 | 9.7 | 9.7 | 10.3 | 10.5 |
| EU28 | 12.3 | 12.6 | 12.9 | 12.9 | 12.9 | 12.9 | 13.0 | 13.0 | 13.0 |

1c.  Current Outstanding debt of taxpayers in Greece (Billions of Euro)

|  | 2010 | 2011 | 2012 | 2013 | 2014 | 2015 | 2016 | 2017 | 2018 |
|---|---|---|---|---|---|---|---|---|---|
| Greece | 40 | 42 | 52 | 62 | 60 | 70 | 80 | 90 | 96 |

**Table 2- Development data for Greece**

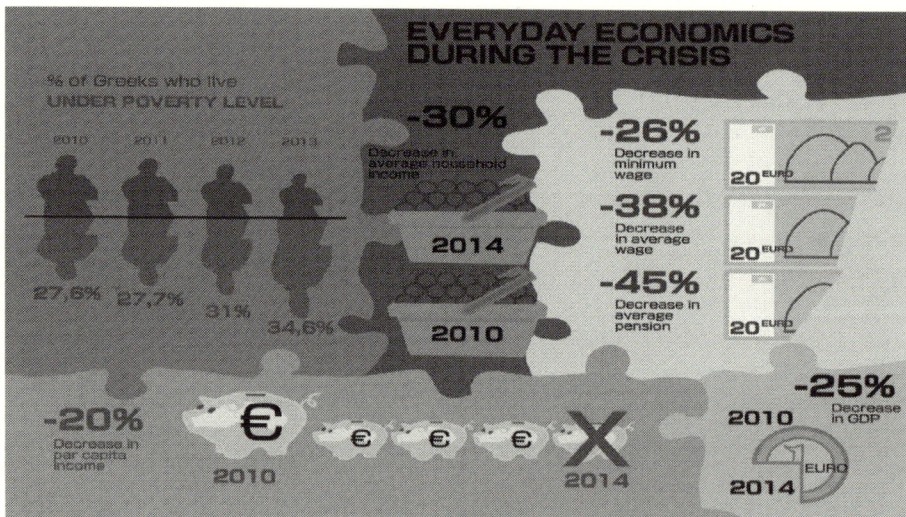

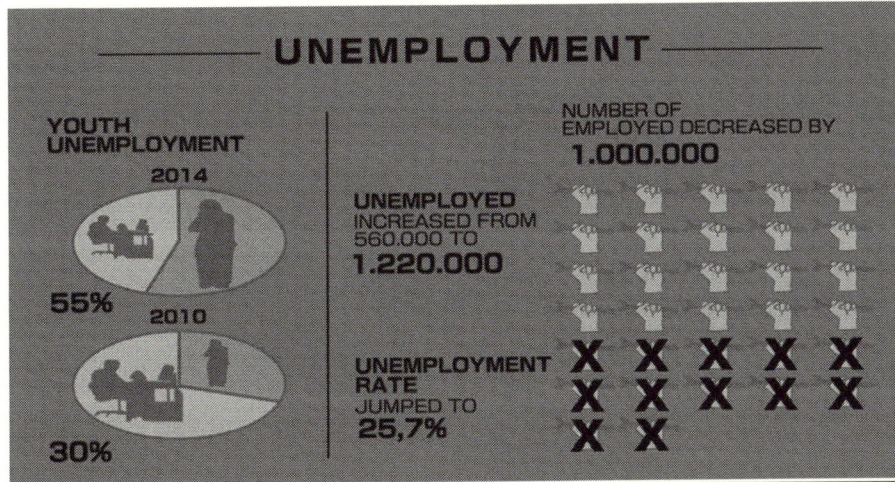

**UNEMPLOYMENT**

YOUTH UNEMPLOYMENT

2014

55%

2010

30%

NUMBER OF EMPLOYED DECREASED BY
**1.000.000**

UNEMPLOYED INCREASED FROM 560.000 TO
**1.220.000**

UNEMPLOYMENT RATE JUMPED TO
**25,7%**

## QUESTIONS

(a)      (i) List 2 functions of the _International Monetary Fund_ (IMF). (Text 1 – paragraph 1[2 marks]

(ii) Define the terms _crowding – ou_t indicated in bold. (Text 1 – paragraph 5)        [2 marks]

(b)s      (i) Using information from Text 2, calculate the value of Greece's Debt (public and private sector) to GDP  ratio.                                                      [3 marks]

(b h    (i) List 3 problems resulting from Greece's very high debt to GDP ratio.            [3 marks]

(b)      (ii) Draw a demand and supply diagram for taxi licenses to explain the effect of not introducing more taxi licenses in 2003. (Text 3 – paragraph 4)            [2 marks]

**(c)**     Using AD / AS, explain how structural adjustment policies can lead to lower level of equilibrium. (Text 1 paragraph 4)                                                                                 [4 marks]

**(d)**     Using an appropriate diagram and Table 1, explain whether Greece's tax system is more or less progressive than the EU 2018 European average.                                                         [4 marks]

**(e)**     Using AD / AS diagram and explain the possible effects of a comprehensive privatisation program on inflation, economic growth and employment levels in Greece.                     [4 marks]

**(f)**     Using a poverty cycle diagram to explain how a rise in youth unemployment can affect the economic development of Greece.                                                                                         [4 marks]

**(g)**     Using information from the texts / data and your knowledge of economics, evaluate the merits of greater foreign direct investment FDI for Greece.                                                   [15 marks]

# ANSWERS:                             9. Greece

**(a)**     **(i) List 2 functions of the _International Monetary Fund_ (IMF). (Text 1 – paragraph 1) [2 marks]**

Two functions of the IMF are: (choose 2 below)

- ▢ Surveillance IMF gathers data and assesses the economic policies of member countries as they try to achieve their macroeconomic objections.
- ▢ Financial Assistance: IMF lends countries funds in order to help them carry out free market reforms.
- ▢ Temporary financial support to members to help than correct fundamental balance of payments disequilibrium.

**(ii) Define the terms _crowding –out_ indicated in bold. (Text 1 – paragraph 5)**     **[2 marks]**

Crowding out:  This is a situation where an economy's limited resources are directed more towards the government sector at the expense of the private sector. This is particularly likely to occur when the economy is at full employment and spare capacity is low.

**(b)s     (i)  Using information from Text 2, calculate the value of Greece's Debt (public and private sector) to GDP  ratio.**     **[3 marks]**

Year 2018 Public Sector debt     =  ($396/$220) x 100 %  = 180%

Private sector debt     =  ($275/$220) x 100%  =  125%

Total Debt to GDP ratio =   180% + 125%   =  **305 %**

**(b)h     (i)  List 3 problems resulting from Greece's very high debt to GDP ratio.**     **[3 marks]**

3 possible problems for Greece.

- Rising debt service costs carry an opportunity cost and more Greece's resources are used to pay interest on debt.
- Loss of national sovereignty as IMF, EU and ECB impose severe restrictions in self-determination.  Greece has no control over its monetary policy.
- Severe cuts in public services.

**(b)     (ii)  Draw a demand and supply diagram for taxi licenses to explain the effect of not introducing more taxi licenses in 2003. (Text 3 – paragraph 4)**     **[2 marks]**

## Taxi Licenses

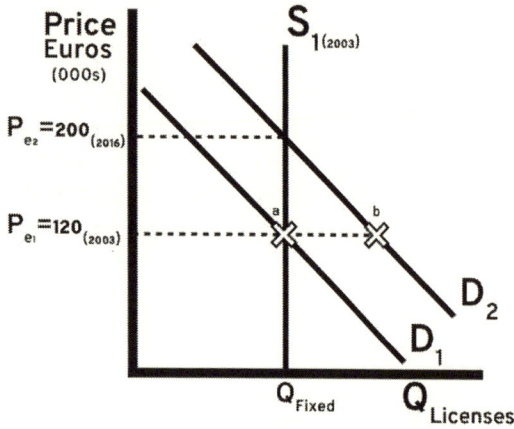

With a growing demand for taxis from tourism the demand for licenses rose (derived demand argument) $D_1$ to $D_2$. At the old price $Pe_1$ = 120000 Euro there was a shortage (ab). The taxi license market cleared at $Pe_2$ = 200000 Euro.

**(c)    Using AD / AS, explain how structural adjustment policies can lead to lower level of equilibrium. (Text 1 paragraph 4)**                                                    **[4 marks]**

### Structured Adjustment Program (SAP)
#### AD/SRAS

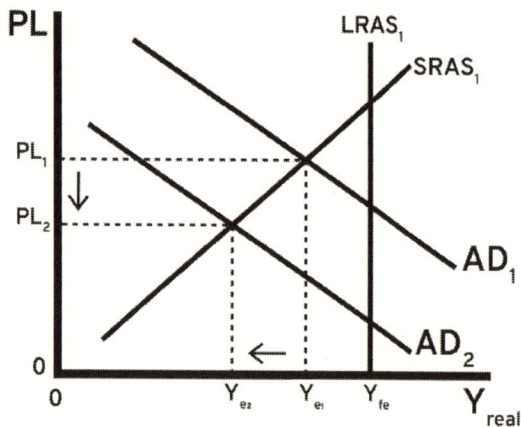

For Greece the SAP imposed by the Troika means a fall in AD. Consumption spending falls due to public sector layoffs and cuts in pensions and other transfer payments. Investment falls as credit availability is restricted. $AD_1$ falls to $AD_2$. At $PL_2$ a new lower level equilibrium is achieved where real output is lower since $Ye_1$ has fallen to $Ye_2$.

**(d)** **Using an appropriate diagram and Table 1, explain whether Greece's tax system is more or less progressive than the EU 2018 European average.** **[4 marks]**

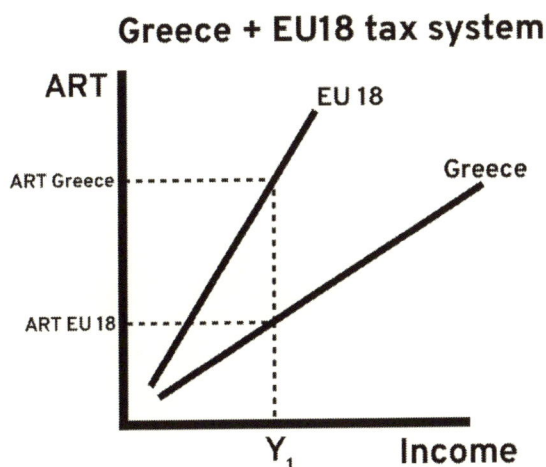

## Greece + EU18 tax system

ART

EU 18

ART Greece

Greece

ART EU 18

$Y_1$     Income

In most OECD countries income tax tends to progressive. This means that the average rate of tax (ART) rises as incomes rise. This tends to be how states raise their funding. Greece is significantly below other Eurozone countries (10.5 % instead of 13 %) in collecting these taxes.

In addition Greece collects proportionately more taxes from VAT than EU 18. Since VAT is an indirect tax and regressive (ART falls as income rises) then Greece's tax system is less progressive and more regressive than the EU 18 average, for a given $Y_1$.

**(e)** **Using AD / AS diagram and explain the possible effects of a comprehensive privatisation program on inflation, economic growth and employment levels in Greece.** **[4 marks]**

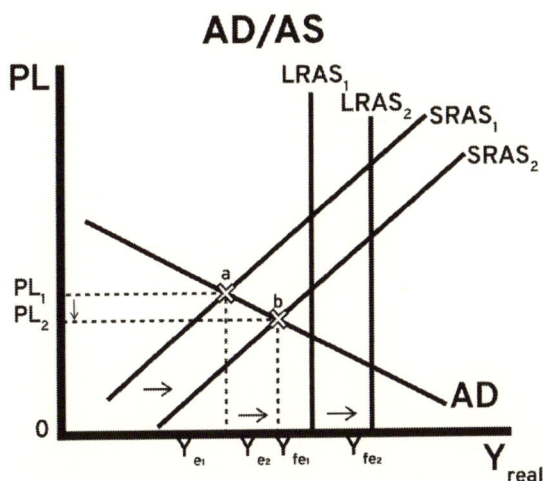

## AD/AS

PL

LRAS$_1$

LRAS$_2$

SRAS$_1$

SRAS$_2$

PL$_1$
PL$_2$

a

b

AD

0

$Y_{e1}$   $Y_{e2}$  $Y_{fe1}$   $Y_{fe2}$   $Y_{real}$

Currently Greece is suffering high unemployment, output well below full capacity (demand deflation), uncompetitive in terms of prices and highly indebted (public and private sector). With deregulation and privatisation where barriers to entry for new firms lower and government budget deficit cut, the intention is to increase SRAS$_1$ to SRAS$_2$. In addition privatisation is brought in to improve competitiveness and productivity and lower prices in the long run (Greece's electricity prices are one of the highest in EU 18). Real output should rise Ye$_1$, to Ye$_2$) production capacity and efficiency will raise LRAS$_1$ to

101

LRAS2 and reduce inflationary pressure $PL_1$ to $PL_2$.

**(f)** **Using a poverty cycle diagram to explain how a rise in youth unemployment can affect the economic development of Greece.** **[4 marks]**

Rising youth unemployment means young people cannot learn on the job skills. Their productivity will be lower resulting in lower earning power and lower level of saving. Further investments in education do not occur. Many leave to find jobs abroad. Family formation rates fall, Greece towns become stagnant, living off state welfare. The old get by on low pensions and the youth become demoralised and reliant low paying service jobs in tourism. A lack of fulfilling jobs leads to low economic growth and development.

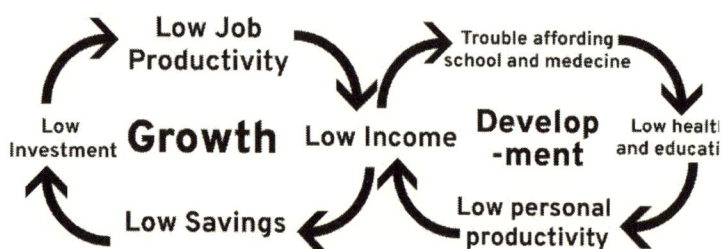

**(g)** **Using information from the texts / data and your knowledge of economics, evaluate the merits of greater foreign direct investment FDI for Greece.** **[15 marks]**

Currently Greece has no control over its monetary policy since it is in a single currency Eurozone. In addition it is forced by the Troika to introduce expansionary fiscal contraction (EFC) where public sector contracts releasing FOPs for the private sector and hence encourage FDI. China's Cosco, Italy's Ferrovie dello Stato, Germany's Deutsche Telecom and Fraport are all FDI ready to take over Greece's assets and introduce new investment. These FDI will have a positive multiplier effect of raise real EDP greater than the initial injection. $AD_1$ rises to $AD_2$ due to approx $ 2 Bn injection. With a multiplier effect $Ye_2$ will rise to $Ye_3$. More jobs, economic growth will be created. In the long run $AS_1$ will rise to $AS_2$ as Greece's capacity to produce rises.

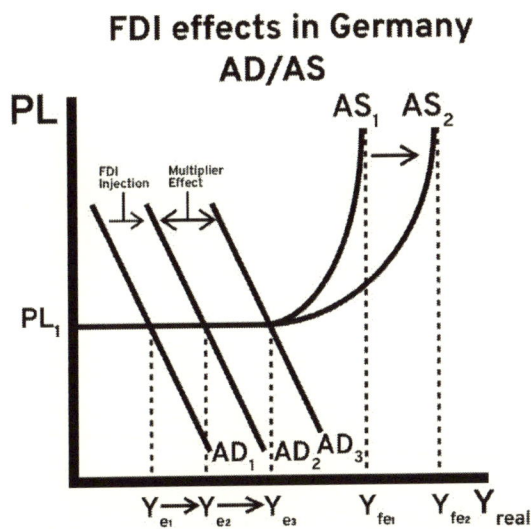

FDI effects in Germany AD/AS

FDIs being in new ideas, new methods of production leading to higher productivity and real wages. The Greek government can collect more taxes to help it reform itself. The ports and airports with their much needed improvements to attract more industry and tourism.

However, it is important to note some of the downsides of FDIs. For Greece with its surplus labour wages may not rise. These foreign companies may demand extensive concessions and preferential treatment from local governments. They may use slash and burn strategies where they asset strip, maximise profits, raise their debt levels and leave.

FDI, expanding and government shrinking means Greece's ability to introduce social programs to help low income households will be restricted. Inequalities may well rise.

## 10.    Bangladesh

*Study the texts and data below and answer the questions that follow.*

### Text 1- Overview of Bangladesh Economy

Soon after its independence from Pakistan in 1971, Bangladesh came to be labeled as a global 'basket case'. It suffered from many natural and man- made disasters. Its starting route to development was marred with cyclones, famines, low human capital, mass poverty, few natural resources and much natural vulnerability caused by low lying flood prone land.

Looking at Bangladesh today, most development economists would consider it a great success story. A precondition for this development has been steady slow economic growth of little over 4% since 1990. This has been driven largely by 3 factors. Firstly, the growing garment exporting industry which has offered employment opportunities to women in the sector. Secondly, a steady flow of remittances which now account for 10% of GDP and finally the introduction of microfinance which has brought access to credit for about 50% of all households. GDP per capita measured in terms of ***purchasing power parity*** has risen by over 300% since 1990. Inflation has been low and household debt low and manageable.

A real striking feature coming out of Bangladesh is its success in turning economic growth into economic development. Since independence male life expectancy has risen by more than 22 years, female fertility rates dropped to 2 from 7 while infant mortality rates fell drastically from 223 to 45. This achievement means Bangladesh is clearly meeting many of its Millennium Development Goals (MDGs) or the more recent ***Sustainable Development Goals (SDGs)***.

The causes of this positive change may well have been the 1974 famine which killed 1.5 million people. Subsequently the ruling class accepted and pursued pro-market, pro-poor development policies which the international community were happy to support and direct more resources. A social contract was established between the well to do and the rest of the community in terms of preventing any subsistence crises. NGOs and other donors were given much more of a free reign to experiment with new initiatives, one of them being the home grown Grameen Bank.

104

## Text 2- Micro Lending in Bangladesh

In the 1970s, the Grameen bank began offering small amounts of credit to poor women in the village of Jobra, Bangladesh, so that they could launch income-generating projects to help support themselves and their families. The Grameen Bank lending model is based on social collateral. References from five unrelated members of the community can help secure a loan of $10 to $500 lasting a year with pay-back is on a weekly basis. The Grameen bank model achieves repayment rates of 99%, much higher than the standard banking model that requires assets as collateral.

The main beneficiaries of the small loans have been women. Decision making has been put in their hands. This sense of empowerment is then instilled in their offspring. The last four decades have brought major poverty reducing changes in Bangladesh especially in terms of household incomes, greater education of girls and smaller family sizes.

Similar micro-lending models have been introduced in parts of the world with varying degrees of success. Research published in the B. E. Journal of Macroeconomics concludes that micro-lending could lift 10.6 million people out of poverty in the developing world. However, the line between more financial inclusion and the risk of borrowers taking on debt that they can't pay back can easily be crossed. Cases of farmers in South India taking out new loans to pay back previous loans have been known to lead to suicides. Without regulation that protects borrowers from taking on debt they can't afford the credit system can quickly degenerate into a type of legal shark lending or payday loans for subprime borrowers.

## Text 3- What is the price of a guarantee?

Readymade IPhones and other smartphones are heavily taxed when imported into Bangladesh. A smartphone with a final price tag of $US898 will carry an import tax of $US180. Bangladesh does not have a 'make in Bangladesh' policy as yet nor do the large smartphone companies like Apple and Samsung seem interested in producing in Bangladesh without receiving significant concessions from the Bangladeshi government along with facilities for re-export and intellectual property protection. Consequently new companies have illegally mushroomed to exploit the possibility of arbitrage. Smartphones are couriered in pieces including the box covers, assembled and sold at $US750 without guarantees. These account for 25% of the $800m mobile phone market.

## Table 1- Economic data for Bangladesh

| Bangladesh Macro Outlook Indicators (annual % change unless indicated otherwise) | | | | | | |
|---|---|---|---|---|---|---|
| | 2014 | 2015 | 2016 | 2017 f | 2018 f | 2019 f |
| **Real GDP growth, at constant market prices** | 6.1 | 6.6 | 7.1 | 6.8 | 6.4 | 6.7 |
| Private Consumption | 4.0 | 5.8 | 3.0 | 4.0 | 5.0 | 5.6 |
| Government Consumption | 7.9 | 8.8 | 8.4 | 10.2 | 9.6 | 8.9 |
| Gross Fixed Capital Investment | 9.9 | 7.1 | 8.9 | 12.0 | 11.1 | 11.0 |
| Exports, Goods and Services | 3.2 | -2.8 | 2.2 | 5.0 | 6.0 | 6.5 |
| Imports, Goods and Services | 1.2 | 3.2 | -7.1 | 6.0 | 10.5 | 11.5 |
| **Real GDP growth, at constant factor prices** | 6.1 | 6.5 | 7.2 | 6.7 | 6.6 | 6.7 |
| Agriculture | 4.4 | 3.3 | 2.8 | 4.1 | 2.5 | 3.3 |
| Industry | 8.2 | 9.7 | 11.1 | 8.9 | 8.3 | 8.9 |
| Services | 5.6 | 5.8 | 6.3 | 6.0 | 6.9 | 6.4 |
| **Inflation (Consumer Price Index)** | 7.3 | 6.4 | 5.9 | 5.6 | 6.3 | 6.3 |
| **Current Account Balance (% of GDP)** | 0.8 | 1.5 | 1.7 | 0.2 | -0.3 | -0.6 |
| **Financial and Capital Account (% of GDP)** | 1.9 | 1.2 | 0.9 | 0.6 | 0.5 | 0.2 |
| Net Foreign Direct Investment (% of GDP) | 0.8 | 0.9 | 0.9 | 1.1 | 0.9 | 1.0 |
| **Fiscal Balance (% of GDP)** | -3.5 | -3.3 | -3.1 | -4.0 | -3.5 | -3.7 |
| **Debt (% of GDP)** | 31.9 | 31.5 | 30.6 | 30.6 | 30.0 | 29.6 |
| **Primary Balance (% of GDP)** | -1.5 | -1.5 | -1.4 | -2.2 | -1.6 | -1.8 |

Sources: World Bacnk, Macroeconomics and Fiscal Managment Global Practice, and Poverty Global Practice.

Notes: e = estimate, f = forecast

**Table 2- Selected development data for Bangladesh**

Development diamond*

Life expectancy

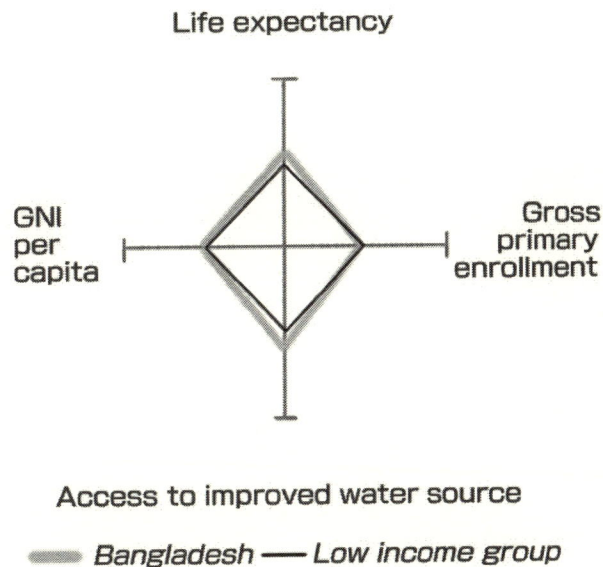

GNI per capita

Gross primary enrollment

Access to improved water source

▬▬ Bangladesh ── Low income group

## QUESTIONS

(a)     (i) List  3 _sustainable development goals_ (SDG). (Text 1 – paragraph 3)          [2 marks]

(ii) Define the term purchasing power parity indicated in bold. (Text 1 – paragraph 2) [2 marks]

**(b)**    **(i) Calculate the level of tariff revenue collected by the Bangladeshi Government on finished imported smartphones. (Text 3)**                                        **[3 marks]**

          **(ii) Use two demand and supply diagrams to explain the emergence of arbitrage in the smartphone market in Bangladesh. (Text 3)**                                  **[2 marks]**

**(c)**    **Draw a tariff diagram to show the tariff revenue on imported smartphones and the allocative inefficiencies this policy causes. (Text 3)**                          **[4 marks]**

**(d)**    **Use a poverty cycle diagram to explain how microloans can help Bangladesh achieve greater income / wealth equality and economic development. (Text 2)**          **[4 marks]**

**(e)**    **Using Table 1 and an AD / AS diagram explain the effects of a sudden severe global slowdown on the economic indicators of Bangladesh.**                          **[4 marks]**

**(f)**    **Using Table 2, draw a new development demand to explain the effects of climate change on Bangladesh's economic development.**                                    **[4 marks]**

**(g)  Bangladesh has set itself the target of achieving the status of middle income country by 2024. Using information from the text / data and your knowledge of economic, evaluate how adopting an export–orientated policy can enable Bangladesh achieve the 2024 target.**          **[15 marks]**

**ANSWERS:**            **10. Bangladesh**

**(a)**      **(i) List 3 _sustainable development goals_ (SDG). (Text 1 – paragraph 3)**      **[2 marks]**

There are 17 SDGs to choose from:

-    No poverty

-    Zero Hunger

-    Good health and well being

-    Gender equality

-    Quality education

           **(ii) Define the term purchasing power parity indicated in bold. (Text 1 – paragraph 2) [2 marks]**

Purchasing power Parity (PPP). This is when monetary values of indicators such as GDP are measured in terms of what amounts of goods and services these values can buy. For Bangladesh today's GDP buys three times as much compared to 1990.

**(b)**      **(i) Calculate the level of tariff revenue collected by the Bangladeshi Government on finished imported smartphones. (Text 3)**      **[3 marks]**

     25 % of 800 m          = $ 200 m value of smartphones non-guaranteed

     75 % of 800 m          = $ 600m value of read made imported smartphones.

Number of imported readymade phones = (600 m)/898 = 668151 smartphones

Total Tariff Revenue = 668151 x $ 180 = **$ 120.3 m   approx tariff revenue**

**(ii) Use two demand and supply diagrams to explain the emergence of arbitrage in the smartphone market in Bangladesh. (Text 3)** **[2 marks]**

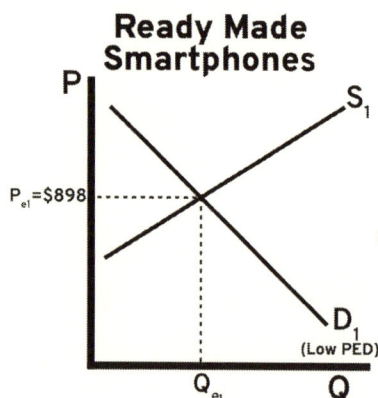

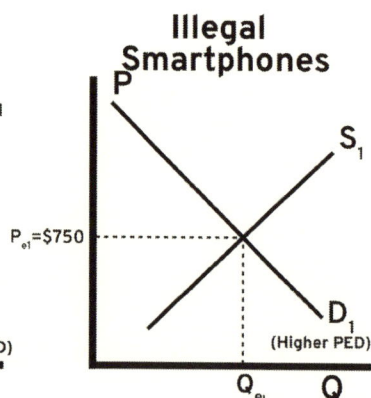

**Ready Made Smartphones**

**Illegal Smartphones**

With huge numbers of lower income consumers the demand for illegal smartphones with no guarantees is high. Local companies are able to change $ 750 and make sufficient profits while Apple and Samsung are not interested in addressing their business strategy for Bangladesh.

**(c)      Draw a tariff diagram to show the tariff revenue on imported smartphones and the allocative inefficiencies this policy causes. (Text 3)                                          [4 marks]**

## Tariff Diagram Smartphones

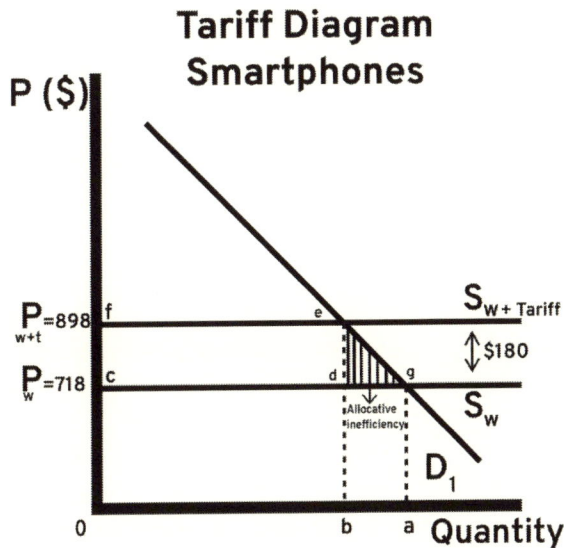

There is no domestic supply since the smartphones are all imported and a tariff of $ 180 imposed on each unit, with no tariff the price Pw = $ 718 and *Oa* is imported. With a tariff of $ 180 per unit the price rises to Pw+t = $ 898 and imports fall to *Ob* units.  Area  *cdef*  is the value of the tariff revenue for the Bangladesh government and triangle *deg* is the dead weight or welfare loss indicating the value of the misallocation of resources due to the $ 180 tariff.

**(d)      Use a poverty cycle diagram to explain how microloans can help Bangladesh achieve greater income / wealth equality and economic development. (Text 2)                      [4 marks]**

Microloans given out by the Grameen Bank allow women access to cheap credit without standard collateral. Women can use this credit to start a small business from home.  The income generated can be used to pay back the loan with interest. The profits empower women. Gender equality rises. Greater spending on health, education and nutrition enable Bangladeshis to meet their SDG targets.

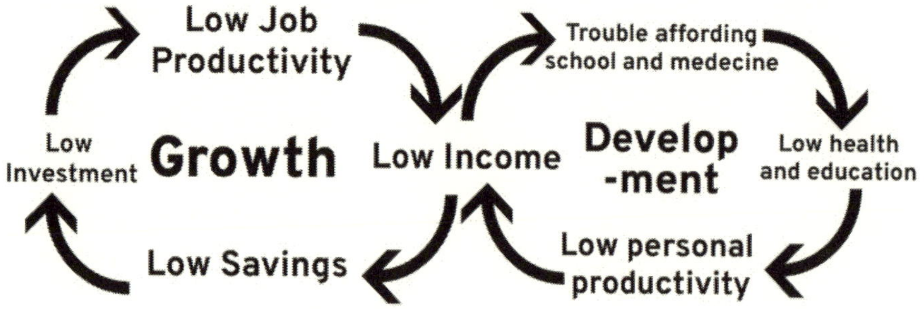


**(e) Using Table 1 and an AD / AS diagram explain the effects of a sudden severe global slowdown on the economic indicators of Bangladesh. [4 marks]**

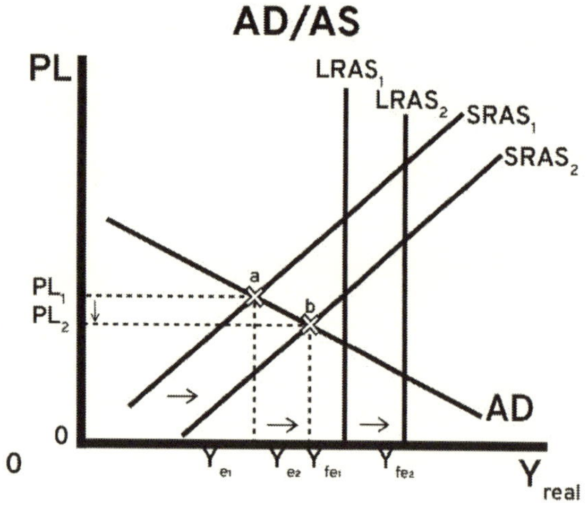


A global slowdown in economic activity usually means that the demand for Bangladesh's textiles way falls. In addition remittances sent by expatriates will be lower as Bangladeshi workers abroad lose their jobs. Together AD1 falls to AD2. Real output may fall Ye2 to Ye1 as production and private consumption within Bangladesh falls. Unemployment may rise. The level of investment will also fall. The government will experience a fall in tariff revenue as well as revenues from consumption. The fiscal balance may worsen beyond -3.7 % of GDP.

**(f)    Using Table 2, draw a new development demand to explain the effects of climate change on Bangladesh's economic development.                                                        [4 marks]**

- ▯   Climate change along with rising sea levels will adversely affect Bangladesh.
- ▯   GNI per capita may well fall as less fertile land is available for productive use. In addition to mitigating the effect of climate change more resources (GNI) will be used in this endeavor. However, with development more contribution will come from secondary and tertiary sectors.
- ▯   Access to good quality water will be more difficult. More resources are required. However, with a higher level of population there will be a greater demand for clean water.
- ▯    More and more GNI will be used to combat the adverse effects on life expectancy. Droughts and ill health due to poor quality water will become more common.

**(g)   Bangladesh has set itself the target of achieving the status of middle- income country by 2024. Using the information from the text / data and your knowledge of economic, evaluate how adopting an export–orientated policy can enable Bangladesh achieve the 2024 target.                [15 marks]**

- ▯   Export oriented strategy implies buying in raw materials, processing them into products such as clothes and export then all over the globe for mass consumption. A clear example is importing cotton to turn into textiles and garments for export. Bangladesh gains from the value added as well as technology transfers and higher productivity from the jobs created.
- ▯   Foreign currency earned can be used to buy in capital goods products unavailable domestically in Bangladesh.
- ▯   With greater in influence from global competition Bangladesh can reduce allocative inefficiency by using free market principles.
- ▯   Bangladeshi's open economy will enable more start-ups to be created.
- ▯   Imprudent or macro-mismanagement may soon be reflected in a depreciating currency.
- ▯   Multinationals are more likely to make new investments if Bangladesh adheres to free market policies.
- ▯   However global competitiveness may well mean lowering of labour rights, lowering of health and safety standards as Bangladeshi firms face margin squeeze from multinational such as

Walmart.

▸ Strong pursuit of profit through efficiency may come at the expense of equity. Corporation may bargain for preferential tax rates.

▸ Governments may be forced to reduce their deficits, to defend the exchange rate by cutting social programs, food subsidies and infrastructure spending.

▸ International free market principles may prevent Bangladesh from diversifying and establishing a new comparative advantage. Higher global oil prices can severely affect Bangladesh through high inflation and stagflation.

## 11.   INDIA

*Study the texts and data below and answer the questions that follow.*

### Text 1- Overview of India

India one of the fastest-growing economy in the world is predicted to be one of the three major economic powers of the world in the next 10 years. It achieved 7.1% increase in its GDP in the past two years. Additionally, as the country improved its trade system, India is experiencing an increase in export revenue. Nonetheless, high levels of imports cause India to suffer from a current account deficit. Furthermore, the country needs to set clear strategies to ensure sustainable economic growth and an equitable distribution of income.  Inequality in India is rising; 1% of its population holds more than 53% of its wealth. Infrastructure spending and facilities are only 10% of what is required when compared to China, a country of similar size..

### Text 2- Malnourishment in India

Despite the improvements and the increase in economic growth and development, one in five Indians is still considered poor. The government is trying to implement policies in order to alleviate poverty by 2030 under the sustainable development goals. India's poverty is mainly caused by the under allocation of food. In 2017 the Global Hunger Index (GHI) ranked India 100 out of 119 countries, with a GHI score of 31.4, placing the country in the "serious" category. India has consistently fallen into the upper half of the "serious" hunger levels category in the past few years. This hunger level has a very important impact on the child mortality rate in the country.

| Indicators | Proportion of undernourished in the population (%) | Prevalence of stunting in children under five years (%) |
|---|---|---|
| 2017 | 14.5 | 38.4 |

The caste system in India is still one of India's biggest reasons for why some minorities have difficulty breaking out of the ***poverty trap.*** These minorities spend proportionately more of their income on necessities such as food and clothing in order to survive, leaving no opportunity to invest in education or healthcare.

In its yearend review 2018, the government has set a target of doubling the incomes of Indian farmers in real terms by the year 2022. It plans to do this by focusing towards income-centeredness rather than the previous production-centeredness. Three of the many initiatives are providing a Minimum Support Price (MSP) for certain crops of at least 150% of the cost of production, bee keeping to increase the productivity of crops through pollination and increase the honey production as an additional source of income of farmers and a scheme that covers various types of risks from pre-sowing to post harvest for which farmers have to pay very nominal premium. However, according to government critics, the problem of exceedingly low farm sizes and hence poor investment possibilities in mechanisation has largely been ignored.

## Text 3- Misery for potato farmers.

In terms of potato production, 2017 has been a good year. For the potato farmer's incomes: not so good. For the crop year between July 2015 and June 2016, India's potato production stood at 43.4 million tonnes. This year's output though is estimated to have touched 47 million tonnes. Prices have fallen from 800 rupees per quintal (100 kilos) down to 450.

One farmer gave a breakdown of his expenses. Costs of buying seeds, pesticides and labour are nearly a hundred rupees per hundred kilos. Then finally, we have to pay 262 rupees to get a quintal (100 kilos) of our potatoes inside the doors of a cold storage facility. Add it all up and our total expense on cultivating and storing one quintal of produce is roughly 450 rupees.

Another potato farmer was saddened by the drastic fall in the price of this output. He says, "We're only getting as much as or less when the wholesalers come to buy our stock. The daily price is anywhere between 350 and 450 rupees a quintal, we're running into losses and going deeper in debt. We aren't getting our dues. The government has to take measures to fix this. It is their responsibility."

The government announced said it would buy 100,000 metric tonnes of potatoes at a rate of Rs 487 per quintal. The move, to be implemented under the Market Intervention Scheme (MIS), was to provide relief to hard-hit potato farmers. The cabinet assured the farmers that potato procurement would begin immediately.

## Text 4- India's strong economic relations

After many economic reforms in the 1990s, India opened up to foreign direct investment (FDI). The country lifted most of its ***import restrictions*** in order to increase their international trade. India's strongest trade relation is with the United States of America.

India's major exports include fish, seafood, different types of metals and precious stones while their imports from the US consist of medicine and other manufactured goods. In order to create the economic growth and development India would need to invest in education and training. This would mean that they would eventually stop exporting primary goods and start exporting manufactured goods, getting a higher yield out of it.

## Text 5- Where's the competition

The Indian government is introducing an anti-profiteering law to protect consumers from exploitative oligopolies in its consumer sector. This is the result of an enquiry looking at consumer complaints and industry data on retail prices. Evidence shows that firms in toiletries such as toothpaste, soaps and detergents have not passed on any gains from falling raw material prices or lower sales taxes. P&G, Nirma and Hindustan Unilever together account for 70% of the Indian market. New comer, Patanjali is unable to make inroads as its marketing budget and distribution is poor. Even after higher labour and costs of compliance profit margins are up from 12.6% 14%. In addition, labour costs as a proportion of sales costs significantly down from 15 % to 13.2%. Government critics are arguing that prices should be left to market forces and bully and micro-managing pricing decisions will simply distort the allocation of resources in terms of efficiency. The enquiry came to the same conclusions when investigating the cars, scooters, mobile phone service and airline sectors.

**Table 1- Rural and Urban Inflation data for India**

## Prices Rise Faster For Rural Consumers in India
Consumer price index for rural and urban (2014-2019)

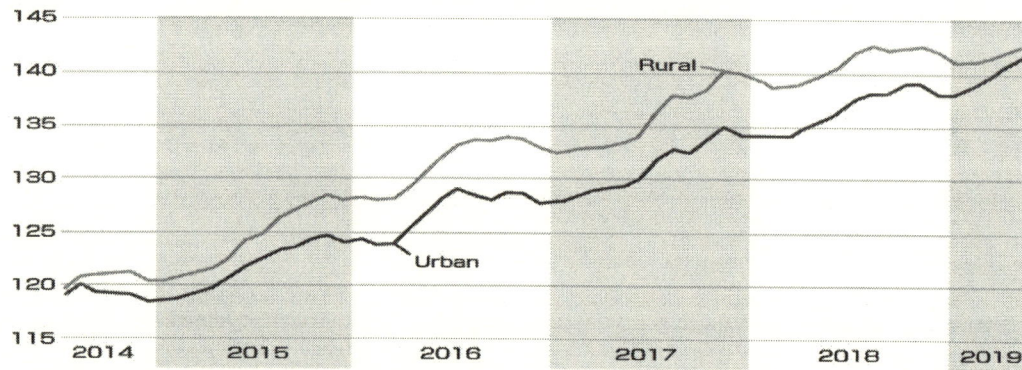

As a base for this consumer price index, 2012 prices equal 100 index
Source: Government of India Ministry of Statistics
and Programme Implementation (MOSPI)

@StatistaCharts

statista

## Table 2- Economic data for India

|  | 2018 Data | Previous Data |
|---|---|---|
| GDP growth rate | 1.8 % | 1.3 % (2016) |
| Unemployment rate | 3.46 % | 4.15 % (2008) |
| Inflation rate | 4.44 % | 1.54 % (2017) |
| Interest rate | 6 % | 8 % (2014) |
| Government debt to GDP | 69. 5 % | 67.5 % (2010) |

Source: India - Economic Indicators, tradingeconomics.com/india/indicators. "India ." India | Data, data.worldbank.org/country/india.

## Table 3:  NOISE POLLUTION

| City ▲ | Country ▲ | Male Hearing Loss (years) ▲ | Female Hearing Loss (years) ▲ | Average Hearing Loss (years) ▼ | Hearing Loss Rank |
|---|---|---|---|---|---|
| Delhi | India | +19.15 | +19.53 | +19.34 | 1 |
| Mumbai | India | +18.40 | +18.77 | +18.58 | 0.98 |
| Istanbul | Turkey | +17.94 | +18.73 | +18.33 | 0.93 |
| Cairo | Egypt | +18.33 | +17.73 | +18.03 | 0.89 |
| Guangzhou | China | +16.89 | +17.98 | +17.43 | 0.82 |
| Saint Petersburg | Russia | +17.24 | +17.06 | +17.15 | 0.78 |
| Taipei | Taiwan | +16.25 | +17.3 | +16.79 | 0.74 |
| Seongnam-si | South Korea | +17.19 | +15.89 | +16.54 | 0.71 |
| Buenos Aires | Argentina | +15.89 | +17.19 | +16.54 | 0.71 |
| Madrid | Spain | +15.34 | +17.18 | +16.26 | 0.68 |

## QUESTIONS

**(a)**    **(i) Define the term _poverty trap_ indicated in bold. (Text 1 – paragraph 2)**          **[2 marks]**

**(ii) Define the term _import restrictions_ indicated in bold. (Text 3 – paragraph 1)**      **[2 marks]**

**(b)s**    **(i) Calculate the price elasticity of supply for the potatoes and comment on the value. (Text 3)**
**[3 marks]**

**(b)h     (i)  Define and state the formula for unemployment rate and suggest one reason why India unemployment rate is likely to be higher than stated in Table 1 for 2018.          [3 marks]**

**(ii) Use demand / supply diagram to explain why primary food prices fluctuate more than manufactured foods.** [3 marks]

**(c)** **Use a poverty cycle diagram to explain the longer-term effects of persistently high rates of hunger and poverty on economic growth and economic development. (Text 2)** [4 marks]

**(d)** **Use a quota diagram to explain 3 benefits of free trade for India. (Text 3)** [4 marks]

**(e)** **Apart from price stability suggest 3 reasons why the Indian Government would like to devote more resources to promoting its exports of both primary and manufacturing goods?** [4 marks]

**(e)h** **Using text 5, explain the features or which seem to indicate that firms in the noted consumer sectors are probably exploitative.** [4 marks]

**(f)** **Using Table 1 and an AD / AS diagram, explain how a fall in the interest rate from 8 % to 6 % can lead to changes in the macro objectives indicators.** [4 marks]

**(g)** **India recently introduced a new policy whereby it no longer accepts bilateral aid from any country. Using the texts/tables and your knowledge of economics, evaluate to what extent is this policy justified in helping India to achieve its sustainable development goals.** [15 marks]

## ANSWERS:                    11. INDIA

**(a)        (i) Define the term _poverty trap_ indicated in bold. (Text 1 – paragraph 2)          [2 marks]**

Poverty trap is a situation where very low income poor groups remain poor, unable to escape the self-reinforcing mechanism. A common example is where poor people lacking asset borrowing at high interest rates which makes even more indebted and poor.

**(ii) Define the term _import restrictions_ indicated in bold. (Text 3 – paragraph 1)      [2 marks]**

Import restrictions are barriers such as tariffs, quotas, subsidies, administrative which prevent free movement of FoPs and final goods / services across international borders.

**(b)s     (i) Calculate the price elasticity of supply for the potatoes and comment on the value. (Text 3)
                                                                                    [3 marks]**

Define PES potatoes  +  State formula

PES potatoes  $= ((47 - 43.4)/43.4)/((450 - 800)/800) = 0.0895/0.4375 = 0.20$

**PES potatoes = 0.20** This means that for every 10% rise in the price of potatoes only 2% more potatoes come on the market to be sold in the short run.

**(b)h**    **(i) Define and state the formula for unemployment rate and suggest one reason why India unemployment rate is likely to be higher than stated in Table 1 for 2018.**    **[3 marks]**

Unemployment can be defined as anyone one who is willing, able and actively seeking work at the current price but cannot find a job. Unemployment Rate = (Number of unemployed)/(Labour Force) 100/1

India's 2018 unemployment rate of 3.46 % is likely to be higher. This may be due to (1) a change in the methodology of calculation (2) high numbers in part time employment who wish to be in full time work (3) growing number of discouraged workers.

   **(ii) Use demand / supply diagram to explain why primary food prices fluctuate more than manufactured foods.**    **[3 marks]**

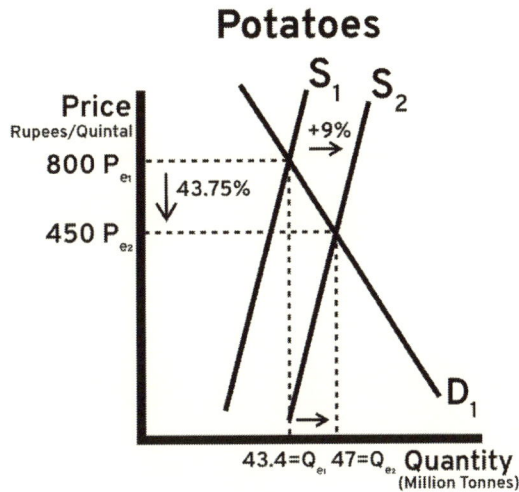

Potatoes

**(c)**    **Use a poverty cycle diagram to explain the longer term effects of persistently high rates of hunger and poverty on economic growth and economic development. (Text 2)**    **[4 marks]**

An increase in supply $S_1$ to $S_2$ (approx + 9%) has led to a huge fall in the price of potatoes $Pe_1$ to $Pe_2$ (approx - 43.75 %). This is due to low PED and low PES for potatoes in India.

123

**(d)** **Use a quota diagram to explain 3 benefits of free trade for India. (Text 3)** **[4 marks]**

**Removal of Quota Medicines**

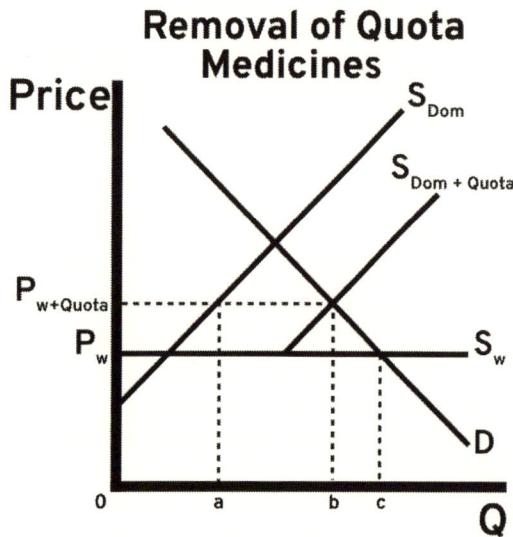

A quota on medicines is a restriction on the volume of imported medicines allowed in India (to protect and help India establish a drug industry)

This import restriction leads to higher prices Pw + quota which subsequently fall when the quota is removed. Quantity imported rises and the total supply on the market rises from Ob to Oc. Foreign companies sell more at a lower price.

3 benefits to choose: Lower prices, more supply and choice, Indian companies can expand and export, more jobs in the health sector, patient care.

**(e)** **Apart from price stability suggest 3 reasons why the Indian Government would like to devote more resources to promoting its exports of both primary and manufacturing goods?** **[4 marks]**

Here are 4 ways how the Indian government can gain from exporting output from primary and manufacturing sectors:

- Gain from foreign currency availability in the Indian banking sector in order to facilitate importers of say capital goods using new technology.
- Global prices tend to be higher than Indian prices even after transportation costs. Export sector creates more, higher value added and higher paying jobs.
- Exporting raw materials or agriculture enables Indian farmers to gain a better price for their produce.
- India can also gain from greater overall production creating more economies of scale

leading to lower average costs.

**(e)h   Using text 5, explain the features or which seem to indicate that firms in the noted consumer sectors are probably exploitative.                                                   [4 marks]**

The oligopolistic market structure in text 5 is exploitative since market is dominated be 3 large players, concentration ratio of 70% for the top 3 firms. Falls in raw material costs have not translated to lower prices. Even the workers are not benefitting as their costs as a % of sales is falling implying higher productivity. New firm, Patanjali is faced with high barriers to entry as it does not have the global marketing budget of P&G. The dominant firms may well also have secured exclusive deals with their retailers to carry only their products.

**(f)   Using Table 1 and an AD / AS diagram, explain how a fall in the interest rate from 8 % to 6 % can lead to changes in the macro objectives indicators.                              [4 marks]**

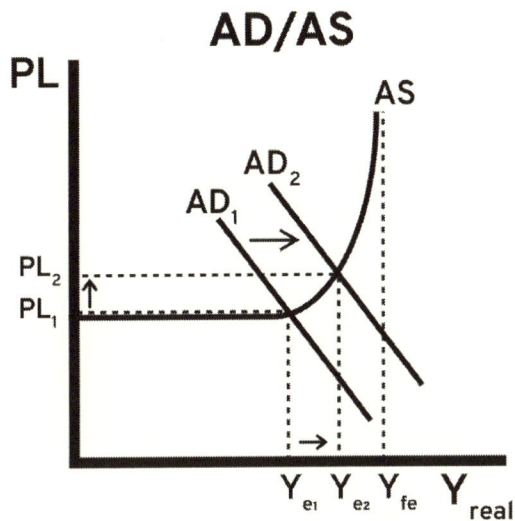

Macroeconomic objectives are low unemployment, low and stable inflation, steady stable economic growth, favourable balance of payments and an equitable distribution of income.

Falling interest rates from 7 % to 6 % can stimulate greater consumer, government and investment borrowing raising debt levels in each of these sectors.

If the economy is close to full employment then inflation may rise from $PL_1$ to $PL_2$. Output may rise but it may be jobless economic growth. Firms may borrow to buy machines which replace labour. The low interest rates may chiefly benefit the high-income groups. Inequalities may rise.

(Rise in all four:  inflation, unemployment, inequality and unsustainable growth)

125

**(g)    India recently introduced a new policy whereby it no longer accepts bilateral aid from any country.  Using the texts/tables and your knowledge of economics, evaluate to what extent is this policy justified in helping India to achieve its sustainable development goals.        (15 marks)**

List some of the relevant SDGs according to the texts and tables.

No poverty.  Zero hunger.  Life on land.  Gender equality.  Clean water and sanitation.  Decent work and economic growth.    Sustainable consumption and production.    Climate action.    Affordable and clean energy

Evaluation of Bilateral Aid

- Aid can fill gaps. Gaps in saving, gaps in foreign currency, gaps in education, gaps in technology, gaps in infrastructure and gap in healthcare. This can be useful for India in achieving its SDG, especially in rural areas where poverty is acute. Water pumps, sanitation basic healthcare, education and agriculture projects.
- However Bilateral Aid is often Aide aid. Doors link aid with large defense contracts. This aid is ripe with corruption and often inefficient, beginning low yield.
- Aid dependency can be a problem.
- Data in table 2 and texts show, India desperately needs technology improvements reducing pollution and producing clean energy in order to meet in SDGs.
- An alternative to consider 'trade for aid'. Across to developed markets will help India increase its income and create jobs and meet its SDGs.
-  The new policy may well be aimed at reducing opportunities for corruption and not suffer from obligations from the developed countries or companies.

## 12.  VENEZUELA

*Study the texts and data below and answer the questions that follow.*

### Text 1- Overview of *Venezuela*

Venezuela is rich in natural resources, including large reserves of petroleum, natural gas, iron ore, gold, bauxite, diamond, and other minerals. It is a member of the Organization of the Petroleum Exporting Countries (OPEC), and its oil production accounts for 96% of all Venezuelan exports, with over 1.8 million barrels of crude oil being produced per day. Venezuela's largest exporting sector is its oil sector. It benefited greatly from high oil prices before the collapse in the international oil price in late 2014. In 2015 it faced a 50% decrease in the price of crude oil. The price of Venezuelan crude oil fell an additional 35% in the first half of 2016 and at the same time as Venezuelan production contracted by around 10% in 2016, from roughly 2.16 million bpd to 1.95 million bpd. Venezuela cannot do anything about the fluctuating oil price, but they could aim to diversify exports.

### Text 2- Economic development and inequality

Venezuela has developed greatly since 1998, with poverty decreasing from 50% in 1998 to 30% in 2013 due to economic growth and redistribution policies from the government. In addition, the government has supplied *'misiones'* or social programs which account for the allocation of fundamental services and transport resources to secluded portions of the population. This also resulted in a change in inequality shown by a change in the Gini index, from 0.49 in 1998 to 0.40 in 2012.

However, this growth was not able to be perpetuated because of the collapse of the international oil price. This, in addition to poor macroeconomic and microeconomic policies caused economic and social performances to decrease significantly. Venezuela now faces major financing needs in the short and medium term, with a fiscal deficit of roughly 20% of the 2015 GDP. External financing requirements are estimated to be between US$25 billion and US35$ billion. Public deficit was largely monetized through borrowing money, and this along with price controls, limitations to foreign currency, and the failure of the private sector to provide basic goods has led to one of the highest inflation rates on a global scale.

Private consumption in Venezuela has diminished greatly due to the erosion of **_real disposable incomes_**. Investment has also plummeted due to rising uncertainty, causing capital stock to shrink. Finally, imports have also collapsed, accompanied by a fall in output because of a severe drought. All of these factors have led to a sharp decline in output, and a sharp decline in aggregate demand, as well as major stagflation. GDP is expected to contract by more than 10% in 2016, accounting for a cumulative reduction of 20% since 2013.

Venezuela faces significant challenges in containing the **_macroeconomic imbalances_** which are reversing previously made social progress. In addition, Venezuela must reestablish the investment climate, and diversify its exports to reduce its vulnerability to fluctuating oil prices. Lastly, the Venezuelan government should seek to implement a macroeconomic policy which protects the portion of the population living in poverty.

### Text 3- Venezuela debt

Venezuela has recently defaulted on its debt, claiming it was unable to pay it. If Venezuelan bondholders demand immediate payment, and Venezuela does not pay, then investors would be entitled to seize any Venezuelan assets – primarily oil. As oil is the primary export of the country, the preexisting food and medical shortages will worsen significantly, as the government will be considerably less able to supply these basic resources.

Venezuela's debt to bondholders alone stands at roughly $60 billion, and its total debt stands at about $196 billion. It currently owes money to China, Russia, oilfield service providers, US airlines, and various other entities. The country's official reserve is reportedly only at $9.6 billion, because it has slowly drained the account to make payments over the years.

The country's current situation can mostly be attributed to the policies the government has implemented since 1999. It fixed the prices of consumer goods such as coffee, gas, and others in an effort to make them more affordable for the masses. Fixed prices resulted in farmer's going out of business because they were forced to sell at a price below production, and imports decreased because importers were forced to sell at lower costs than the cost of tariffs. Furthermore, the regime decided to fix the exchange rate of the Bolivar. Food shortages spurred the growth of a black market, resulting in the value of the Bolivar to plummet, leaving it almost worthless. At the beginning of the year, one US dollar was worth roughly 3,200 Bolivars, but now one dollar will buy roughly 55,200 Bolivars, demonstrating massive inflation. The inflation rate is expected to rise from 650% this year to roughly 2,300% in 2018.

## Text 4- Humanitarian crisis

Venezuela is currently in a humanitarian crisis and in dire need of aid. Roughly 470,000 Venezuelans have fled across the border to Colombia, due to food shortages, high levels of crime, political unrest, and other economic issues. This, among other factors, has led to the poverty rate of Venezuela rising to 86%, and facilitated a rise in other statistics such as the neonatal death rate, which is now at 2.06%. The United Nations has pledged to donate more resources to Colombia to help them deal with this crisis.

**TABLE 1**

| | 2011 | 2012 | 2013 | 2014 | 2015 | 2016 | 2017 | 2018 | 2019 |
|---|---|---|---|---|---|---|---|---|---|
| **Interest Rates %** | 18.11 | 16.75 | 15.63 | 16.57 | 19.46 | 21.36 | 21.57 | 22.64 | 30.62 |
| **Consumer Price Index** | 26.1 | 21.1 | 40.3 | 302 | 480 | 720 | 652.7 | 140000 | 282973 |

**TABLE 2**

# How Venezuela Looked 10 Years Ago
Key economic/social data about Venezuela

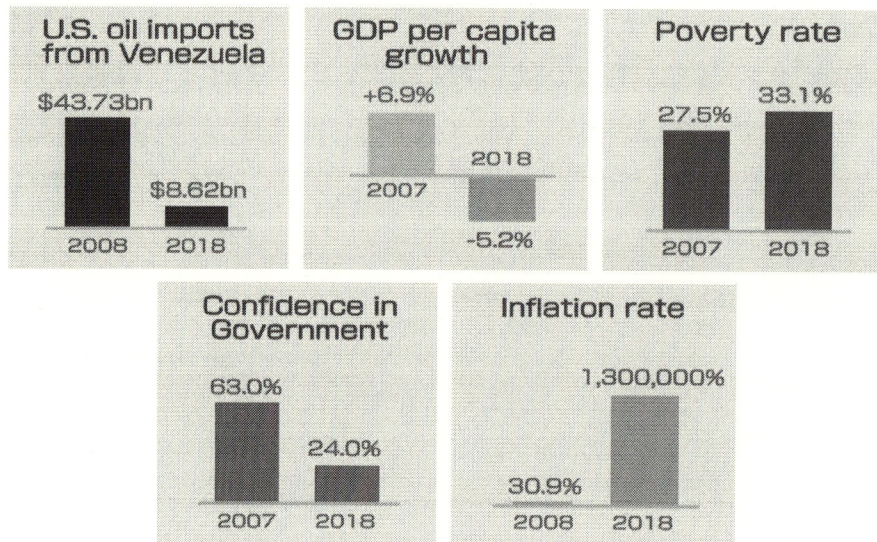

| U.S. oil imports from Venezuela | GDP per capita growth | Poverty rate |
|---|---|---|
| $43.73bn (2008) / $8.62bn (2018) | +6.9% (2007) / -5.2% (2018) | 27.5% (2007) / 33.1% (2018) |

| Confidence in Government | Inflation rate |
|---|---|
| 63.0% (2007) / 24.0% (2018) | 30.9% (2008) / 1,300,000% (2018) |

@StatistaCharts     Sources: New York Times, IMF, USTradeNumbers, Legatum Institute, World     statista

## QUESTIONS

**(a)**     **(i) Define the term _real disposable incomes_ indicated in bold. (Text 2 – paragraph 3)   [2 marks]**

**(ii) Define the term _macroeconomic imbalances_ indicated in bold. (Text 2 – paragraph 4)**
**[2 marks]**

**(b)** **(i)** Draw a Lorenz Curve to illustrate the change in the level of inequality in Venezuela. (Text 2 –paragraph 1) [3 marks]

**(ii)** State the Gini coefficient formula and explain the meaning of the change in the values of the Gini index. (Text 2 – paragraph 1) [2 marks]

**(c)** Use a demand and supply diagram to explain the effect of following official reserves on Venezuela's exchange rate against the US dollar. (Text 3 – paragraph 2) [4 marks]

**(d)** Use a demand and supply diagram and the concept of elasticity to explain the large fluctuations in oil prices and oil revenues for Venezuela. (Text 1) [4 marks]

**(e)** Use an AD/SRAS diagram to explain how Venezuela's rising foreign debt can increase poverty and inequality in the country. (Text 3) [4 marks]

**(f)** Using the information in Text 2 and Text 3, explain why accelerating rates of inflation in Venezuela is most likely to lead to falls in the country's capital stock. [4 marks]

**(g)** Using the text / tables and your knowledge of economics, evaluate economic policies the Venezuelan Government can introduce to reverse the decline in the economic development of the country. [15 marks]

## ANSWERS:                    12. Venezuela

**(a)       (i) Define the term _real disposable incomes_ indicated in bold. (Text 2 – paragraph 3)   [2 marks]**

Real disposable income is the buying power of a worker's earnings after paying income tax and removing the effect of inflation.

**(ii) Define the term _macroeconomic imbalances_ indicated in bold. (Text 2 – paragraph 4)**
**[2 marks]**

Macroeconomic imbalance is the condition where inflation and unemployment are rising above target levels. Economic growth is falling below the long term trend. Inequalities are rising and the balance of payments deficits are becoming unfavourable.

**(b)       (i) Draw a Lorenz Curve to illustrate the change in the level of inequality in Venezuela. (Text 2 –paragraph 1)                                                    [3 marks]**

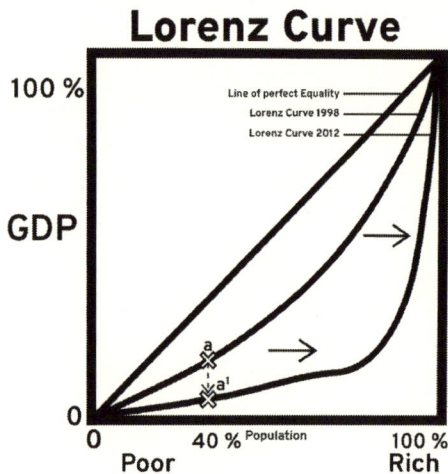

Lorenz Curve measures the distribution of income of a population. For Venezuela, given the current economic problems and the cutbacks in government social programs of price controls on essentials, the poorest 40 % of population command only 'a' portion of the national income when previously they had 'a' portion.

**(ii) State the Gini coefficient formula and explain the meaning of the change in the values of the Gini index. (Text 2 – paragraph 1)** [2 marks]

Gini coefficient formula = (Area  a)/(Area  (a +  b))

With perfect equality the Gini Coefficient  =  0

With perfect inequality the Gini Coefficient  =  1

Venezuela's Gini coefficient has risen from 0.40 to 049. This means the level of income inequality has risen significantly. This inequality is probably an underestimate given the current dire situation.

**(c)    Use a demand and supply diagram to explain the effect of following official reserves on Venezuela's exchange rate against the US dollar. (Text 3 – paragraph 2)** [4 marks]

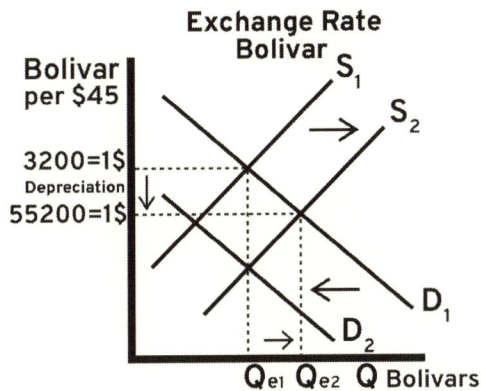

With hyperinflation (650 %, 2300 %) there is little faith in the Bolivar. Foreigners have reduced their demand for Bolivars $D_1$ falls to $D_2$ as it will drastically lose its purchasing power and Venezuelans earning in Bolivars prefer to sell the currency as soon as possible, $S_1$ falls to $S_2$. The currency dramatically depreciates quickly draining away US $ reserves.

(d)s     Use a demand and supply diagram and the concept of elasticity to explain the large
fluctuations in oil prices and oil revenues for Venezuela. (Text 1)                              [4 marks]

Price of oil

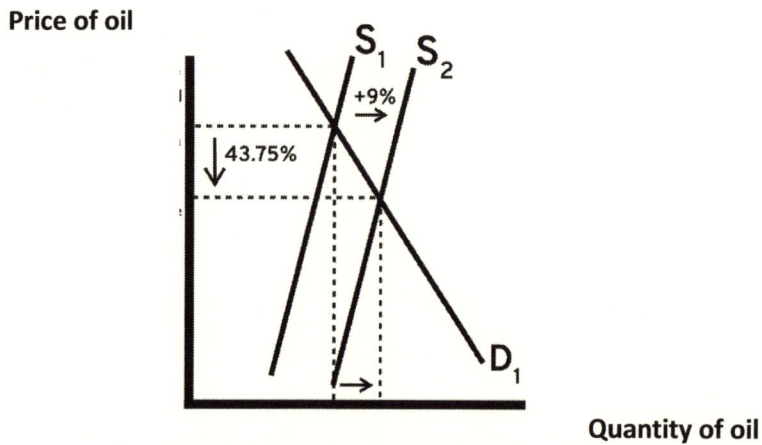

Quantity of oil

Above we can say that with low PED and low PES an increase in global supply of 9% will lead to a large
fall in price of 43.75%. Total oil revenue (PxQ) will clearly fall.

**(d)h     Use a production possibility frontier (ppf) to explain how Venezuela like many other oil rich often specialize mostly on oil to gain foreign currency revenues to import goods such as medicines. (Text 1)                                                    [4 marks]**

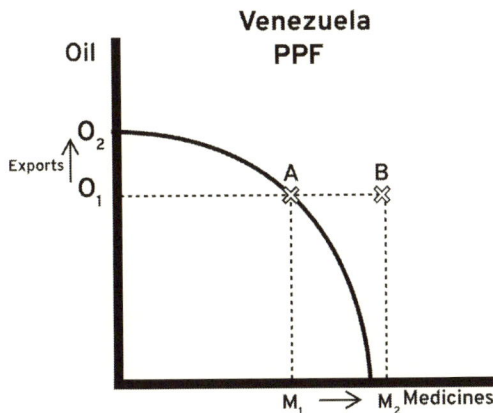

If initially before specialisation and trade, Venezuela was at point A, producing and consuming $O_1$ and M1, then by completely specialising in oil it produces $O_2$. Venezuela can still consume $O_1$, export $(O_2 - O_1)$ and use the earnings to buy medicines from abroad. With the gains from specialisation it can consume $OM_2$ instead of $OM_1$.  This means Venezuela applying comparative advantage trade theory is able to <u>produce</u> on its PPC while <u>consuming</u> beyond its PPC.

**(e)     Use an AD/SRAS diagram to explain how Venezuela's rising foreign debt can increase poverty and inequality in the country. (Text 3)                                         [4 marks]**

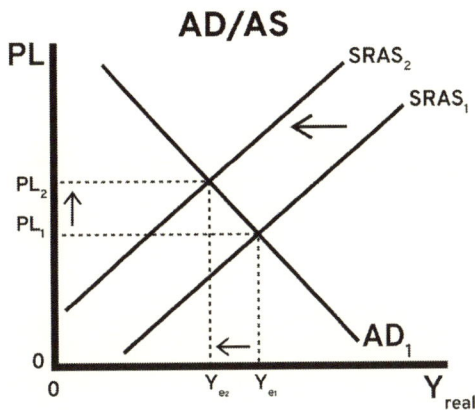

Most of Venezuela's foreign debt is in US$ or other more stable foreign countries. With a rapidly depreciating currency, more and more Venezuela's output has to be diverted away from the domestic economy, $SRAS_1$ falls to $SRAS_2$, to be sold abroad to earn foreign exchange to service the debt (Principal of the loan + interest).

Domestically $AD_1$ > $SRAS_2$ at price level $PL_1$. Price rise $PL_1$ to $PL_2$. The situation worsens if Venezuela's government prints more Bolivars without a corresponding increase in output to match. Poverty and inequality worsens are most workers earn in local currency and their purchasing power is rapidly diminishing. Inflation acts as a massive stealth tax. The high-income groups often earn their incomes in foreign currencies as they own assets which bring returns in those foreign currencies.

**(f)      Using the information in Text 2 and Text 3, explain why accelerating rates  of inflation in Venezuela is most likely to lead to falls in the country's capital stock.                    [4 marks]**

- Accelerating rates of inflation ends up as hyperinflation where the buying power of the money is less than the paper value of the Bolivar currency. (Inflation rising from 650 % to 2300 %)
- With hyperinflation new investment (domestic and foreign) will fall rapidly. This is because future profits are extremely difficult to calculate since future revenues and costs are impossible to calculate and uncertain.
- The replacement investment (wear and tear) may also stop as customers for the products are unable to pay for the goods / services produced by the machinery.
- Owners of capital goods, hotels, factories, apartments are probably keen to sell as profits turn into losses. They are probably willing to lower their prices if payments are made in a more stable currency.
- Those owners who are unable / unwilling to sell their assets often strip the assets and sell the components. Criminality increases leaving Venezuela with a diminished level of capital stock and no investment. This is clearly shown in the fall in oil production figures. (2.16 BPD to 1.95 BPD)
- Rising interest rates in Table 1 show that it is unlikely currently that a wave of optimism will take over business sentiment and spur any new investment.

**(g)      Using the text / tables and your knowledge of economics, evaluate economic policies the Venezuelan Government can introduce to reverse the decline in the economic development of the country.                                                                    [15 marks]**

- Summarise the current situation using the information in the question:
- As Per inflation, economic depression, falling exports, rising poverty rates, greater inequality, falling investment, massive budget deficits and rising debt, rising interest rates and falling confidence in the government.
- Venezuela may have to adopt drastic policies simultaneously. To stabilise the value and faith in

136

the Bolivar, Venezuela may need to peg its currency to a more stable one. This could be with its neighbour Columbia or the US$. This will mean savings in Bolivar will lose more of their purchasing power. Focus will be upon promoting exports to gain foreign currency. Great hardship domestically for those who have no access to foreign currency. Large members of citizens, workers may leave to earn foreign currency abroad. Government's access to foreign currency could be used alleviates the immediate poverty. Export sector will expand beyond oil.

- A stable currency will subsequently lead new domestic industries growing, such as food and drink. This can help Venezuela become loss specialised, more diversifies and self-reliant.
- Macro imbalances can gradually improve with this reset. Remittances from workers abroad will help to rebuild the nation.
- It is important to note that the oil sector may need new investment and the required funds may be hard to find without severe conditions.

## 13.    QATAR

*Study the texts and data below and answer the questions that follow.*

### Text 1- Overview of Qatar

Qatar's economic climb of recent years has few equals. Its abundant carbon resources did not destine it, nor did it happen merely by chance. Other countries with equal natural endowment have not been able to develop and grow economically. The reason for Qatar's leading economic situation is due to the wise and committed national leadership, strong and reciprocally rewarding relationships with international partners, and vigorous execution. Qatar has set in place a long-term development strategy under the National Vision 2030 to diversify its economy and investment in infrastructure. Improving its transport, education, sports, healthcare, telecommunication and hospitality are a key part of this plan. Healthy economic growth in times of weaker oil prices is a demonstration that the strategy of ***economic diversification*** is already proving successful.

Qatar's real GDP expanded from 2000 and 2011 by 13.1% on average a year. Between 2004 and 2011 GDP yearly growth averaged 15.9%. On an international level, Qatar's economic growth has outperformed even that of China (Figure 1) below.

**Figure 1**

Real GDP: Qatar and selected economies since 2000

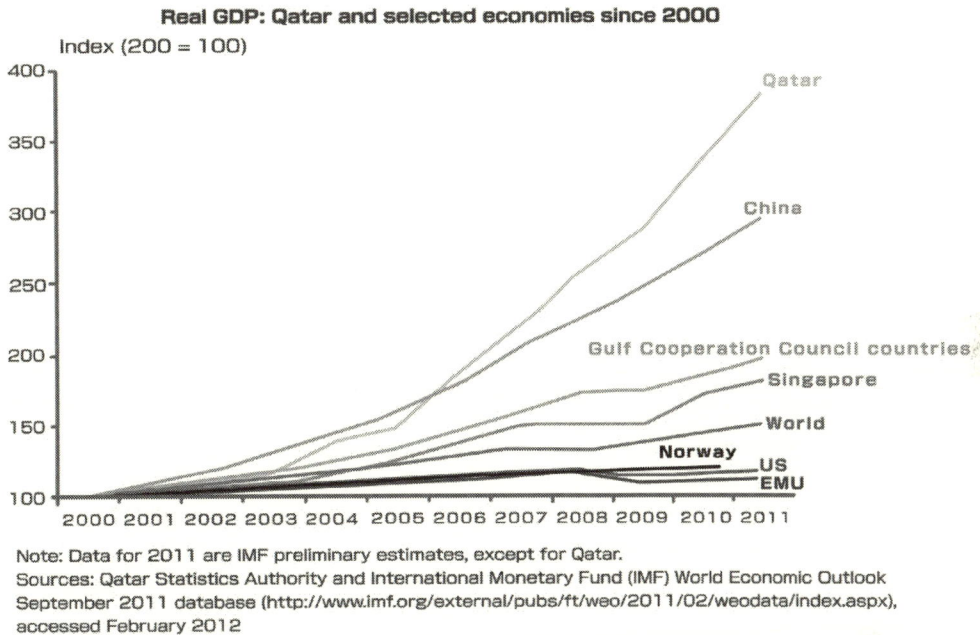

Note: Data for 2011 are IMF preliminary estimates, except for Qatar.
Sources: Qatar Statistics Authority and International Monetary Fund (IMF) World Economic Outlook
September 2011 database (http://www.imf.org/external/pubs/ft/weo/2011/02/weodata/index.aspx),
accessed February 2012

A fall in the oil and gas prices has led to a contraction in the revenue from these exports but other sectors growth is strong and expected to be around 5.7% in 2017, contributing to an overall GDP growth of just under 3%. Qatar's non-oil and gas economy has also grown rapidly, averaging nearly 20% from 2004 to 2011. But much of this expansion would not have occurred without hydrocarbons. Countries that heavily rely on oil exports, and did not diversify its exports are now forced into making government spending cuts.

Qatar has consistently had ***current account surpluses***, often surpassing 10% of GDP. Its total saving has averaged 56% of GDP and investment around 33% over the same period. In recent years, Qatar has been investing 10% of GDP on economic and social infrastructure.

Behind these favorable indicators lies progress on policy and institutional reform. Qatar is an open economy with few impediments to trade or investment. Qatar maintains low nominal tariffs on imports, with most tariff lines at 5% or less. In 2000, Qatar began to ease restrictions on direct foreign investment (outside of oil and gas). Although majority Qatari ownership is required in some sectors, 100% foreign ownership is permitted.

The 2018 trade embargo led by Saudi Arabia led to a sudden downturn in the economy. Panic ensued and there was a significant liquidation of assets leading to capital flight. Using its vast reserves of foreign currency gained from the sales of petroleum, the Qatar Central Bank stabilised the Qatari Riyal by injecting $38.5bn.

## Text 2- Milk shortage in Qatar

Due to Qatar's alleged support of terrorism Arab states – Saudi Arabia, Bahrain, United Egypt and Arab Emirates are boycotting Qatar and obstructing the import of necessity goods. Sea, air and land blockades are causing severe scarcity of food; Qatar depends on imports to meet the needs of the population. The first 126 cows of the anticipated 4000 arrived in Doha to tackle the dairy shortage caused by the blockade of the country. The shortage lasted only a few weeks as the supply chain adjusted. Power International, the Qatari firm that initiated this Qatari dairy farming project, estimates that, once all the cows have been flown in, it will be able to meet 30% of the demand in one year. A further 10000 cows are planned to arrive in the next 3 years to ensure complete dairy self-sufficiency in 5 years in Qatar.

## Text 3- 6th Sustainable development goal 2030 MET

The Minister for Energy and Industry, Dr. Mohamed bin Saleh al-Sada, announced that Qatar has met the sixth sustainable development goal by insuring that the entire population has now access to clean water and sanitation facilities. Good water management is essential on both a social as well as an economic level. During the conference on International Decade for Action in Dushanbe, Tajikistan the Minister mentioned the launch of the Permanent Water Resources Strategy Committee and Qatar's National Water Act, which aim to insure the supply of clean water for future generations. Due to the high population growth, it is essential to invest in strategies of integrated water management and recycling.

## Text 4- CPI inflation edges down 0.3% in May this year

CPI falls 0.3% in May from the previous month due to a fall in the prices of food, housing and utilities. However, compared to the previous year the CPI for May 2018 has increased by 0.5% to 108.20 (**base**

**year 2013**).

## Table 1

| | 2018 Q2 | 2018 Q3 | 2019 Q2 | 2019 Q3 |
|---|---|---|---|---|
| GDP (Billions QR) | 170.6 | 179.9 | 181.3 | 182.1 |
| Inflation Rate y-o-y | 0.2 | 0.2 | −0.3 | −1.4 |
| Budget Surplus (Deficit)/GDP | 3.6 | 1.0 | 3.4 | 3.0 |
| Current Account/GDP | 8.8 | 8.0 | 9.1 | 9.8 |

## Table 2A

**Human Capital Index (gender)**

| | 2014 | | | 2019 | | |
|---|---|---|---|---|---|---|
| | Male + Female | Male | Female | Male + Female | Male | Female |
| Human Capital Index (HCI) | 0.57 | 0.54 | 0.62 | 0.61 | 0.59 | 0.65 |

**Table 2B**

**Human Capital Index for Selected Countries 2019**

| Male + Female 2019 | Qatar | Europe | Latin America | Middle-East | US | South Asia |
|---|---|---|---|---|---|---|
| **Human Capital Index (HCI)** | 0.61 | 0.70 | 0.55 | 0.57 | 0.78 | 0.46 |

(World Bank)

**Table 3**

## Economic Sectors

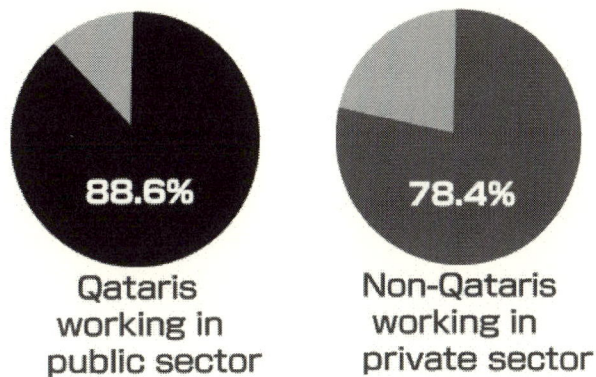

88.6%

Qataris
working in
public sector

78.4%

Non-Qataris
working in
private sector

Source: Qatar Statistics Authority

**GDP - composition by sector: agriculture: 0.2%, industry: 50.3%, services: 49.5% (2017 est.)**

**Definition: The distribution gives the percentage contribution of agriculture, industry, and services to total GDP. Agriculture includes farming, fishing, and forestry. Industry includes mining, manufacturing, energy production, and construction. Services cover government activities, communications, transportation, finance, and all other private economic activities that do not produce material goods.**

## QUESTIONS

(a)     (i) Define the term *economic diversification* indicated in bold (Text 1 – paragraph 1)  [2 marks]

(ii)  Define the term *current account surpluses* indicated in bold (Text 1 – paragraph 4)2 marks]

**(b)** **(i) Calculate the CPI value for May 2017. (Text 4)** [3 marks]

**(ii) Using Table 1 identify <u>three</u> groups in Qatar that might be adversely affected by a negative rate of inflation.** [2 marks]

**(C)** **Use a production possibility curve (PPC) to illustrate how changes in Qatar's Human Capital Index (HCI) can affect its economy. (Table 2)** [4 marks]

**(d)** **Suggest and explain 2 reasons why hydrocarbon dominated country like Qatar may grow significantly faster than Norway, another oil exporting country. (Figure 1)** [4 marks]

**(e)** **Use an AD / AS diagram to explain Qatar's economic growth and falling month to month CPI (April to May 2018) at the same time. (Figure 1 and Table 1)** [4 marks]

**(f)** **Use a demand and supply diagram and the concept of elasticity of the boycott on the price and quantity of milk in Qatar in the short and long run.** [4 marks]

**(g)** **Using the texts / tables and your knowledge of economics, evaluate the view that for Qatar to grow sustainability, it must diversify extensively in all sectors.** [15 marks]

**ANSWERS:**             **14. Qatar**

**(a)**      **(i) Define the term _economic diversification_ indicated in bold (Text 1 – paragraph 1) [2 marks]**

Economic diversification is FOPs are used to develop many sectors of the economy at the same time. Total output increases and a downturn in any sector can be compensated by growth in another sector thereby lowering risk of economic collapse.

            **(ii) Define the term _current account surpluses_ indicated in bold (Text 1 – paragraph 4)**
            **[2 marks]**

Current account surplus is when the value of export of food services, income from FOPs abroad and transfers are greater than the corresponding imports.

**(b)**      **(i) Calculate the CPI value for May 2017. (Text 4)**             **[3 marks]**

CPI value for May 2017

$$\text{CPI } 2017 + 0.5\% \text{ of CPI } 2017 \ = 108.20$$

$$1.005 \text{ CPI } 2017 \ = 108.20$$

$$\text{CPI } 2017 \ = 108.20/1.005 \ = \ \underline{\mathbf{107.66}}$$

This means prices overall have by 7.66 % from 2013, the base year.

**(ii) Using Table 1 identify <u>three</u> groups in Qatar that might be adversely affected by a negative rate of inflation.** **[2 marks]**

Negative inflation rate means falling general prices compared to the previous period. Three groups adversely affected are:

(1)  Shopkeepers as their profit margins fall
(2)  Borrowers since their real value of debt rises and
(3)  Savers likely to receive lower interest rates.

**(C)     Use a production possibility curve (PPC) to illustrate how changes in Qatar's Human Capital Index (HCI) can affect its economy. (Table 2)** **[4 marks]**

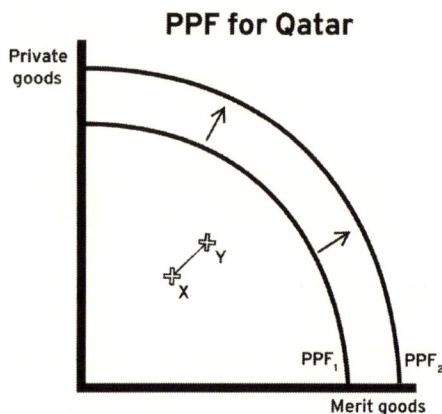

**PPF for Qatar**

A higher HCI means human capital depending. Each worker has more skills to apply. This raises the productivity of workers and translates into higher production potential for the economy PPC$_1$ rises to PPC$_2$ and all its sectors.

In addition the process of acquiring the skills creates more jobs, more spending and output, combination X rises to combination Y.

**(d)** **Suggest and explain 2 reasons why hydrocarbon dominated country like Qatar may grow significantly faster than Norway, another oil exporting country. (Figure 1)** **[4 marks]**

Figure 1 shows that Qatar has grown significantly faster than Norway between the years 2000 and 2011, 200 percent compared to 50 percent rise in Real GDP. There are several reasons for this:

- ▢ Qatar is a less matured economy with lots of unused capacity and hence it is easier to expand from a low base than a high base.
- ▢ Qatar's region of the world is fast expanding and hence Qatar is closer at hand than Norway to supplying the expanding countries with hydrocarbons.
- ▢ Qatar has relatively speaking only recently started to reform its institutions and subsequently attract major FDI. Text 1 paragraph 5.

**(e)** **Use an AD / AS diagram to explain Qatar's economic growth and falling month to month CPI (April to May 2018) at the same time. (Figure 1 and Table 1)** **[4 marks]**

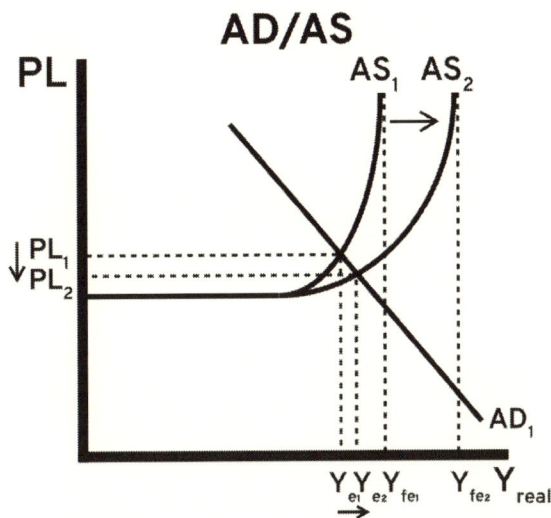

Qatar's rising real economic growth can be seen by rise in Ye1 to Ye2. The aggregate supply has risen from AS1 to AS2 to enable this.

With a strong current account surplus, the Qatari Riyal may well have appreciated against other currencies such as the Indian Rupee since the Riyal is pegged against the US$. This makes prices of imports fall and subsequently the price level may drop, $PL_1$ to $PL_2$ causing deflation as table 1 shows.

**(f)** **Use a demand and supply diagram and the concept of elasticity of the boycott on the price and quantity of milk in Qatar in the short and long run.** **[4 marks]**

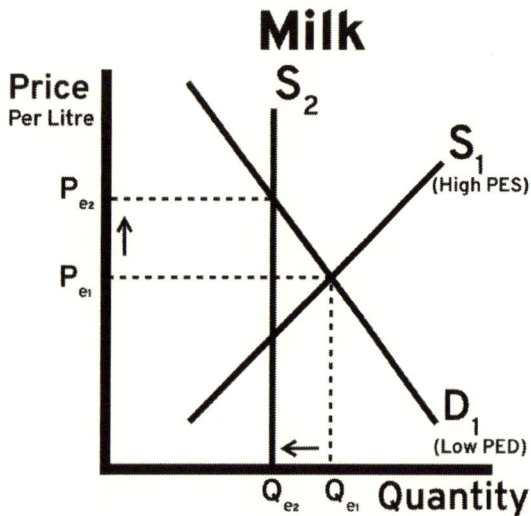

The PED for milk in Qatar is low since milk probably takes up a small percent of average income and it is habit forming. The PES is much higher since Qatar, prior to the boycott, had ample access to imported milk.

Any supply shock $S_1$ to $S_2$ can dramatically increase the price of milk Pe1 to Pe2. However as new suppliers of milk are found and the supply chain readjusted new supply comes on the market. S2 rises and price falls below Pe2. In the long run power international's project of dairy farming in Qatar may well bring some national food security. However, the price of milk may be permanently higher if power International remains uncompetitive. Alternatively a domestic subsidy may be required if the Qatar government wants to make a political point to its neighbours.

**(g)      Using the texts / tables and your knowledge of economics, evaluate the view that for Qatar to grow sustainability, it must diversify extensively in all sectors.                    [15 marks]**

Diversification is an economic strategy of widening the range of goods and services produced in the economy. For Qatar this means moving away from being heavily dependent on hydrocarbons.

For Qatar diversification means less vulnerability to fluctuations in primary commodities. (could use a demand – supply diagram)

Strategic diversification in say port facilities may take advantage of potential comparative advantage (define). Here Qatar can follow Singapore's example.

Diversification can result in import substitution. This is argument behind Qatar starting dairy farming as part of national food security.

A lack of diversification means Qatar risks future growth if the world quickly moves away from fossil fuels.

There are however many problems Qatar faces in diversifying.

- Qatar loses the gains accrued from international specialisation. Milk will be most costly to produce.
- Diversification into products Qatar lacks comparative advantage worsens the global allocation of resources.
- Qatar lacks the economies of scale since its population is too small.
- Most of Qatar's population is imported labour. Diversification is not possible using Qataris only.
- The quickest route to diversification is permitting multinational corporations to invest (PDI). This has its own set of disadvantages, even though it may be very useful.

Overall if it is not too costly some limited diversification may be possible for Qatar. However given the geographical position of Qatar and the current institutions it is unlikely the Qatar will benefit much beyond political prowess.  Qatar's vast resources of money and oil allow it promote this nationalistic view against its neighbours.

## 14.   THAILAND

*Study the texts and data below and answer the questions that follow.*

### Text 1- Overview of *Thailand*

In 2019 the GDP of Thailand was at $387bn with a GDP per capita at $5,780. While the average annual growth rate in real GDP since 2014 to 2019 has been 2.9%, however, World Bank forecasts Thailand's economy to reach 3.2% economic growth in 2020. Thailand is very much dependent on international trade as exports account for ⅔ of the GDP. The main exports include machinery, manufactured goods, processed foods, tourism and chemicals. Thailand's greatest problem, poverty, has reduced significantly over the last 30 years from 67% in 1986 to 7.2% in 2019. However, Thailand's poverty rates can rise if economic growth falls along with falling agricultural prices and droughts. Thailand's inequality is worse than many East Asian countries. In 2017, more than 80% of the country's poor population lived in rural areas. A continuous growing disparity in consumption and household income between the wealthy North, North East and Far South with the rest of the regions is a growing problem. For the past 20 years.

Thailand has imposed many significant reforms in order to obtain the developed nation status in the long term. These reforms are set to focus on human capital, equal economic opportunities, environmental sustainability, competitiveness, and economic stability. However, long term issues such as an ageing population, labour shortages, rising domestic debt levels, and political uncertainty might pose a threat on growth. Although economic growth has slowed down in recent years due to sluggish global demand, Thailand's economic foundation is robust with a low inflation rate (0.2%), a low unemployment rate (0.9%) and reasonable public and ***external debt***.

### Text 2- Electric car industry

Thailand is a regional manufacturing hub and export base for the world's top carmakers. The auto industry accounts for about 10 percent of the country's gross domestic product. As the industry goes towards the production and consumption of electric vehicles (EVs) there is  going to be ***market-failure*** from negative externalities to positive externalities in the market for electric vehicles. Since driving EVs produces no carbon emissions which do not contribute to pollution when consuming, Thailand's two state owned enterprises; Gulf Group (largest electricity provider in Thailand) and PTT Group (the largest energy company based in Thailand) initiated an investment plan worth a combined 4.65 billion US dollars in two electricity generating projects. Tax incentives have also been approved to promote the production of three types of electric vehicles. This allows the electric vehicle manufacturing firms to benefit greatly hence becoming more competitive and able to develop better quality EVs at a lower price.

## Text 3- Fall in Consumer Prices

In the month of June 2017, deflation occurred again as consumer prices fell to -0.1%. Policy makers are having a tough time to get inflation into the 1 percent to 4 percent target rate. Nevertheless, The Bank of Thailand has remained reluctant to decrease below the benchmark interest rate any further at 1.5% despite having a strong currency. Policy makers are optimistic about the economic future by raising growth estimates.

## Text 4 - Currency Aid from the IMF

The Asian crisis first emerged in Thailand in 1997 as the Thai baht came under a series of increasingly serious speculative attacks while confidence in Thai markets was diminishing. On August 20th, 1997, the IMF's Executive Board approved financial support for Thailand of up to 2.9 billion worth of special drawing right (SDR), or about US$4 billion, over a 34-month period. The total amount of bilateral and multilateral assistance to Thailand came to US$17.2 billion. Thailand drew US$14.1 billion of that amount before announcing in September 1999 that it did not plan to draw anymore of the remaining balance, due to improved economic situation.

## Text 5 – Thai Rice Exports to Decrease

Thailand is the largest rice exporter after India, however, it is expected in 2020 that rice exports will fall by 4% due to the increased competition of Vietnam. Last year, rice exports from Thailand totaled 9.88 million tonnes, whilst in 2018, rice exports were 9.5 million tonnes according to Chookiat Ophaswongse, the honorary president of the Thai Rice Exporters Association. In addition, the price of rice is expected to fall between 5 to 10 percent due to a lack of global demand for Thai rice. Lastly, according to the USDA, world rice production will increase by 1.6 percent to 480 million tons while consumption will rise by 1.5 percent to 477.8 million tons.

## Table 1- Economic Data for Thailand*

| | 2019 Data | 2018 Data |
|---|---|---|
| GDP (real growth rate) | 3.2% | 2.9% |
| GDP per capita (PPP) | $16,900 | $16,400 |
| Unemployment rate | 0.9% | 0.9% |
| Inflation rate | 0.2% | -0.9% |
| Central bank interest rate | 1.5% | 1.5% |
| Current account balance | $46.41 billion | $32.15 billion |
| Exchange rate (Baht per US$) | 35.3 | 34.25 |
| External debt | $131.4 billion | $131.4 billion |
| Foreign Direct Investment (FDI) net inflows | $197.4 billion | $188.9 billion |

*All figures are in US dollars *Source Adapted from The CIA World†Factbook*

Data Response-Paper 2

## Table 2A- Development Data for Thailand

|  | Previous Years | 2018 |
|---|---|---|
| Human Development Index | 0.686 (2005) | 0.740 |
| Gini Coefficient | 40.45 (1998) | 44.5 |
| Life expectancy at birth (years) | 72.160 (2005) | 75.068 |
| Adult literacy rate (% of ages 15 and older) | 93.51% (2005) | 93.98% |

**Source Adapted from The World Bank,**

## Table 2B – International Data for Thailand

| Exports | $228.2 billion (2017) |
|---|---|
| Imports | $190 billion (2017) |
| Reserves of foreign exchange and gold | $193.5 billion (2017) |
| Exchange rate | 34.34 baht for $1 |
| External debt | $135.5 billion (Dec. 2017) |
| Current Account Balance | $44 billion (2017) |

*Source: Adapted from The CIA World Factbook*)

**(a)** (i) Define the term _external debt_ indicated in bold. (Text 1 - paragraph 2)     **[2 marks]**

(ii) Define the term _market failure_ indicated in bold. (Text 2 - paragraph 1)     **[2 marks]**

**(b)** (i) From text 1 calculate the population of Thailand in 2019. (Text 1 – paragraph)     **[3 marks]**

(ii) Draw an appropriate diagram illustrating the positive externalities accrued as a result of more electric vehicles on the streets of Thailand.  (Text 2 – paragraph 1)     **[2 marks]**

**(c)s**     Suggest 3 reasons why Thailand may wish to put a limit on the amount of FDI coming into the country.     **[4 marks]**

**(c)h**     To what extent does the data support the assertions of the Marshall – Lerner Theorem? (Table  1)     **[4 marks]**

**(d)**     Distinguish between GDP per capita and GDP capita PPP and decide with an explanation if the Thai currency is overvalued or under – valued against the US$.     **[4 marks]**

**(e)**     Using a demand and supply exchanged rate diagram, explain the effect on the Thai Baht / US$ exchange rate of a serious speculative attack like the one in 1997. (Text 4)     **[4 marks]**

**(f)**     Calculate the price elasticity of demand for Thailand's rice on the global market and suggest 2 reasons why income elasticity of demand for Thailand's rice is likely to be inelastic. (Text 5)   **[4 marks]**

**(g)**     Using the text / tables and your knowledge of economics, evaluate the possible consequences on Thailand's economic development if the Thai Baht significantly appreciates over the next decade against all other currencies.     **[15 marks]**

**ANSWERS:**                    **14. THAILAND**

**(a)**       **(i) Define the term _external debt_ indicated in bold. (Text 1 - paragraph 2)**          **[2 marks]**

External debt is the value of borrowed money by a country's commercial banks, government, companies from foreign lenders. This usually comes with interest which needs to be repaid.

       **(ii) Define the term _market failure_ indicated in bold. (Text 2 - paragraph 1)**          **[2 marks]**

Market Failure is when the full benefits of an additional unit of activity [(marginal social benefit (MSB)] does not equal to the full costs [(marginal social costs (MSC)] of that unit of activity. MSB = marginal private benefit + external / 3$^{rd}$ party benefit MSC = marginal private cost + external / 3$^{rd}$ party cost.

**(b)**       **(i) From text 1 calculate the population of Thailand in 2019. (Text 1 – paragraph)**          **[3 marks]**

In 2019  GDP = $ 387 Bn        GDP/POP = $ 5780

       Population of Thailand in 2019  =  ($ 387 Bn)/($ 5780)= **$ 66955017**

**(ii) Draw an appropriate diagram illustrating the positive externalities accrued as a result of more electric vehicles on the streets of Thailand. (Text 2 – paragraph 1)** **[2 marks]**

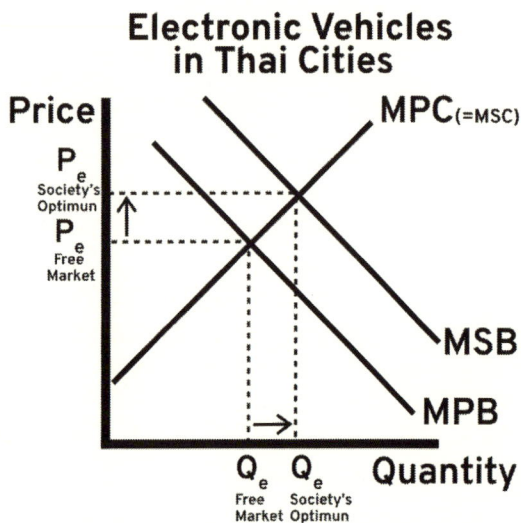

**Electronic Vehicles in Thai Cities**

Free market equilibrium only considers private benefits and private costs. However, the introduction of electric vehicles will reduce pollution and noise and raise the well-being of the rest of society or 3rd party. Free market here under producers the number of electric vehicles in comparison to society's optimum.

〖Qe〗 (Free market) < 〖Qe〗 (society's optimum).

**(c)s** **Suggest 3 reasons why Thailand may wish to put a limit on the amount of FDI coming into the country.** **[4 marks]**

3 reasons for Thailand concerned about FDI.

- Thailand may not wish to give concessions such as tax breaks or other preferential treatment to foreign companies.
- FDI can flood into Thailand's stock market and artificially raise share prices and appreciate currency. The reverse is true also. (Speculative motive)
- FDI tends to capital intensive. If may not create many jobs and may even reduce the number of workers.
- FDI can also influence local politics, culture and traditions.

**(c)h    To what extent does the data support the assertions of the Marshall – Lerner Theorem? (Table 1)**                                                                                 **[4 marks]**

Table 1 shows that Fran 2015 to 2019 the Thai Baht has depreciated from 34.25 per $ to 35.3 Thai Baht per $. During this period the current account surplus rose from $ 32.15 BN to $ 46.41 BN.

The Marshall Lerner Theorem is satisfied by the above figures provided PED exports + PED inputs > 1

If Thailand's data shows  PEDx + PEDm  less or equal to  1   then the Marshall Lerner theorem does not support Thailand's situation.

**(d)     Distinguish between GDP per capita and GDP capita PPP and decide with an explanation if the Thai currency is overvalued or under – valued against the US$.**                       **[4 marks]**

For 2019, GDP per capita in market terms is 5780 US$. The GDP per capita in PPP (Purchasing Power Parity) terms is $ 16900. There is clearly a huge difference between the 2 values.

The PPP method values GDP figure in terms of what goods and services 5780 US$ can actually buy in Thailand. Each US$ buys more goods / services in Thailand than in the US.

It is likely that with such low inflation rate the Thai Baht is significantly undervalued compared to the US$.

**(e)     Using a demand and supply exchanged rate diagram, explain the effect on the Thai Baht / US$ exchange rate of a serious speculative attack like the one in 1997. (Text 4)          [4 marks]**

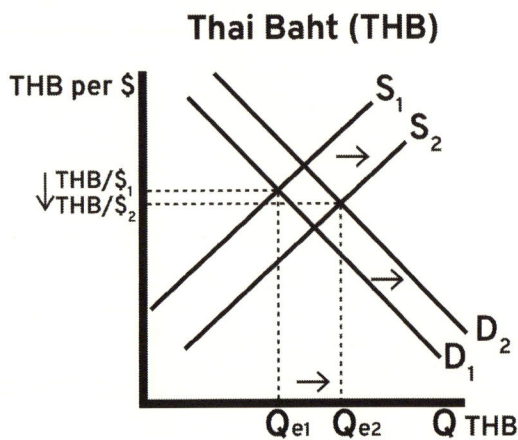

**Thai Baht (THB)**

Speculative attack on Thai Baht means holders of Thai currency sell their holding $S_1$ to $S_2$ quickly as they anticipate further depreciation of the Thb. Thb / $ starts depreciating at an accelerating rate.

The Thai Central Bank and the Government have a decision to take. Allow the Thb to depreciate and find a new free market equilibrium or intervene and stabilise the drop by intervening and buying up the Thb on the foreign exchange market, $D_1$ to $D_2$.

It was not until September 1999 through significant intervention that the Thai authorities finally managed to stabilise the currency at Thb / $2 rate. However their foreign exchange reserves had been depleted and now they were low in debt with the IMF and other lenders.

**(f)     Calculate the price elasticity of demand for Thailand's rice on the global market and suggest 2 reasons why income elasticity of demand for Thailand's rice is likely to be inelastic. (Text 5)   [4 marks]**

PES$_{rice}$ = (percent change in QS for Thai rice)/(Percent change in P of Thai rice)

= (4 %)/(5 % to  10 %)    = 4/5  to  4/10

0.4  <  PES $_{Thai Rice}$  <  0.8          Thai Rice is supply price inelastic.

Income elasticity of demand for Thai rice measures the degree of responsiveness in the demand for Thai rice as a result of a change in the price of Thai rice.

YED $_{Thai Rice}$   = (percentage change QD Thai Rice)/(Percent change in P Thai Rice)

0 < YED < 1 inelastic, This is probably because :

As global incomes, incomes rise, the demand for rice as a commodity does not rise as fast. The demand

158

for Fancy and more convenient forms of consumption rises. (Value added argument)

**(g)     Using the text / tables and your knowledge of economics, evaluate the possible consequences on Thailand's economic development if the Thai Baht significantly appreciates over the next decade against all other currencies.**
**[15 marks]**

A stronger currency buys more units of another currency than before.

- ☐   Define economic development.
- ☐   Imports become cheaper, imported inflation rates fall. Cheaper oil, machinery enables Thai industry to expand. More jobs may be created. If prosperity not shared inequality will rise further as Gini coefficient value rising Fran 0.40 to 0.44 indicates. The migration to urban areas will create new health problems of overcrowding and congestion.
- ☐   Higher incomes allow workers to invest in education and health and this raises HDI for Thailand further. (HDI has risen from 0.68 to 0.74)
- ☐   Low inflation due to stronger. Thai Baht enables low interest rates which creates additional C, I and G. Aggregate demand rises to raise economic growth. There may well be rising asset prices and debt levels which may be become unsustainable.
- ☐   Government tax revenues may rise due to greater activity.
- ☐   Stranger Baht make Thailand's export more expensive and less price comparative Globally. Rice prices fall in Baht terms. Export industries may be required to improve productivity which is more difficult in the short run.
- ☐   Current account balance may worsen if PED X  +  PED  >  1. However Thailand is running a surplus at the moment any way. (there is some room to manoeuvre)
- ☐   New FDI may be reluctant to enter Thailand as Thai assets may be too expensive. FDI may go instead to cheaper neighbouring countries. Tourist industry will lose price competitiveness.

In conclusion, Thai government may need to introduce new policies which provide a greater safety net to alleviate the inequalities which may be caused as well as promote industries which value add (electric vehicles) and export (electric vehicles) along with improving levels of human capital.

## 15.   NIGERIA

*Study the texts and data below and answer the questions that follow.*

### Text 1- Overview of Nigeria

Nigeria is one of the most populous countries in Africa and accounts for 47% of West Africa's population. Nigeria is a country composed of a plethora of natural resources and is Africa's most prominent oil exporter by virtue of having the biggest natural gas reserves in Africa. Powered by one of the largest populations of youth in the world, Nigeria has the tools necessary to become at the forefront of the continent.

Economic growth rate is estimated to have been 2.7% in 2015, a substantial fall from 6.3% in 2014. This has mainly been because of the significant hit taken by oil industry due to a persistent fall in the prices of oil. 2016 has been worse; Nigeria's economy has continued to worsen by recording ***real negative growth rates*** resulting in a recession.

Lower oil prices still pose a threat to the economy.  Shortages of power and fuel coupled with a decrease of foreign exchange are expected to further reduce GDP. Inflation increased in 2016 to 18.8% approximately doubled from 9.6% (CPI of 130 in 2015) in the previous year. This is because of electricity price increases due to the aforementioned shortage of fuel and the ***depreciation of the Naira***, Nigeria's currency, throughout the year. Inflation is now projected to continue to remain in double digits over 2017/2018.

As Nigeria's core business, oil, suffers, the government aims to diversify the economy, by promoting growth in the private sector and trying to increase the number of jobs in the economy by investing into newer industries

Nigeria aims to recover by stabilizing the economy and looking towards long term growth. There are important areas for growth and missed opportunities that the government can use to improve. The private sector's immediate problem is lack of regulation and access to finance. Improvements in these areas will open the sector to smaller businesses.

Nigeria's youth remain frustrated with the slow job creation and inequality still remains high. There is a deep divide socioeconomically from the North and the South of the country due to Boko Haram. Health inequalities along with access to basic education and water still are lacking. Nigeria despite its great potential, risks losing it through lackluster efforts to provide basic amenities and infrastructure greatly required by the populace is looking towards creating cogent policy aimed at tackling obstacles to Nigeria's prosperity.

## Text 2- Overview of Nigeria

Nigeria's booming population puts pressure on the land and due to a lack of resources available to the public through the government, a type of economic market failure known as the "Tragedy of the Commons" takes place. The irony is that a great number of Nigerians depend on the forest ecosystem for food and other crucial resources. Hence, Nigeria with the highest rate of deforestation of its primary forests is hampering the wellbeing of its own citizens in order to achieve economic growth. 50% of Nigeria's forests have been lost to unstable logging, agriculture and fuel-wood collection.

Nigeria has lost 139067 hectares of forest area from 1990-2005. Currently, only 12% of the country's landmass is forest and at the current rate of deforestation, Nigeria looks to deplete all its forest land by 2052.

The government introduced measures to counter this rapid deforestation and thus depletion of land by creating the national forestry action plan (NFAP). Whilst NFAP is making progress, the aforementioned political instability and lack of political consolidation and support makes it hard for the organization to continue preventing the harmful deforestation of its lands.

The forest is primarily being cleared for Nigeria's agriculture industry which is looking to use the fertile land gained from cutting those trees. In the long run, it will be that same industry that suffers as once all the forests are cut down, there will be no further land to exploit leading to lackluster growth. In order for Nigeria to continue growing such a key industry, technological improvements need to be made to till the land in a sustainable manner.

## Text 3- Lowering Interest Rates in Nigeria

A prominent economics Dr. Bongo Adi from the Lagos Business School has urged the government to lower its interest rates from 14% to 12%. He believes that the government no longer needs to keep the former interest rate as it has worked in reducing inflation.

As of October 2017, the inflation rate has stood at 15.91%, its ninth consecutive decline since the beginning of the year. However, due to the lackluster growth of the manufacturing sector, Dr. Adi asks for the government to reduce its interest rates to promote growth in that sector. Growth in the manufacturing sector will increase the quality and quantity of capital in the economy leading to an increase in aggregate supply, lower prices even further and promote growth. An increase in real output that does not result in inflation has many beneficial outcomes for the economy. Nigeria will be able to take advantage of its large and youthful population and employ them to increase the productivity of the economy and decrease the high unemployment rate.

## Text 4- Nigeria restriction on food imports

Nigeria has been suffering from food deprivation for its citizens for a long time. It has recently caught up to the world standard of 2630 calories per day. However, food production has lulled behind and has not caught up with the increased technological improvements of the industry.

Furthermore, Nigeria implements high tariffs and other forms of protectionist policies which according to the Brookings Institute adversely affect the well-being of Nigerians. The reason for this high level of protection is because Nigeria wants to stop being dependent on foreign countries and diversify and grow its own domestic industry especially by taking advantage of the rich resources the country has in oil and land.

The government does gain revenue by imposing tariffs and as of 2014, tariffs are ranked second in contribution to government revenue, superseded only by more key industries such as oil. Furthermore, the government wants to keep foreign currency which is far more valuable than domestic currency within the country. In order to do this, President Muhammadu Buhari has restricted foreign exchange access for 41 important goods, including staples such as wheat.

The tariffs on rice range from 30-50% while flour imports are completely banned. This has done little to domestic firms as they lag behind technologically and the restrictions increase the price of inputs for the food industry.

**Table 1- Development data for Nigeria**

| Year | 2015 |
|---|---|
| Human Development Index | 0.527 |
| Gini Coefficient | 43 |
| Life expectancy at birth (years) | 53.1 |
| Adult Literacy Rate | 59.6% |
| Maternal Mortality Ratio (deaths per 1000 live births) | 814 |
| Adolescent Birth Rate (births per 1000 women aged 15-19) | 110.6 |
| Share of Seats Held in Parliament (% held by women) | 5.8 |
| Labour force participation rate (% ages 15 and older) | **Female: 48.4** **Male: 64.0** |

## QUESTIONS

**(a)**      **(i) Define the term _real negative growth rates_ indicated in bold (Text 1 - paragraph1) [2 marks]**

         **(ii) Define the term _depreciation of the Naira_ indicated in bold (Text 2 - paragraph2)  [2 marks]**

**(b)s**     **(i) Using information from Text 1, paragraph 3, calculate the CPI value for Nigeria for 2016.**
                                                        **[3 marks]**

**(b)h**     **(i)  State 2 reasons why the labour force participation rate (LFPR) for females is lower than males especially in rural areas. (Table 1)**                           **[3 marks]**

         **(ii) Identify 3 possible problems for Nigeria resulting from high levels of youth unemployment. (Text 1-paragraph 6)**                        **[2 marks]**

**(c)**      **Use an AD/AS diagram to explain Dr Bongo Ali's view that dropping interest rates will promote growth of the manufacturing sector in Nigeria.  (Text 3 - paragraph 2]**       **[4 marks]**

**(d)**      **Draw a production possibility curve to explain the effects of the 'Tragedy of the Commons'. (Text 2-paragraph 1)**                           **[4 marks]**

(e)      Draw a poverty cycle diagram to show the effects on economic development of poor access to basic education and health facilities.  (Text 1 - paragraph 6)                    [4 marks]

(f)      Draw a tariff diagram to explain the revenue gains for the Nigerian Government and losses for the Nigerian consumer from imposing high tariffs.  (Text 4- paragraph 3)                    [4 marks]

(g)      Using the texts/tables and your knowledge of economics, evaluate the view that Nigeria is justified in maintaining its high tariffs and other barriers to international trade to promote economic development.                                                          [15 marks]

## ANSWERS:               15. NIGERIA.

**(a)**      **(i) Define the term _real negative growth rates_ indicated in bold (Text 1 - paragraph1) [2 marks]**

Economic growth is the rise in the real value of final goods and services produced in an economy over a given period of time. This value is calculated after removing the effect of inflation. Real negative growth rate is the percentage fall, after removing inflation, in value of this economic activity. This is measured by a negative GDP percentage value.

          **(ii) Define the term _depreciation of the Naira_ indicated in bold (Text 2 - paragraph2)  [2 marks]**

Depreciation of the Naira means in a freely floating exchange rate regime, each unit of the Nigerian currency, Naira, buys less foreign currency such as the US $.

**(b)s**     **(i) Using information from Text 1, paragraph 3,  calculate the CPI value for Nigeria for 2016.**
                                                           **[3 marks]**

CPI 2015 = 130

$$CPI\ 2016 = CPI\ 2015 + 18.8\%\ of\ CPI\ 2015$$

$$CPI\ 2016 = 130 + 24.44$$

$$= \underline{\mathbf{154.44}}$$

**(b)h     (i)  State 2 reasons why the labour force participation rate (LFPR) for females is lower than males especially in rural areas. (Table 1)                                        [3 marks]**

LFPR for females is most likely to be lower than males, especially in rural areas because:

- There is a lack of formal jobs in the rural areas.
- Lack of transport and allied infrastructure in rural areas makes it difficult for women to get to work places easily and cheaply.
- Lack of jobs and child care facilities makes it more likely that women drop out of the labour force.
- Lack of corporate involvement and acknowledgement of the issue and responsibility.
- Traditions and culture.

**(ii) Identify 3 possible problems for Nigeria resulting from high levels of youth unemployment. (Text 1-paragraph 6)                                        [2 marks]**

3 problems from high youth unemployment in Nigeria are :

- Higher crime rates and anti-social behaviour.
- Fall in household formation rates leading to less social cohesion in communities.
- Low spending and consumption rates adversely affecting economic growth and jobs.
- Lower rates return from education and human capital.
- Greater government resources required to integrate the disenfranchised youth.

**(c)    Use an AD/AS diagram to explain Dr Bongo Ali's view that dropping interest rates will promote growth of the manufacturing sector in Nigeria.  (Text 3 - paragraph 2)          [4 marks]**

## AD/AS Nigeria

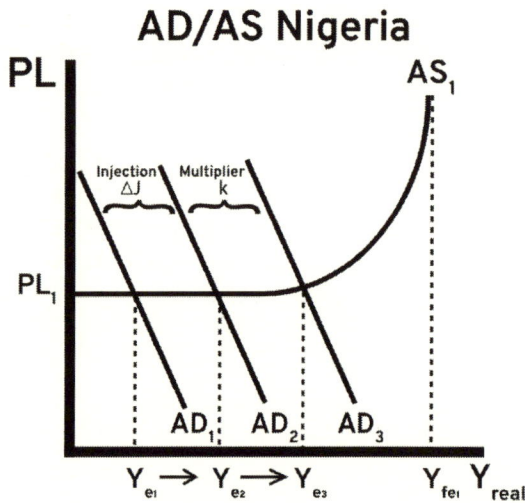

A loose monetary policy of dropping interest rates and increasing credit supply means :

▪    Rise in C spending through greater credit card usage on manufactured output.

▪    Rise in I spending OS costs of production fall and rates of return to new I rises. New factories may be built.

▪    Rise in G spending through higher government borrowing through the issue of bonds carrying lower yields.

▪    In the foreign sector export demand will rise while imports fall when the Naira depreciates.

An initial injection will raise AD1 to AD2 and with a positive multiplier 'k' effect AD2 rises further to AD3.

If the economy is in severe recession (Text 1) then the expansion may not lead to inflation. It is also worth noting that according to Text 3, that if there is inflation then greater investment in manufacturing will increase capacity, AS shifts right and price level may be prevented from rising.

**(d)**    **Draw a production possibility curve to explain the effects of the 'Tragedy of the Commons'. (Text 2-paragraph 1)**                                                                   **[4 marks]**

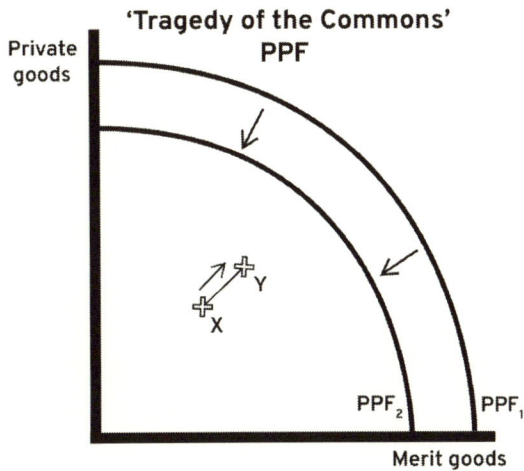

'Tragedy of the Commons' PPF

Deforestation in the short run increases economic activity as more output and jobs occur. X rises to Y with more private goods and merit goods.

However, in the long run, deforestation kills the 'Goose that lays the golden egg.' The potential to produce in the future falls. PPC1 falls to PPC2. Tragedy of the commons is the result of overuse of a common resource due to ill-defined property rights.

**(e)**    **Draw a poverty cycle diagram to show the effects on economic development of poor access to basic education and health facilities.  (Text 1 - paragraph 6)**                         **[4 marks]**

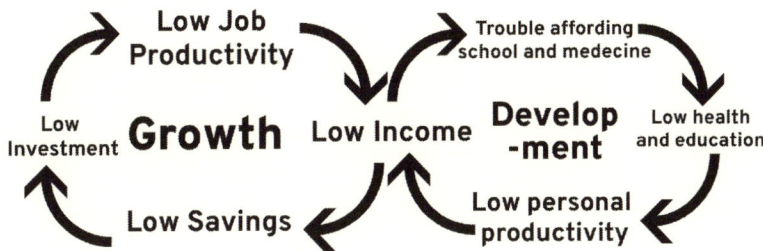

Poor access to basic education and health facilities will mean low human capital will result in low job productivity and low income. Households will have trouble affording school and medicine. This reduces the well-being of families.

Poor health leads to poor productivity at work as absenteeism rises. This low personal productivity leads to low income. The cycle of poverty continues as economic development falls in Nigeria.

**(f)** **Draw a tariff diagram to explain the revenue gains for the Nigerian Government and losses for the Nigerian consumer from imposing high tariffs. (Text 4- paragraph 3)** **[4 marks]**

## Tariff on Rice

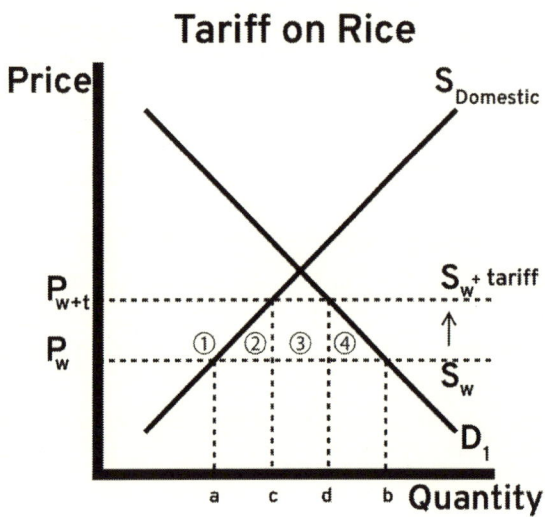

A rice tariff means that a tax is imposed on the value of rice coming into Nigeria from abroad.

The Nigerian passes on the tax to the consumer through higher prices. The loss of consumer surplus is given are areas 1 + 2 + 3 + 4.

The Nigerian Government collects the tariff revenue area 3. Imports of rice clearly fall from (ab) to (cd).

**(g)** **Using the texts/tables and your knowledge of economics, evaluate the view that Nigeria is justified in maintaining its high tariffs and other barriers to international trade to promote economic development.** **[15 marks]**

Define economic development:

Arguments for Nigeria maintaining its high tariffs and barriers:

- National Food security (Text 4)
- Develop its own food industry (Text 4) similar to India and China, the other populous countries. This development creates jobs, on the job training for its huge unemployed army of workers.
- Nigeria can use more of its land to grow food instead of the more destructive dumber industry. (Text 2) Nigeria has plethora of resources (Text 1 paragraph 1).
- Domestic food industry can expand and achieve economies of scale and keep the value added internally.
- Less pressure for Nigeria to export to earn foreign currency (Text 4, paragraph 3)
- Diversification from oil, reduces risk, and less vulnerability to fluctuating oil prices. (Text 1).
- Agriculture and manufacturing spread all over Nigeria can help to reduce regional inequalities, improve, rural infrastructure and enable new investment in health and rural facilities. It can kick-start. Arthur Lewis's dual sector growth model. (Table 1)
- Strong empirical Japan, Switzerland, India, China and the US suggest that in the early stages of development strong barriers are needed to achieve critical mass for domestic industries before opening up to free trade.

Arguments against tariff and other barriers:

- These barriers generally raise prices and reduce choice for Nigerians. (Text 1 - paragraph 3)
- There is deadweight loss or inefficiency caused by the misallocation of resources.
- Greater likelihood of corruption.
- Invites retaliation from other countries.
- FDI may be deferred from Nigeria as the tariff rates and other rules many create uncertainty.
- Foreign imports forces Nigeria to export more and more especially if the Naira is depreciating and more foreign currency is required to import non-essentials.
- Free market policies mean Nigerian government does not have sufficient revenue to finance social programs to raise the well-being of its rural citizens. Gini coefficient will rise above 0.43. (Text - 4, Table 1)
- Deforestation may accelerate to order to expert and earn foreign currency. (Text 2)

171

## 16.    Malaysia

*Study the texts and data below and answer the questions that follow.*

### Text 1- Overview of Malaysia

With a population of 31.9 million people, Malaysia is at the forefront of Southeast Asia, averaging an astonishing growth of more than 7 percent every year for the past 25 years. With an economy led by the production of raw materials, today, Malaysia has become one of the leading exporters of electrical parts, components and appliances, as well as natural gas and palm oil. Suffering a financial crisis through 1997 to 1998 as well as in 2009, Malaysia has shown incredible growth in its economy at an average rate of 5.5 percent through the years of 2000 to 2008, and an average of 5.7 percent since 2010.

Although Malaysia being an upper-middle income economy, they have managed to almost eradicate **absolute poverty** by reducing its percentage to under 1 percent for those households living with low incomes. However, the income inequality still remains high, towards which the Malaysian government has now implemented policies and redirected its subsidies on basic food staples and medicines to try and address the needs of the poorest 40 percent of its population. From 2009 to 2014, the average household income of Malaysia's bottom 40 percent increased by 11.9 percent per year, compared to the 7.9 percent growth for the total population, thus slowly closing the income gap.

Alongside these policies, the government has also made reforms in its fiscal position to limit its fiscal deficit to the targeted 3 percent of the GDP of 2017. However to uphold future growth, the Malaysian government may require more series of reforms with the forecasted plateau in the collection of taxes, and a narrowing of expenditure in the public sector this is going to become more and more unlikely. With a fast growing economy, the government should focus more on social policies to create programs in which they support vulnerable households, as well as boost the productivity of the public sector and the use of public spending. While Malaysia's economy experienced extreme growth, they must aim to grow its productivity even more by implementing productivity-enhancing reforms to compete against other regional countries and to narrow the gap between high-income economies.

### Text 2- Increase in crude palm oil tax

In February 2017, Malaysia raised its export tax on palm oil for shipments to 8 percent per tonne from 4.5% previously. Being the world's second largest crude palm oil exporter, the increase in tax was implemented due to palm oil's increase in price from $655 per tonne to $825 per tonne year on year. Export demand by volume also rose during this time from 16.5 million tonnes to 17.3 million tonnes.

Malaysia's oil palms trees yield more oil per acre than do other crops. But soaring demand for the world's most popular vegetable oil has led to extensive deforestation and loss of wildlife in Indonesia and Malaysia, the biggest producers.

### Text 3- Bank Negara Malaysia keeps its 3% rate

Following the depreciation of the Malaysian ringgit by 6 percent following the election of Donald Trump, an increase in the interest rate was projected to limit the damage from offshore foreign-exchange trading. However, the Bank Negara Malaysia (BNM) has kept its 3 percent key rate to strengthen its currency in preparation of stricter US monetary policies.

### Text 4- UK's FDI into Malaysia in tech sector to grow stronger

From October 2016, Malaysia has the potential to receive over RM 270million in investments in the technology sector from the UK in the next 15 months. 42 UK tech companies are expected to partner with Malaysia, which will be the largest UK tech delegation to Malaysia.

Two strategic plans were implemented with first being formed by UK's Action Starter and CAS Analytics Sdn. of Malaysia. The second plan was between UK's Kino-mo and People n Rich Holdings to advertise new tech innovations. These plans will bolster employment, training and development issues, and the UK will hope to use Malaysia as a means to access more emerging markets in the ASEAN.

During his first tenure as Malaysia's prime minister, Mahathir Mohammad, introduced several capital controls to stop the speculative attacks on the Ringgit and stem the decline of Malaysia's economy during the 1997-1999 Asian financial crisis. The controls included the repatriation of all ringgit assets held abroad and the elimination of offshore ringgit trading to contain speculation and capital outflows.

The controls effectively saw Malaysia shift from a liberalised to a highly regulated market.

In 2005 Malaysia returned to the floating exchange rate regime.  This provides the country the flexibility to adjust to international economic and financial developments.

**Table 1**

| | New Data | Previous Data |
|---|---|---|
| GDP (Real growth rate) | 4.2% (2016) | 4,3% |
| GDP per Capita (ppp) | $9503 (2016) | $10,540 |
| Unemployment rate | 3.45% (2016) | 3,1% |
| Inflation rate | 2.09% (2016) | 3,1% |
| Central bank interest rate | 3.125% (2016) | 3,19% |
| Current account balance | $6.92 billion (2016) | $9.06 billion (2015) |
| Exchange rate (Malaysian ringgit per US$) | 4.456133 (December 2016) | 4.280748 (December 2015) |
| External Debt | $213 billion (31 December 2017) | $195.3 billion (31 December 2016) |
| Foreign Direct Investment (FDI) net inflows | $13.51 billion (2016) | $9.85 billion (2015) |

Source: Adapted from the World Bank: http://www.worldbank.org/ and CIA Country Profile: https://www.cia.gov/library/publications/the-world-factbook/(docs/profileguide.html

**Economic data for Malaysia**

**Table 2- Development data for Malaysia**

|  | New Data | Previous Data |
|---|---|---|
| Population | 31,382,000 (2016) | 31,634,000 (2015) |
| Human Development Index | 57th (2018) | 60th (2015) |
| Gini Coefficient | 39 (2017) | 37.16 (2010) |

**Source: Adapted from the World Bank and CIA Country Profile**

## QUESTIONS

(a)     (i) Define the term *absolute poverty* indicated in bold. (Text 1 – paragraph 2)          [2 marks]

        (ii) Define the term *interest rate* indicated in bold. (Text 3 – paragraph 3)          [2 marks]

(b)s     (i) Calculate the change in the export revenue collected by the Malaysian government as a result of the rise in the tax rate. (Text 2)                                        [3 marks]

**(b)h** **(i) Explain why a higher price for palm oil and simultaneously a higher demand for Malaysian palm oil exports does not necessarily contradict the law of demand. (Text 2)** **[3 marks]**

**(ii) Suggest 2 risks that Malaysia may risk if it maintains the interest rate at 3 % even when its currency the Malaysian Ringgit has depreciated by 6 % against the US $. (Text 3 – paragraph 1)** **(2 marks]**

**(c)** **Using the data, draw an AD / AS diagram to explain the effects of Foreign Direct Investment (FDI) on the macroeconomic indicators of Malaysia. (Table1)** **[4 marks]**

**(d)** **Draw a demand / supply diagram to explain the changes in consumer and producer surplus as a result of introducing a 20 % subsidy on basic food staples. (Text 1 – paragraph 2)** **[4 marks]**

**(e)** **(i) Using data on GDP and population in Table 1 and Table 2, explain any changes in inequality.** **[4 marks]**

**(f)** **Using an appropriate market failure diagram, show how an indirect tax in Malaysia alone will not be sufficient as a measure to protect the endangered wildlife. (Text 1 – paragraph 2)** **[4 marks]**

**(g)** **Using the information in the texts and tables discuss to what extent can further fiscal consolidation aimed at balancing the Malaysia Government's budget lead to further economic development.** **[15 marks]**

## ANSWERS:           16.  MALAYSIA.

**(a)**     **(i) Define the term _absolute poverty_ indicated in bold. (Text 1 – paragraph 2)**       **[2 marks]**

Absolute poverty is when individuals / households are not able to access even the minimum levels of food, clothing and shelter required to survive.

    **(ii) Define the term _interest rate_ indicated in bold. (Text 3 – paragraph 3)**       **[2 marks]**

The intended rate is the price of borrowing or lending credit. The keyr base rate is set by the control like the BNM and the other financial institutions follow the trend set by the BN[1]. For savers the interest rate is a reward for being patient as for borrower it is the price for being impatient in spending.

**(b)s**     **(i) Calculate the change in the export revenue collected by the Malaysian government as a result of the rise in the tax rate. (Text 2)**       **[3 marks]**

Export tax revenue change:

| | | |
|---|---|---|
| Export tax revenue Before | = | tax per unit  x  number of units |
| | = | 4.5 %  of 655  x  16.5 million |
| | = | 28.575  x  16.5 m |
| | = | $ 471,487,500 |
| Export tax revenue after | = | 8 % of $ 825  x  17.3 million |
| | = | 66  x  17.3 m |
| | = | 1,141,800,000 |
| Change | = | 1,141,800,000  - 471,487,500 |

**$ 670.31 m approx increase in export revenues**.

**(b)h** **(i) Explain why a higher price for palm oil and simultaneously a higher demand for Malaysian palm oil exports does not necessarily contradict the law of demand. (Text 2)** **[3 marks]**

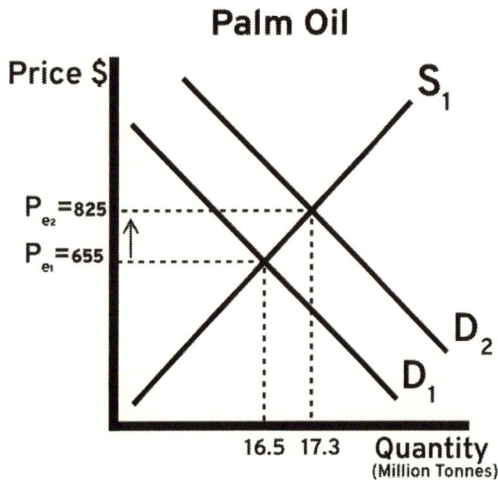

The Law of demand says that as the price of palm oil rises, the quantity demand for palm oil will assuming, all other factors remain constant (ceteris paribus). In text 2, it seems that factors such as global income and tastes and preferences may have changed and the demand for Malaysia's palm oil may have risen.

Here the equilibrium price has risen from $ 655 to $ 825 per tonne because of the rise in global demand resulting in S, accommodating this rise from 16.5 to 17.3 million tonnes.

**(ii) Suggest 2 risks that Malaysia may risk if it maintains the interest rate at 3 % even when its currency the Malaysian Ringgit has depreciated by 6 % against the US $. (Text 3 – paragraph 1)** **[2 marks]**

Interest rate maintained at 3% when the Malaysian Ringgit has depreciated by 6 & could lead to:

A further depreciation in the Ringgit will occur if US interest rates rise. A speculative attack will mean business or currency speculators who have borrowed in US $ and bought Ringgits in the past will now reverse their actions. Sell Ringgits and buy US $ to pay back their dollar loans.

International buyers of Malaysian government or corporate bonds will reduce their demand for these bonds and switch towards US bonds if the US is planning to raise its interest rates. Malaysia may find it harder to borrow money externally through Ringgit land sales.

**(c)      Using the data, draw an AD / AS diagram to explain the effects of Foreign Direct Investment (FDI) on the macroeconomic indicators of Malaysia. (Table1)                            [4 marks]**

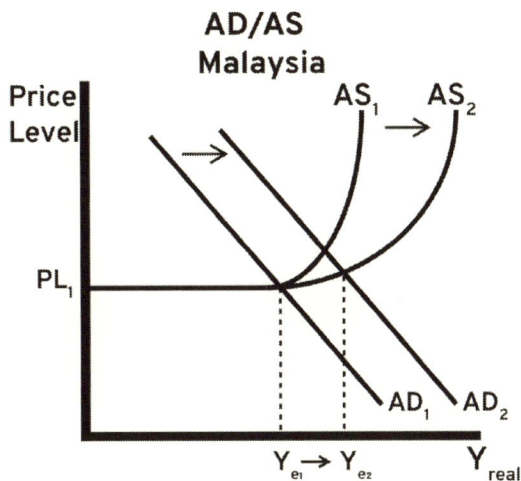

Using Text 4 and Table 1, draw an AD / AS diagram to explain the macroeconomic effects a move in 2005 to restore a freely floating exchange rate refine may have had on Malaysia.

Empirically in the short run a restoration of a freely floating regime, forces of demand and supply determining the exchange rate, usually, depreciates the currency. This is because of Malaysia's per up demand for imports. Ringgits are sold in favour of major global currencies.

Over time with stability FDI inflows will rise. $AD_1$ rises t $AD_2$. There is imported inflation due to a depreciated currency, output rises, and more jobs created along with technological transfers and higher productivity levels. $AS_1$ rises to $AS_2$ with growing capacity and $Ye_1$ rises to $Ye_2$. Table 1 shows the long term results where FDI has risen and current account is now in surplus. However, external debt is higher indicating greater integration of Malaysia in the global economy.

179

**(d)** **Draw a demand / supply diagram to explain the changes in consumer and producer surplus as a result of introducing a 20 % subsidy on basic food staples. (Text 1 – paragraph 2)** **[4 marks]**

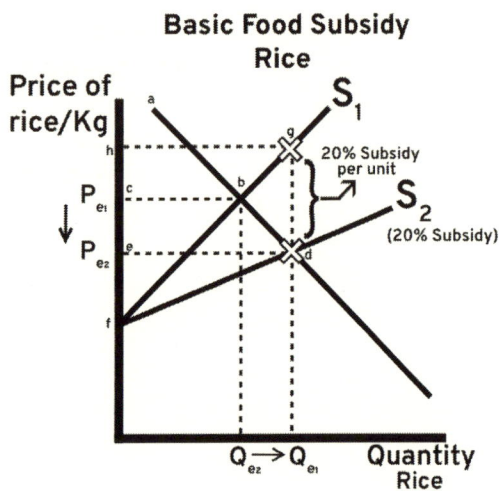

Basic Food Subsidy
Rice

Consumer surplus is the difference between the price the consumer is willing to pay and the market price. At initial price Pe1 the value of the consumer surplus is given by area (*abc*). After the 20 % subsidy the price falls to Pe2 and the consumer surplus rises to area (*ade*).

Producer surplus is the difference between the minimum price the seller is willing to accept and the equilibrium price. Before the subsidy the producer surplus is area (*bcf*). After the subsidy the producer surplus rises to area (*fgh*).

Price at point *h* is the price the producer receives.

**(e)** **(i) Using data on GDP and population in Table 1 and Table 2, explain any changes in inequality.** **[4 marks]**

From Table 1, the GDP per capita for 2016 in terms of the buying power of the US $ has fallen by about 10 %. The population has fallen during this time. This means that economic activity has fallen more than the population.

The inequality of income during this decade using the Gini coefficient has risen significantly from 37.16 (2010) to 39 (2017).

The two sets of data point to an economically slowing Malaysia with a disproportionately higher levels of suffering among the lower income groups.

**(f)     Using an appropriate market failure diagram, show how an indirect tax in Malaysia alone will not be sufficient as a measure to protect the endangered wildlife. (Text 1 – paragraph 2)      [4 marks]**

## Malaysia Palm Oil
(Market Failure)

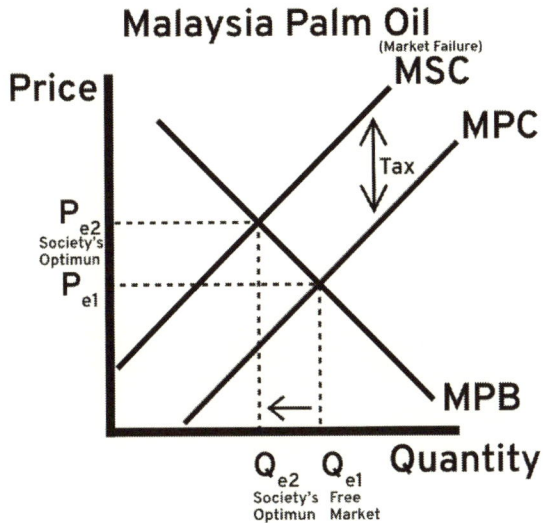

The diagram shows that market failure (MSB $^1$ MSC) occurs in the production method of palm oil. Marginal social cost of production > Marginal private cost of production of palm oil. The environmental damage of destroying biodiversity and natural habitat has not been internalised. The free market overproduces and under-prices compared to society's optimum.

$$(Qe_1 \text{ free market} > Qe_2 \text{ society's optimum})$$

$$(Pe_1 \text{ free market} < Pe_2 \text{ society's optimum})$$

An indirect tax may be seen to correct this market failure in Malaysia but globally the destruction may well continue as Indonesia may simply crank up production and destruction. The global price of palm oil may rise due to efforts made by Malaysia. This will incentivize Indonesia and other countries to expand production. A more global effort is hence required.

**(g)      Using the information in the texts and tables discuss to what extent can further fiscal consolidation aimed at balancing the Malaysia Government's budget lead to further economic development.                                                                                      [15 marks]**

Currently Malaysian is running a government budget deficit over 3 % of GDP. This means Government spending > Government revenues by more than 3 % of the total value of final goods / services.

It has to finance this deficit by selling bonds have and abroad. If sold abroad the size of borrowing adds to external debt which has risen by another 10 %. ($ 213.5bn from 195.3bn)

The Malaysian Government now wants to important austerity policies disguised as reforms to bring down public sector. This can be done by raising takes or reducing Government services. Social programs may be trimmed. This may result in rising inequality.

The Gini coefficient figures in Table 2 may worsen. The Human Development Index (HDI define) has improved from 62$^{nd}$ to 59$^{th}$ but this can go into reverse.

Alternatively, Malaysia may be hoping to reduce the deficit through focusing on economic growth policies and allocating greater FDI (text 4). The subsequent expansion in output, jobs, incomes and tax receipts can go towards reducing the debt. The success of this strategy depends upon raising the level of human capital and convincing the private sector to expand. Climate change obligation may mean Malaysia has to 'taper' its agriculture sector. Raising the level of human capital and productivity requires a long term resource commitment which the Malaysian Government may be weary of.

## 17.    Myanmar

*Study the texts and data below and answer the questions that follow.*

### Text 1- Overview of Myanmar

Myanmar is one of the fastest growing economies in Asia with a population of 52.89 million, despite being one of the most prone countries to natural disasters. With that, major flooding in recent years has decreased GDP growth from 2016 to 2017 down to 5.9% due to difficult recovery coming from long standing productivity issues in the agricultural sector which accounts for 37.8 % of Myanmar's GDP.

With a government undergoing a democratic transition, the concerns remain the political instability, achieving peace agreements with multiple armed ethnic organizations and how to address the question of Rakhine state, a large state bordering China, where independence movements have arisen.

With the lowest life expectancy and second highest child mortality rate of the ASEAN countries, Myanmar's development is severely threatened. However, other indicators like a poverty analysis conducted by the World Bank show that poverty declined from 32.1%in 2004/05 to 25.6% in 2009/10 and 19.4% in 2015. Though these figures were revised to 44.5% in 2004 to 37.5% in 2009/10 and 26.1% in 2015, they still show progress and a substantial amount of poverty remaining notably in poorer regions relying mostly on agriculture, making them all the more exposed to economic shocks.

Basic infrastructure is still lacking in Myanmar, with only one third of the population having access to national electricity and road density within the country only reaches 219.8 kilometers per 1,000 square kilometers of land area. Although some areas have improved thanks to the ***liberalization*** of the telecommunication sector making mobile and internet penetration increased significantly from less than 20% and 10% in 2014, to 60% and 25% respectively in 2015.

Education in rural areas is also a major concern as the dropout rate is very high, 6 out of 10 children who start first grade drop out before the end of middle school, this figure is 7 out of 10 in poorer circles.

## Text 2- The tourism industry in Myanmar

With the recent encouragement of tourism in Burma by the government after over 50 years of military rule has come a whole new wave of ***investment*** in the sector. There is significant job creation opportunity and poverty alleviation potential with tourism. But whether or not this it is sustainable for the country is what will determine its long-term effects.

Numbers are increasing, although the figure of three million arrivals in 2014, up from two million in 2013, may not reflect real tourists and may include day visitors, business people, returning Burmese, and others entering on a tourist visa, in addition to genuine tourists spending over 24 hours in-country. Myanmar's infrastructure and society is poorly prepared to receive a large number of foreign tourists or for an expansion of domestic tourism.

## Text 3- Solar panels

Like many developing countries, it is possible for Myanmar to skip using wasteful and unsustainable energies and move straight to using clean ones such as solar power. But experts say unsupportive government policies and lack of political will are hampering these developments.

With more than two thirds of Myanmar's people not having access to affordable and reliable energy, the perfect solution seems to be sustainable and long term solutions which would make each village more self-sufficient. And yet the government has focused on hydropower, gas and coal.

Due to an over dependence on hydropower in some areas, there has been a plague of blackouts throughout Myanmar during the dry season and has pushed people to find their own solutions such as solar power.
According to Myanmar's 2014 census, about 178,000 households used private water mills as a primary source of lighting, while 945,000 used solar, and 1 million used diesel generators.

One hour of diesel power in rural Myanmar costs roughly the same as 24 hours of power in Yangon, the commercial capital. Myanmar's Energy Master Plan, drawn up with the Asian Development Bank (ADB), projects a significant increase in coal's share of national electricity output by 2030, to almost 30 percent from less than 2 percent in 2015.

Meanwhile, the $5.8-billion National Electrification Plan (NEP) - which aims to bring power to all of Myanmar by 2030 and overwhelmingly favors grid extension - is starting with a $400 million loan from the World Bank, which said the money is not funding coal or hydropower projects.

## Table 1- Economic data for *country*

|  | 2016 | Previous years |
|---|---|---|
| GDP (real growth rate) | 1,275.02 USD | 987.74 USD (2010) |
| GDP per capita (PPP) | 1,275.02 USD | 987.74 USD (2010) |
| Unemployment rate | 0.8% | 0.8% (2010) |
| Inflation rate | 6.77% | 2.83% (2012) |
| Current account balance | 3.9 bn USD | -4.14 bn USD |

*Sources: World Bank*
*-https://www.statista.com/statistics/525775/unemployment-rate-in-myanmar/*
*-https://www.statista.com/statistics/526525/trade-balance-of-myanmar/*

## Table 2- Development data for Myanmar

|  | 2016 | 2010 |
|---|---|---|
| Population | 52.89 million | 50.16 million |
| Human Development Index (rank) | 0.556 (145) | 0.526 (149) |
| Life expectancy at birth (years) | 66.1 | 64.92 |
| Adult literacy rate % (aged 15 and older) | 93.1 | 89 |

Sources: World Bank & UNDP http://hdr.undp.org/en/countries/profiles/MMR

## QUESTIONS

(a)    (i) Define the term _liberalization_ indicated in bold. (Text 1 – paragraph 4)        [2 marks]

(ii) Define the term _Investment_ indicated in bold. (Text 2 – paragraph 1)        [2 marks]

(b)s    (i) Calculate the change in real GDP. (Table 1 and Table 2)        [3 marks]

(b)h    (i) Suggest 2 reasons why the unemployment level in Myanmar is significantly under-estimated. (Table 1)        [3 marks]

(ii) Identify 3 characteristics suggesting that Myanmar is a developing country. (Text 1)
        [2 marks]

**(c)** Use a production possibility curve to show the effect of extensive flooding and other natural disasters on Myanmar. **[4 marks]**

**(d)** Draw an appropriate market failure diagram for unsustainable energy (diesel) to show the effect of increasing use of removable sources of energy. (Text 3 – paragraph 1) **[4 marks]**

**(e)** Use a circular flow of income to explain the effect of significant numbers of foreign tourists in Myanmar on the Government sector and foreign sector. (Text 2) **[4 marks]**

**(f)** Draw a foreign exchange market diagram to explain the effect of the change in the current account balance on Myanmar's rate of exchange against the US$. (Table 1) **[4 marks]**

**(g)** Using the information in the texts and tables evaluate the short term and long term effects on the economic development of Myanmar of the National Electrification Plan. **[15 marks]**

## ANSWERS:                    17.  MYANMAR

**(a)       (i) Define the term _liberalization_ indicated in bold. (Text 1 – paragraph 4)          [2 marks]**

Liberalisation is removal of all barriers to trade across frontiers as well as adopting a freely floating exchange rate regime.

**(ii) Define the term _Investment_ indicated in bold. (Text 2 – paragraph 1)          [2 marks]**

Investment is the expenditure on capital goods over a given period of time. Capital goods / services go to make consumer goods / services.

**(b)s      (i) Calculate the change in real GDP. (Table 1 and Table 2)          [3 marks]**

Real GDP is the value of all final goods / services produced in an economy over a given period of time after removing the effect of inflation.

Real GDP before (2010)        =        GDP real per capita x population (2010)

Before        =        $ 49545038400

Similarly Real GDP after (2016) =        $67435807800

Change in Real GDP   = 17890769400 = **$ 17.89bn**

**(b)h** **(i) Suggest 2 reasons why the unemployment level in Myanmar is significantly under-estimated. (Table 1)** **[3 marks]**

Myanmar's official unemployment of 0.8 % is significantly underestimated because:

- ⬚ Huge informal economy
- ⬚ Methods of collecting data politicised
- ⬚ Regular changes in methodology, sampling
- ⬚ Over manning in public sector. Using 3 workers when only one is needed.
- ⬚ Under employment

**(ii) Identify 3 characteristics suggesting that Myanmar is a developing country. (Text 1)**
**[2 marks]**

3 Characteristics of a less developed country:

Low life expectancy, high percentage of labour force in agriculture, high growth rate, high incidence of poverty, high infant mortality rate, poor infrastructure such as roads, electricity and internet penetration, fewer resources to deal with natural disasters

**(c)** **Use a production possibility curve to show the effect of extensive flooding and other natural disasters on Myanmar.** **[4 marks]**

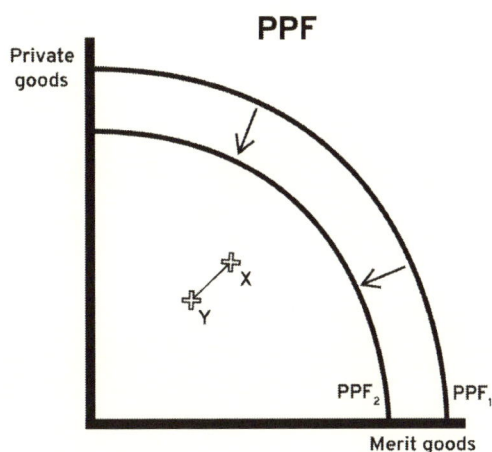

A natural disaster can reduce the production capabilities of Myanmar as large areas of land can become useless and be reclaimed by the sea due to climate change PPC1 falls to PPC2. Movement from X to Y means that in current time production of private goods and merit goods can both fall due to the disruption.

It is perhaps worth noting that as some form or rebuilding occurs more economic activity takes place and Y can reverse back to X.

**(d)     Draw an appropriate market failure diagram for unsustainable energy (diesel) to show the effect of increasing use of removable sources of energy. (Text 3 – paragraph 1)          [4 marks]**

### Diesel

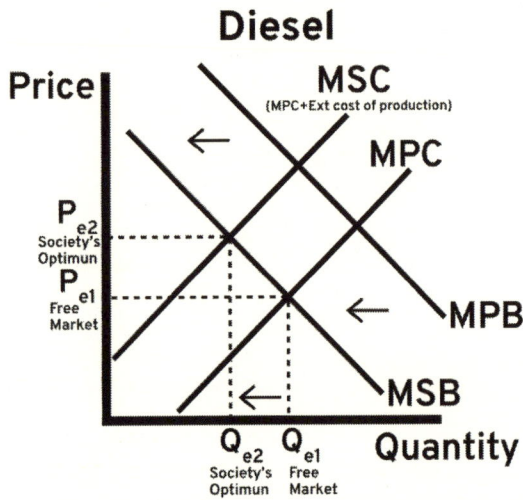

Currently the free market price $Pe_1$ is below the society optimum $Pe_2$ and there is overproduction $Qe_1 > Qe_2$ and hence market failure (MSC does not equal MSB). Note Diesel produces negative externalities at both production and consumption ends.

Greater use of renewable in Myanmar will reduce the use of diesel especially in the rural areas (1 hour of diesel in rural costs 24 hours of power in the city) will shift MPB and MSB left and $Qe_1$ output will fall.

**(e)     Use a circular flow of income to explain the effect of significant numbers of foreign tourists in Myanmar on the Government sector and foreign sector. (Text 2)          [4 marks]**

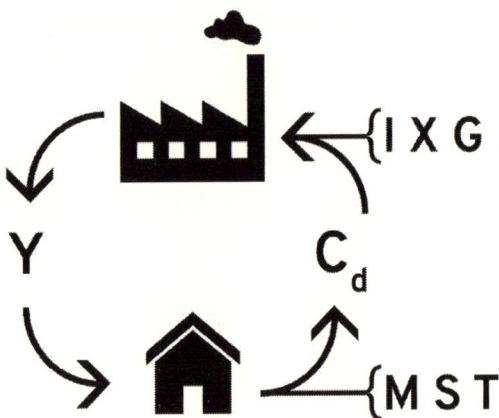

Foreign tourists bring in foreign currency and by spending bring in tax revenue for the Myanmar Government. The Myanmar Government can then buy goods / services from private sector which can expand and sue more FOPs.

The households receive income which can then he put in the banking sector, domestic consumption and Government sector. The tourists can also create a positive multiplier effect by buying goods / services from the private sector which turn expands through

190

greater investment. The circular of income expands as a result of more tourism.

**(f)** **Draw a foreign exchange market diagram to explain the effect of the change in the current account balance on Myanmar's rate of exchange against the US$. (Table 1)** **[4 marks]**

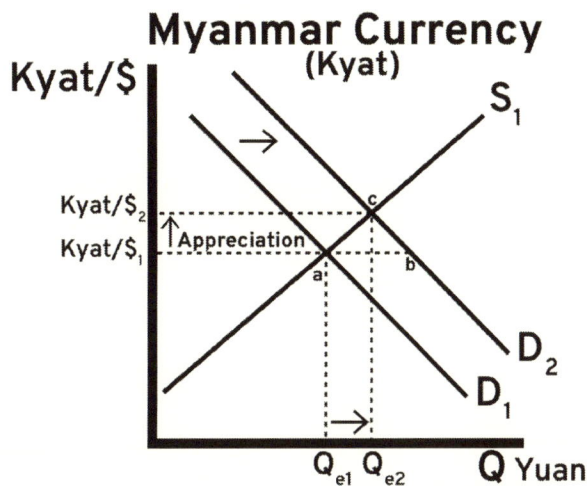

Define current account balance.

The current account has progressed from a deficit to a surplus in recent years. (-$4.14bn to + $3.95 bn).

A current balance of + 3.9 Bn $ means that at Kyat / $_1$ the demand for Kyat is rising as foreigners become more interested in trading with Myanmar. $D_1$ rises to $D_2$. There is a shortage of Kyat of (*ab*). The market clears as the Kyat appreciates against the US $ until point C. A new equilibrium Kyat / $_2$, Qe$_2$ is established.

Myanmar Currency (Kyat) diagram: Kyat/$ on vertical axis, Q Yuan on horizontal axis, with $S_1$, $D_1$, $D_2$, Appreciation arrow, points Kyat/$_2$, Kyat/$_1$, $Q_{e1}$, $Q_{e2}$.

**(g)** **Using the information in the texts and tables evaluate the short term and long term effects on the economic development of Myanmar of the National Electrification Plan.** **[15 marks]**

National Electrification Program $5.8 Bn

Define economic development and its measurement. For Myanmar this has improved through it is me of the poorest countries in the world.

A national electrical grid will be a massive injection creating lots of economic activity at the household and producer / retail level. New goods/services (refrigeration), jobs can bring massive benefits and economic development. Unemployment and inflation rate can fall in the rural areas. Health care and education facilities can certainly improve along with real incomes. The gains are widespread as experience from history clearly shows. Both short term and long-term improvements. Both AD and LRAS will rise.

**Myanmar National Electrification Plan**

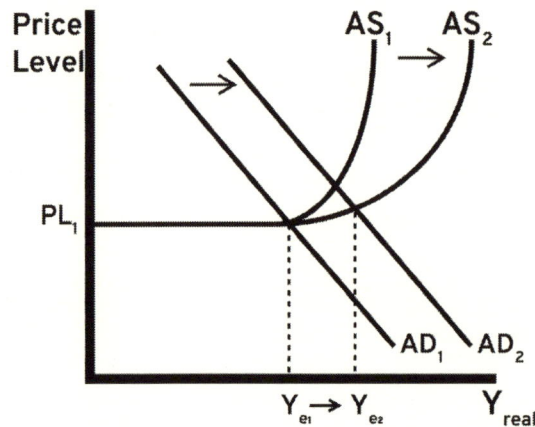

However it's not clear how electricity will be generated. The ADB seems to promote greater use of fossil fuel. This can really increase the pollution levels as FDI come into cheap Myanmar to expand manufacturing. Cars and congestion and the entire problems found in other cities of Asia will come to Myanmar.

Myanmar could skip and make a leap towards renewables and replicate the Bhutan model of economic development.

## 18.   Vietnam

*Study the texts and data below and answer the questions that follow.*

### Text 1- Overview of Vietnam

As of 2014 Vietnam has a population of 91.7 million people, of which around 33.6% live in urban areas. As Vietnam is not particularly a large country in terms of landmass, it has a very high population density at around 672 people per square mile.

The GDP of Vietnam has been continuously growing and has averaged a growth rate of around 5.7% from 2008 to 2013. By far, the largest component of Vietnam's GDP has been private consumption, which makes up for around 63% of its total GDP. This is followed by investment, which makes up for 27% and public consumption which makes up for 6%. Additionally, Vietnam has maintained a ***favourable balance of trade***.

Vietnam's principal imports are machinery & equipment. These complement its large industrial based economy. Currently, Vietnam's biggest exports are textiles and garments, footwear and crude oil. Its largest trade partners include China, South Korea and Japan, although the United States are large consumers of Vietnam's exports. The total value of Vietnam's exports adds up to around $132.7 billion, however, they are still heavily reliant on other countries, spending about $131.9 billion on imports yearly.

Vietnam's economy also relies heavily on agriculture, which constitutes 47.4% of all employment. The second largest sector of the economy is services and finally industry, which make up for 31.5% and 21.1% of the economy respectively. Vietnam has managed to maintain a relatively low unemployment rate with just 2% of the population being unemployed as of 2013. Some business economists comment that Vietnam as an attractive destination for foreign businesses is more about ***absolute advantage*** and less about ***comparative advantage***.

Vietnam is currently governed by the Communist Party of Vietnam who continually try to regulate the spread of propaganda against the state. They have, however, been known to repress freedom of speech and freedom of the press. Many bloggers as well as human rights activists have been sanctioned or received jail time for supposedly campaigning against the state. The ***socialist state*** however retains a high literacy rate and life expectancy.

## Text 2- Expanding Economic growth

Vietnam has been taking advantage of the recovering global economy with an increase in economic growth of 5.7% since late 2016. The economy is focused largely on domestic demand and the export of manufactured goods such as broadcasting equipment, computers and cellphones. Consistent growth in these sectors has played a large role in the Vietnam's increasing GDP. The domestic demand increased mainly thanks to growth in the service sector caused by an increase in retail trade. The sector makes up approximately 42% of Vietnam's GDP.

The State Bank of Vietnam decreased the base rates in summer 2017 for the first time in 3 years with the goal of maintaining growth and stability. The new interest rate charged by the commercial banks was set at 6.25% and the new base interest rate was set at 4.25%, a drop of 1% in both cases. Although this is an effective way of increasing the aggregate demand of an economy there have also been concerns over credit. Large Vietnamese companies are known to rely heavily on bank loans and the economy is currently still recovering from high levels of debt. This means banks will now focus more on the creditworthiness of consumers when making loans.

## Text 3- Misallocation of resources

Since 2006 private Vietnamese firms have started to suffer from lack of productivity and falling efficiency due outdated, tired machinery. Additionally, structural problems have caused inflation rates to increase drastically to the point where they have become unstable. In 2011, a money loaning scandal emerged where swindlers borrowed money from banks at the standard interest rate of around 20% and later loaned that money to other consumers at much higher rates of up to 90% interest. The scandal cost investors up to $190 million.

## Table 1- Economic data for Vietnam

| Year | 1999 | 2002 | 2005 | 2007 | 2010 | 2012 | 2014 | 2016 | 2018 |
|---|---|---|---|---|---|---|---|---|---|
| GDP current prices. US$ billion | 28.64 | 35.06 | 57.63 | 77.41 | 115.93 | 155.93 | 186.21 | 205.28 | 244.92 |
| Population (millions) | 79 | 81.5 | 83.8 | 85.4 | 88 | 89.8 | 91.7 | 93.6 | 95.5 |
| GNI current prices US$ billion | 28.30 | 37.38 | 56.58 | 75.24 | 111.51 | 149.57 | 177.36 | 196.69 | 231.48 |
| Producer Price Index | 104 | 107 | 112 | 115 | 117.2 | 118.78 | 121.6 | 132.6 | 133.2 |
| $CO_2$ emissions per capita (metric tonnes) | 0.6 | 0.87 | 1.17 | 1.23 | 1.62 | 1.58 | 1.82 | 1.97 | 2.06 |

Source: World Bank

**Table 2- Development data for Vietnam**

Economic growth in Vietnam is low due to macro instability, high energy consumption and low productivity. There are also environmental issues caused by outdated and overused materials. High poverty rates of ethnic minorities due to natural disasters, pandemics and the market economy. Education is lower than the development expectations because of bad school materials. To resolve this Vietnam receives bilateral aid from Australia. This comes in the form of project and monetary aid. The aid is focused on education, gender equality, infrastructure and trade.

| HDI | 0.683 |
|---|---|
| Life expectancy | 75.9 |
| Expected years of schooling | 12.6 |
| GDP median | $5,335 |
| GDP per capita | $6.010 |
| Employment rate | 76.7% |

**QUESTIONS**

**(a)s**    **(i) Define the term _favourable balance of trade_ indicated in bold. (Text 1 – paragraph 2)**
[2 marks]

**(ii) Define the term _socialist state_ indicated in bold. (Text 1 – paragraph 5)**    **[2 marks]**

**(a)h** **(i) Define the term _absolute advantage_ indicated in bold. (Text 1 – paragraph 4)** **[2 marks]**

**(ii) Define the term _comparative advantage_ indicated in bold. (Text 1 – paragraph 4)** **[2 marks]**

**(b)s** **(i) Calculate Vietnam's balance of trade. (Text 1 – paragraph 4)** **[3 marks]**

**(b)h** **(i) Identify 3 benefits for Vietnam's Government arising from an increase in private consumption. (Text 1 – paragraph 2)** **[3 marks]**

**(ii) Draw a demand and supply diagram for loans to explain how a fall in interest rate can occur. (Text 2 – paragraph 2)** **[2 marks]**

**(c)** **Use an AD / AS diagram to illustrate the effect on the Vietnamese economy of a global economic recession. (text 2 – paragraph 1)** **[4 marks]**

**(d)** **Using an AD / AS diagram explain the rate of inflation that Vietnam suffered in 2016. (Text 3)** **[4 marks]**

**(e)s** **With reference to Table 2, explain briefly the difference between GDP per capita and GDP median and then explain why Vietnam may have a lower global ranking in the HDI compared to GDP per capita.** **[4 marks]**

**(e)h** **Using a PPC (opportunity cost diagram), show how Vietnam when compared to Bangladesh has an absolute advantage in both shoes and shirts and a comparative advantage in shirts. Explain then why Nike might choose to put its factories in Vietnam to produce shoes.** **[4 marks]**

**(f)**     **Explain two shortcomings of the data in Table which suggest very high connection between economic activity and $CO_2$ emissions. (Table 1)**                          **[4 marks]**

**(g)**     **Using information from the texts and tables evaluate the view that Vietnam needs to adopt an export orientated industrial strategy to an even greater degree of it wants to aspire towards being another Singapore.**                          **[15 marks]**

**ANSWERS:**                 **18. VIETNAM**

**(a)s**     **(i) Define the term _favourable balance of trade_ indicated in bold. (Text 1 – paragraph 2)**
                                                         **[2 marks]**

This is value of exports exceeds the value of imports, slightly. The surplus does not adversely affect the country's exchange rate or price competitiveness on the global market.

     **(ii) Define the term _socialist state_ indicated in bold. (Text 1 – paragraph 5)**     **[2 marks]**

In a socialist state large parts of the economy's GDP is controlled by the government. Greater degree of ownership of factors of production is under the control of the government.

**(a)h**     **(i) Define the term _absolute advantage_ indicated in bold. (Text 1 – paragraph 4)**     **[2 marks]**

Absolute advantage is when a country can produce a good at a lower cost than another country.

     **(ii) Define the term _comparative advantage_ indicated in bold. (Text 1 – paragraph 4) [2 marks]**

Comparative advantage is when a country produces good or service for a lower opportunity cost (it has fewer sacrifices in terms of FOPs to make to produce the food compared to other countries.)

**(b)s**     **(i) Calculate Vietnam's balance of trade. (Text 1 – paragraph 4)**             **[3 marks]**

     Balance of Trade = Value of exports of goods - value of imports of goods

                        = \$ 132.7bn- \$ 131.9bn

                        = **+ \$ 0.6bn surplus**

**(b)h** **(i) Identify 3 benefits for Vietnam's Government arising from an increase in private consumption. (Text 1 – paragraph 2)** **[3 marks]**

Vietnamese Government benefits from rising private consumption in 3 ways:

- More jobs created which help Government to fulfill its macroeconomic more date of low unemployment.
- More direct and indirect tax revenue to help fund Government services such as basic health care and education.
- Fewer resources used up in dealing with social problems caused by unemployment particularly growth unemployment.

**(ii) Draw a demand and supply diagram for loans to explain how a fall in interest rate can occur. (Text 2 – paragraph 2)** **[2 marks]**

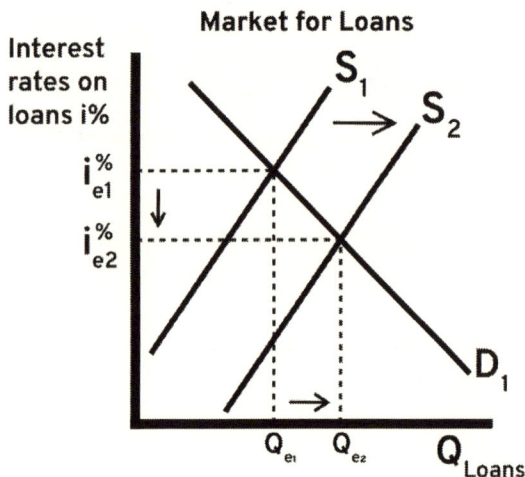

Market for Loans

When the Central Bank of Vietnam reduce base rate to 4.25 %, the commercial banks create loans and focus on finding credit worthy customers. At $i_{e1}$ % the supply of loans exceeds the demand for loans. (Surplus of loans available). With competition among the commercial banks, the take up of new loans will probably occur at a lower interest rate. A new equilibrium will occur at $i_{e1}$ %, $Qe_2$.

**(c)     Use an AD / AS diagram to illustrate the effect on the Vietnamese economy of a global economic recession. (text 2 – paragraph 1)                              [4 marks]**

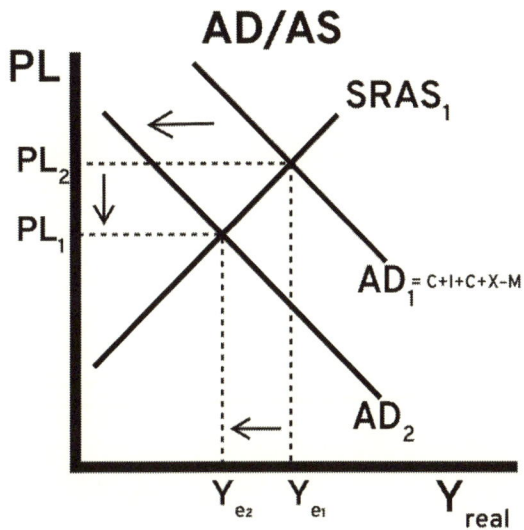

Define recession: Point out Vietnam is an open economy. Foreign sector (Exports $ 133 Bn, Imports $ 132 Bn) is relatively high as a percentage of GDP (GDP = $ 244 Bn)

A global recession will mean demand for Vietnamese exports of discretionary goods and services will fall. In addition Vietnamese factories will import in fewer inputs. $AD_1$ falls to $Ad_2$. The price level $PL_1$ will be pressured down wards as excess surplus of goods / services will need to be sold. With a negative multiplier real output falls from $Ye_1$ to $Ye_2$. Jobs will be lost, government revenues may suffer.

**(d)** **Using an AD / AS diagram explain the rate of inflation that Vietnam suffered in 2016. (Text 3)**

**[4 marks]**

## AD/AS for 2016

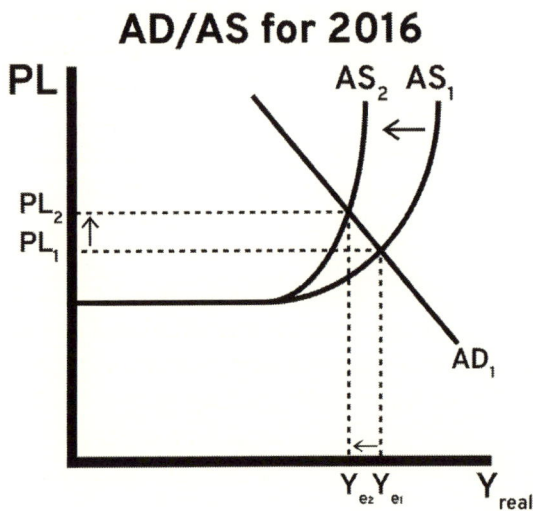

Text 5 implies fall production efficiency will shift $AS_1$ to $AS_2$. The PPI rose drastically from 121. to 132.6 from 2014 to 2016 (Table 1). These higher costs of production can be caused by bottlenecks and result in structural inflation or cost push inflation. $Pl_1$ rises to $Pl_2$. Producing and delivering each unit of goods is more costly.

**(e)s** **With reference to Table 2, explain briefly the difference between GDP per capita and GDP median and then explain why Vietnam may have a lower global ranking in the HDI compared to GDP per capita.** **[4 marks]**

GDP per capita = GDP/ population whereas GDP median states the contribution of the 50$^{th}$ percentile. A per capita figure distorts the true picture by including the extreme rich and extreme poor. For Vietnam (GDP median $5335 < GDP per capta $6,010) implies there are some extremely rich Vietnamese causing inequalities in income.

If Vietnam ranks lower in global HDI than in GDP per capita then it probably due to the mal-distribution resources devoted to healthcare and education and fairness in income distribution.

**(e)h     Using a PPC (opportunity cost diagram), show how Vietnam when compared to Bangladesh has an absolute advantage in both shoes and shirts and a comparative advantage in shirts.  Explain then why Nike might choose to put its factories in Vietnam to produce shoes.          [4 marks]**

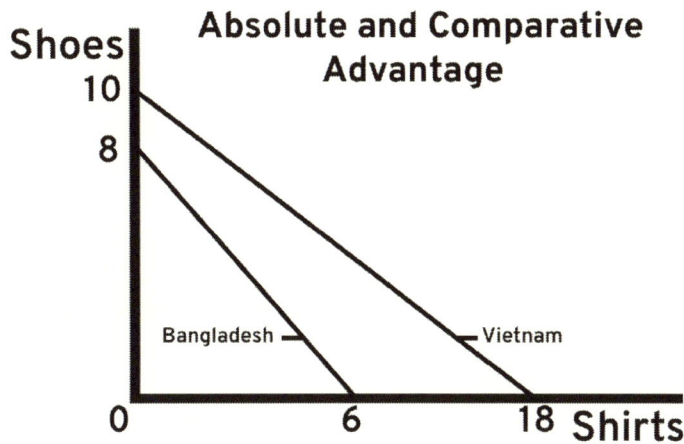

The diagram shows Vietnam is 3 times more efficient at producing shirts and only 25 % more efficient at producing shoes compared to Bangladesh. Vietnam is also able to produce more shoes and shirts per unit of FOP than Bangladesh (Absolute advantage).

Nike may still choose Vietnam become firms are more interested in absolute advantage in their product. Nike can clearly gain by getting more output per unit of input in Vietnam than Bangladesh (10 units instead of 8). Alternatively, lower costs of production per pair of shoes. The above model is also unrealistic as it is hardly realistic to assume 2 countries, 2 products.

**(f)     Explain two shortcomings of the data in Table which suggest very high connection between economic activity and $CO_2$ emissions. (Table 1)                                    [4 marks]**

Generally speaking greater economic activity leads to higher CO2 emissions. This is become we use energy to achieve economic activity.  However, the data in table 1 needs to be modified to give a better picture.

Currently it seems that an 800 % increase in GDP leads to CO2 emissions rising by 350%. However, there is inflation. The figures for GDP current have to be changed and put in terms of Real GDP.

Secondly there has been a rise in population from 79 m to 95.5. The Real GDP could be changed to Real GDP per capita.  Another point to consider is that Vietnam is more globalised in 2018 than in 1999. This means it is polluting more on behalf of the world than it is doing it for domestic demand.

**(g)** **Using information from the texts and tables evaluate the view that Vietnam needs to adopt an export orientated industrial strategy to an even greater degree of it wants to aspire towards being another Singapore.** **[15 marks]**

An outward export oriented strategy of industrialisation for Vietnam will promote exports and an openness to the world economy even more by promoting inward direct foreign investment to help make the transition to widespread manufacturing and service industry. This may involve FDI controlling more than 50 % of shares in Vietnamese companies.

**Advantages:**

- Vietnam has the same comparative advantage in manufacturing on which it can build upon. (Text 2)
- This policy will force Vietnamese infant industries to become more competitive, otherwise they will fail and lose government support.
- Multinationals could turn Vietnam into a hub, bring technology and global consumer knowledge to help Vietnam fine tune it's manufacturing to what the global wants, adding value.
- Economics of scale are more likely.
- More financial capital and foreign currency which can help finance domestic infrastructure projects and reduce debt burden.

**Disadvantages of expanding outwards orientation policy:**

- Number of jobs created with capital intensive technology may not be sufficient for a growing population.
- Higher degree of economic activity can turn Vietnam into a global Dump yard.
- Citizen's Health and safety conditions may be traded for jobs.
- Foreign multinationals may demand further concessions or threaten to leave.
- Manufacturing may take up lots of water and land and thus deprive the agriculture sector and undermine national food security. Singapore has no agriculture to speak of. (Text 1 - paragraph 4)
- The education and health system in Vietnam may not be able to cope with the demands of the labour market in terms of quality of the workforce. (Table 2)
- Inequality may rise if the gains are not shared equitably.
- There may well be more rural to urban migration that will result in asset price inflation and negative externalities of pollution, congestion, noise and poor sanitation. (Text 1 - Paragraph 1)

## 19.    United Kingdom

*Study the texts and data below and answer the questions that follow.*

**Text 1- United Kingdom**

Since the 2016 referendum, Britain has been struggling to find and agree on ways in which it can leave the European Union (EU) single market economic and social agreements without causing adversity. The uncertainty regarding the new rules of trading and the likely disruption this change may cause will manifest itself indirectly in investment and production and subsequently employment decisions for both large and small firms. The day to day decisions currently made by consumers, producers and the government is on a business as usual basis.

The IMF in their October 2019 World Economic Outlook has forecasted further slowdown in growth in 2020 for the UK of 1.0% from 1.3% in 2019 and 1.5% in 2018.  The UK growth rate since the 2016 referendum has moved from the top to near the bottom of the Group of Seven growth tables. Upon leaving the EU and reverting to the global standard ***WTO trade rules*** will diminish the UK GDP by around 5 to 8 percent according to the IMF forecast. The UK will then be subjected to higher import tariff and ***non-tariff trade barriers***, lower net inward migration of labour, and reduced domestic and foreign direct investment as large companies rethink their location strategy.

Inflation for both 2018 and 2019 as measured by The Consumer Prices Index (CPI) was still above the Bank of England's 2% inflation target while wages are only now rising above inflation. The fall in sterling (UK pound currency) over the recent years shows no sign of reversing.

The labour market offers lots of work opportunities in terms of quantity but little in terms of quality. Workers terms and conditions have deteriorated significantly over the last two decades even though the unemployment rate is at a 43 year low of 4%. UK's unemployment rate is above the rate of the US (3.9%), below that of France (9.0%) but above that of Germany (3.4%). Like in most other developed countries youth (aged 15-24) UK unemployment rate remains at 11%.

## Text 2- UK

The steady downward drop in interest rates down to 0.5% and ultra-loose credit or lending conditions has encouraged some stakeholders to take on more debt and discouraged other stakeholders from saving. Household debt peaked in Q2 2008 at 148% of household disposable income. It then declined to 127% by late 2015. It has remained steady at around 135% of GDP since. The cost of servicing debt for households remains relatively low, due to very low interest rates, including mortgage rates. However, there has been a surge in unsecured consumer borrowing (credit card use, car and personal loans) where the ability to repay is highly sensitive to changes in interest rates, real incomes and jobs. Asset prices have risen well above rates of CPI and wages leading some economists to conclude that a severe recession is imminent as a rebalancing of the economy occurs.

## Text 3- Easyjet

Johan Lundgren, the CEO of Easyjet, the low cost short haul airline, has defended the company's high ticket prices to fly to Madrid for the Champions League final between Tottenham and Liverpool on 1 June 2019.

Football fans complained that flights normally priced £250 are now being offered at £1,000. Mr Lundgren said the price was higher than average because there had been an "enormous" surge in demand. "That is actually how the system works," he said.

"The whole pricing picture is very dynamic," he said, adding that at peak booking times. Normally our algorithm quickly matches demand with supply in real time to arrive at multiple equilibrium prices as the seats are sold. "But there's no doubt that this was an occasion where the prices went very high because the demand was enormous." The EasyJet economy class only flight with 175 seat carrying capacity took only six seconds to fill up. Other airlines serving the same route did exactly the same

**Text 3  Minimum Price of Alcohol**

In May 2018 Scotland introduced a $0.70 a unit minimum price on alcohol.  This meant on average the price of alcohol rose by 30%.  Today a year later, the effects can be seen through a fall in the sales volume of 3%.  The Scottish health secretary, Jeane Freeman, welcomed the figures stating that alcohol sales are the lowest in 25 years. She added further that, "Given the clear and proven link between consumption and harm, minimum unit pricing is the most effective and efficient way to tackle the cheap, high-strength alcohol that causes so much harm to so many families.  There are, on average, 22 alcohol-specific deaths every week in Scotland, and 683 hospital admissions, and behind every one of these statistics is a person, a family, and a community badly affected by alcohol harm."

In Scotland, supermarkets and other outlets are not permitted to sell cheap or discounted alcohol but online retailers outside Scotland are exempted.  The Scots still drank an average of 9.9 litres per year or 19 units of pure alcohol per week before the new regulation.  Scotland's chief medical officer's advice is while abstinence is best, it is safest not to drink more than 14 units a week to keep the risks low.

In England and Wales the current average cost per unit of alcohol is $0.65 and now both are considering introducing a minimum price to prevent retailers from creating loss leaders for alcoholic drinks to entice consumers.   The Scottish Whisky Association has been battling the Scottish Government in court since 2012 to prevent the implementation the $0.70 new pricing regulation.  The many court appeals and delays have subsequently diluted the effectiveness of the $0.70 per unit minimum price as it has not been keeping up with inflation.  A further rise is now being planned next year.

**Table 1- Economic data for *country***

## UK Consumer Confidence Index (Source: OECD)

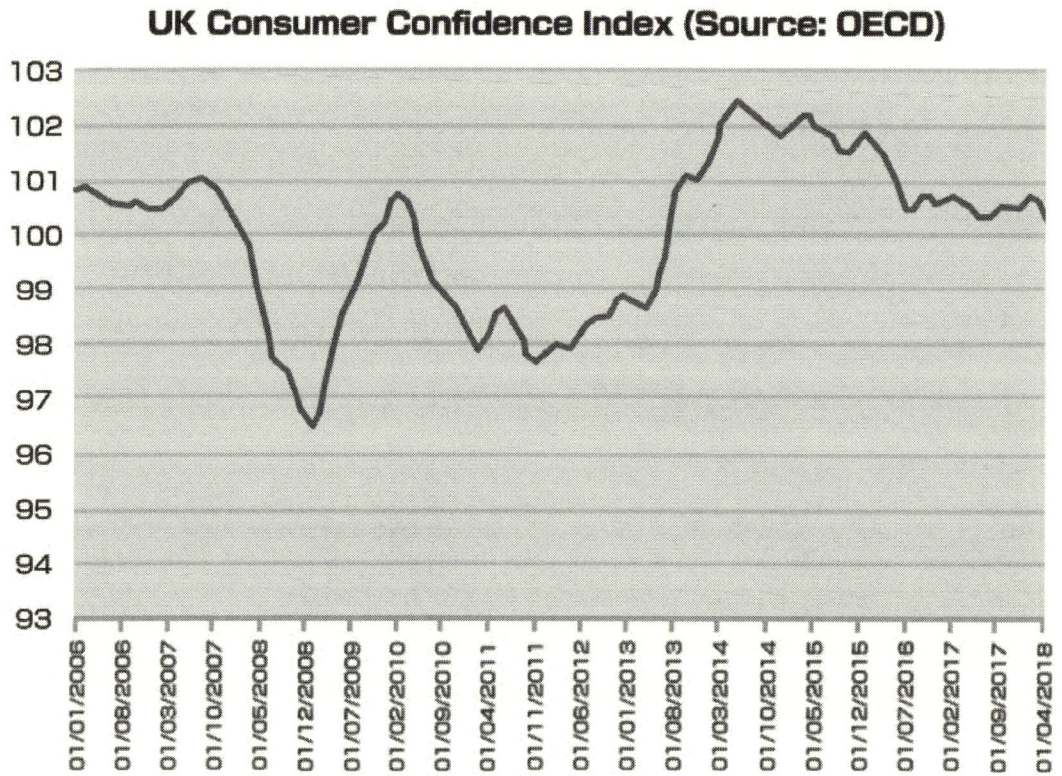

## Table 2- Savings Ratio

Households (s.14): Households' saving ratio (per cent): Current price: £m: SA

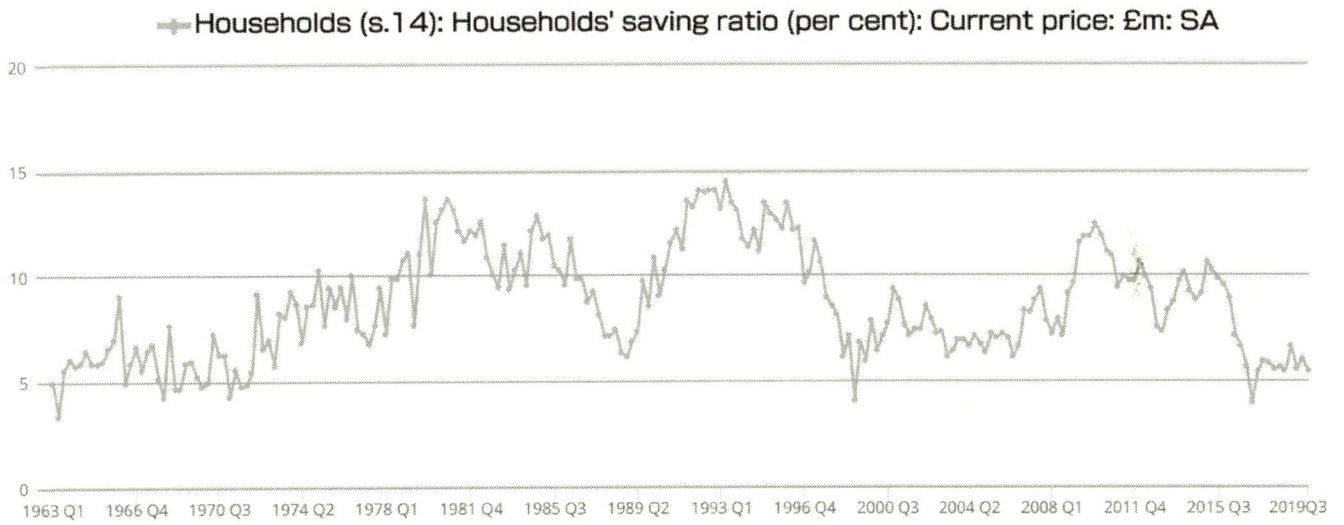

## Table 3- Economic data for *United Kingdom*

| Annual % change unless stated | 2016 | 2017 | 2018 Forecast |
|---|---|---|---|
| Gross domestic product (GDP) | 1.9 | 1.7 | 1.5 |
| GDP per capita | 1.1 | 1.1 | 0.9 |
| Household consumption | 2.9 | 1.7 | 0.9 |
| Buisness investment | -0.5 | 2.2 | 1.7 |
| Consumer Price Inflation | 0.7 | 2.7 | 2.4 |
| Employment (millions) | 31.7 | 32.1 | 32.1 |
| Average earnings | 2.7 | 2.6 | 2.7 |
| LFS unemployment (rate, per cent) | 4.9 | 4.4 | 4.4 |
| Current account (BoP) (% of GDP) | -5.6% | -4.1% | -3.7 |
| Fiscal balance (% of GDP) | -2.3% | -2.2% | -1.8% |

Source: Office of National Statistics

## QUESTIONS

(a)      (i) Define the term *non-tariff trade barriers* indicated in bold. (Text 1 – paragraph 2)  [2 marks]

       (ii) Identify 2 functions of the World Trade Organisation (WTO) indicated in bold. (Text 1 – paragraph 2)                                                                [2 marks]

(b)s      (i) Calculate the Price Elasticity of Demand (PED) for alcohol in Scotland and comment on the result. (Text 4)                                                          [3 marks]

**(b)h** **(i) Draw a demand - supply diagram to show a rise in minimum price from $ 0.55 to $ 0.70 per unit of alcohol has led to a fall in demand of 3 % and the change in consumer and producer surplus. (Text 3)** **[3 marks]**

**(ii) Identify 3 externalities arising from alcohol abuse in Scotland. (Text 3)** **[2 marks]**

**(c)** **Use a demand and supply to explain surge pricing and calculate the change in total revenue from surge pricing.** **[4 marks]**

**(d)** **Draw a trade creation diagram to illustrate the net benefits for a less economically developed country joining a more economically developed European Union (EU).** **[4 marks]**

**(e)** **(i) Use a tariff diagram to explain the effect on UK stakeholders of importing German Cars under WTO rules of 15 % tariff on Cars. (Text 1 – paragraph 1)** **[4 marks]**

**(f)** **Use an AD / AS diagram to explain how a tightening of UK monetary policy will likely lead to a recession. (Text 2)** **[4 marks]**

**(g)** **Using the information in the text/tables and your knowledge of economics evaluate the proposition that second largest member of the E.U. ,the United Kingdom will gain more from Economic Sovereignty than lose from the binding ties of a larger European Union.** **[15 marks]**

**ANSWERS:**                     **19. UNITED KINGDOM**

**(a)**        **(i) Define the term _non-tariff trade barriers_ indicated in bold. (Text 1 – paragraph 2) [2 marks]**

Non-tariff barriers are obstructions to cross border international trade which do not involve a tax or duty. Examples of these types of barriers are quotas, administrative barriers, health and safety requirements, embargoes, sanctions.

       **(ii) Identify 2 functions of the World Trade Organisation (WTO) indicated in bold. (Text 1 – paragraph 2)**                                          **[2 marks]**

Functions of WTO are:

- Providing a form for trade negotiations between members
- Administering the WTO trade agreements which are already in place.
- Handling trade disputes.
- Providing technical assistance and training to developing countries.

**(b)s**     **(i) Calculate the Price Elasticity of Demand (PED) for alcohol in Scotland and comment on the result. (Text 4)**                                                         **[3 marks]**

$$PED_{alcohol} = (\text{\% change of QD for alcohol})/(\text{\% change of Price for alcohol})$$

$$PED_{alcohol} = (3\%)/(+30\%) = \mathbf{\underline{0.1}}$$

PED = 0.1 implies that the demand for alcohol is highly price insensitive. This may be due to Scotland's unique cultural problem compared to most other countries.

212

**(b)h** **(i) Draw a demand - supply diagram to show a rise in minimum price from $ 0.55 to $ 0.70 per unit of alcohol has led to a fall in demand of 3 % and the change in consumer and producer surplus. (Text 3)** **[3 marks]**

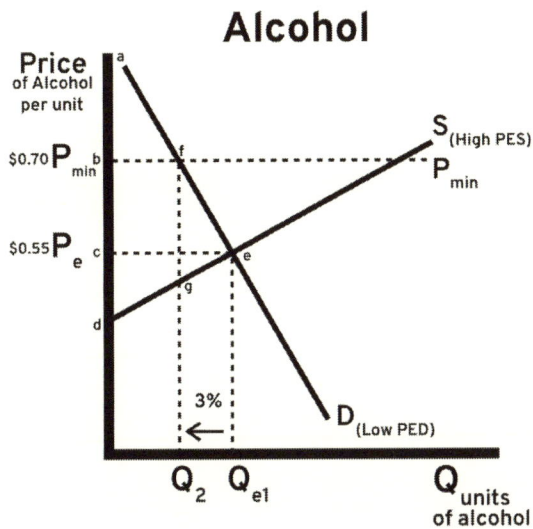

The PED for alcohol in Scotland is low due to cultural reasons whereas the PES as alcohol is essentially manufactured and easy to increase or decrease.

The minimum price of each unit of alcohol is set above the free market equilibrium $ 0.55. This is about 30 % above the equilibrium and now so far has reduced demand by only 3 %.

Consumer Surplus (define). It falls from area (*ace*) to area (*abc*).

Producer surplus (define). It changes from area (*cde*) to area (*bdfg*). Without actual numbers it is not possible to say if it will rise or fall.

**(ii) Identify 3 externalities arising from alcohol abuse in Scotland. (Text 3)** **[2 marks]**

3 externalities from alcohol abuse are :

☐ Cost to the UK National Health Service for treatment paid by 3rd parties. (UK tax payer)
☐ Cost to the police in dealing with antisocial behaviour. (Paid by UK tax-payer)
☐ Loss of output and tax revenue to society due to early deaths and absenteeism and loss of productivity.

Data Response-Paper 2

**(c)** **Use a demand and supply to explain surge pricing and calculate the change in total revenue from surge pricing.** **[4 marks]**

### Easyjet Flights

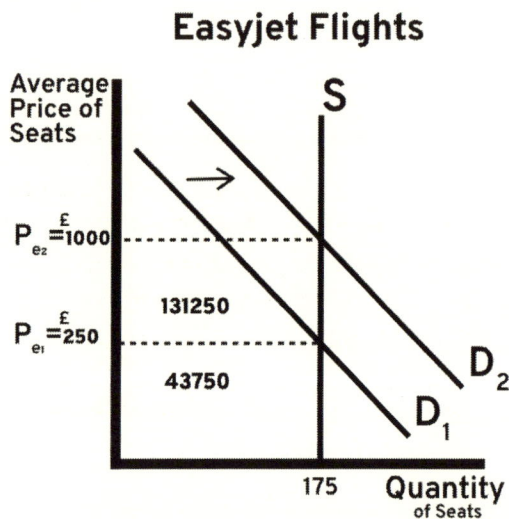

Total Revenue before the surge = £ 250 x £ 175 seats = £ 43,750

Total Revenue for Easy jet as a result of the price surge

£ 1000 x 175 seats = £ 175000

Change in Total Revenue = **£ 131250**

Instant (6 seconds) rise in demand due to announcement of Champion League Final Meant $D_1$ rises to $D_2$ for the same 175 seats causing huge rise in total revenue

214

**(d)** **Draw a trade creation diagram to illustrate the net benefits for a less economically developed country joining a more economically developed European Union (EU).** **[4 marks]**

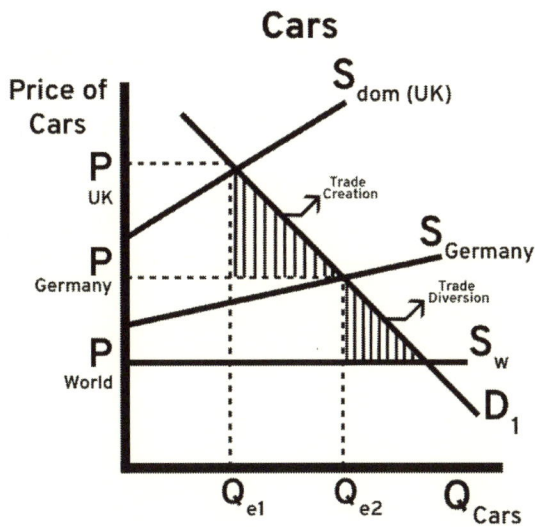

The above diagram shows that by joining the EU Britain gains more from 'Trade Creation', benefits of preferential treatment, than it loses 'Trade Diversion', loss from losing access to cheaper products from the rest of the world.

Trade Creation is greater than Trade Diversion, the more Germany is able to produce at Pw.

**(e)** **(i) Use a tariff diagram to explain the effect on UK stakeholders of importing German Cars under WTO rules of 15 % tariff on Cars. (Text 1 – paragraph 1)** **[4 marks]**

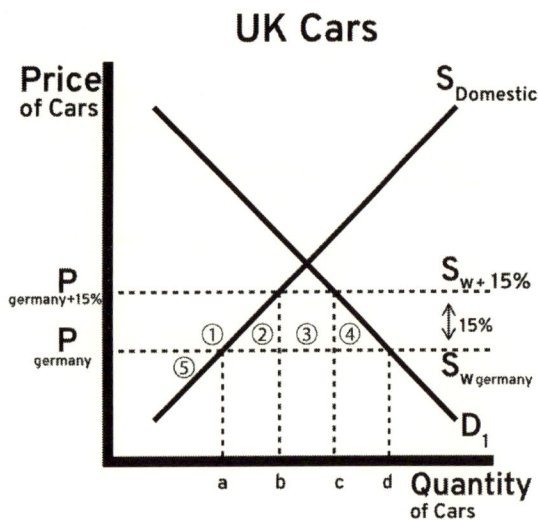

## UK Cars

A 15 % tariff under WTO rules nears German Car prices in the UK will rise P germany + 15 %, imports of German cars will fall from (ad) to (bc).

UK consumers pay a higher price and there is less choice. Consumer surplus falls by (1) + (2) + (3) + (4).

UK Car producers gain from selling more cars (Oa) to (Ob). Producer surplus to (1) + (5) area.

UK car workers may be more in demand.

UK Government collects tax revenue area (3) Germany will no doubt retaliate against British products.

This is a misallocation of resources (welfare or deadweight loss) of area (2) + (4)

UK exporter may be disadvantaged. According to trade theory there is a net loss globally.

**(f)** **Use an AD / AS diagram to explain how a tightening of UK monetary policy will likely lead to a recession. (Text 2)** **[4 marks]**

## AD/AS

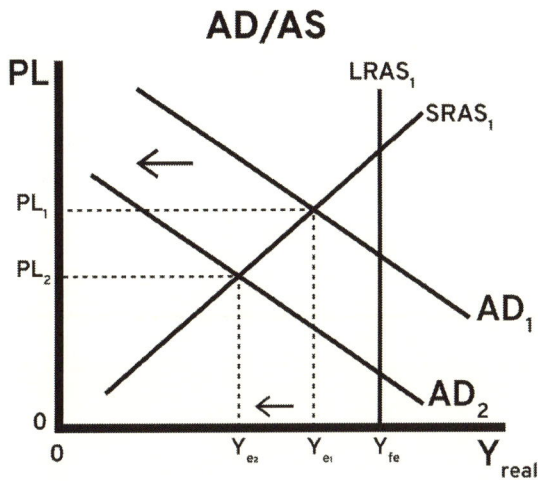

Define recession.

Tightening monetary Policy means rising interest rates and less access to cheap credit.

Currently UK unemployment is very low ($Y_{e1}$ close $Y_{fe}$). If $i$% rise (C falls, I falls, G falls, (X − M) falls) Overall fall in AD from $AD_1$ to $AD_2$.

Saving rate may rise as banks offer higher rates. However, according to the text many households will not be able to service their debts. They may severely reduce their spending or default on their loans. Firms may also default on their loans and go bankrupt.

Output fall Ye1 to Ye2, unemployment may rise. Price level may fall to PL2 and government finances worsen.

**(g)    Using the information in the text/tables and your knowledge of economics evaluate the proposition that second largest member of the E.U., the United Kingdom, will gain more from Economic Sovereignty than lose from the binding ties of a larger European Union.          [15 marks]**

Will the UK gain or lose from Brexit is currently difficult to say.

Most economists wisely argue that the UK currently already benefits greatly from the EU in terms of preferential trading arrangements:

- Free movement of capital, labour, technology.
- Larger market to sell its products even though its products may not be the cheapest in the world. A common external tariff in the EU protects loss efficient UK companies from global competition which is fiercer.
- UK retains its currency and monetary policy sovereignty unlike Eurozone countries which have a single currency, Euro and a single central bank, heavily biased by the biggest economy, Germany.
- So leaving the EU will be a major blow to the UK economy. Many UK companies may more to EU because of free access. Jobs, output will be lost. The city of London will lose some Euro currency trading. A recession may be imminent.

Some economists focus on the long term re adjustment process, Restructuring of the UK economy can be beneficial for the following reasons:

- Less dependency on London and concentration on the financial sector. (London = 23 % of UK GDP)
- More diversification of industry reduces long term risk and creates new comparative advantages.
- Greater geographical use of FOPs and job creation.
- Revival of depressed areas leading to more balanced growth.
- New relationships with rest of world.
- Greater ability of UK to offer global companies preferential deals to complete with EU.
- Rights of workers and health and safety regulations can be changed (for better or for worse) to

suit British ruling parties.

## 20.    China 2

*Study the texts and data below and answer the questions that follow.*

### Text 1- Overview of China

China is an emerging economy with a population of 1,385.6 million people. Main industries of China include electrical goods at 292.6 billion dollars and telecoms equipment at 257.8 billion dollars. China has one of the biggest economies in the world with a total GDP of $9.240 tn.  China thrives off its exports with 16.7% of GDP exported to the United States alone and 17.4% of GDP goods going to the rest of the World.. China's greatest import is electrical machinery at $356.8 billion, in order to insure their factors of production are sufficient to keep up with their exports. Currently China is in the frontline suffering from the major effects of the Corona Virus.  The City of Wuhan is in a lockdown and economic activity throughout China has slowed down significantly and this may well lead to China's first ***recession*** after decades of economic growth.
.

### Text 2- Air pollution

As China is one of the biggest manufacturers across the globe there is an unhealthy level of air pollution directly linked to the amount of production that goes on within China's borders. Companies around the world look to China to outsource their production as factors of production are less costly and therefore outsourcing leads to lower average costs for firms. This however holds great implications for the nation as air pollution is a **negative externality of production** and issues such as health from smoke inhalation arise as well as damages caused by increased greenhouse gases which has implications for the whole planet. The effect this has is 5.6% of the GDP being allocated to health spending, although other factors dilute this figure away from the air pollution. The fact that air pollution causes deaths of 1.1 million Chinese citizens each year shows the size of China's problem.

## Text 3- Chinese currency exchange troubles

As China relies heavily on its export industry, currency exchange has great influence over the economy. This is due to the fact that if the Yuan were to appreciate too greatly, importing would be relatively more expensive for foreign countries and therefore the Chinese economy would be affected to a large extent. Since the beginning of 2019, the Yuan has revalued 7.8% against the US dollar. This contrasts with previous year's devaluation of 6.5% however new problems arise from this increase. Although this unwanted appreciation can be solved by buying dollars with their Yuan and thus increase their reserve of US dollars; the United States under Mr. Trump's leadership have begun to question China's currency adjustment practices. Bad relations with their trading partner is cannot be afforded and therefore the appreciation of the Yuan poses a great risk to the Chinese economy.

## Text 4- Literacy rate

In China, the number of citizens who cannot read or write has been cut by an impressive 40 million between 1990 and 2000 alone. The disparities across gender and ethnic minorities can be highlighted by the fact that 70% of the illiterate population is women with Tibetan dense regions having an illiteracy rate of 42%. With each year of education, one can expect an 8% overall increase in incomes later on in life. This highlights that although China appears to be a more and more economically prominent in the world economy, it must be remembered that their population is immense and disparities are hidden.

## Table 1- Economic data for China

|  | 2014 | 2016 |
|---|---|---|
| GDP | $9.240 trillion | $11.2 trillion |
| GNI | $12.36 trillion | $15.65 trillion |
| GDP per capita | $6,810 | $8,123 |
| Unemployment Rate | 4.0% | 4.04% |
| Inflation Rate | 2.0% | 2.0% |
| Central bank interest rate | 6% | 4.35% |

**Table 2-Global CO2 Emissions**

# The Global Disparity in Carbon Footprints

Per capita $CO_2$ emmisions in the world's largest economies in 2016* (in metric tons)

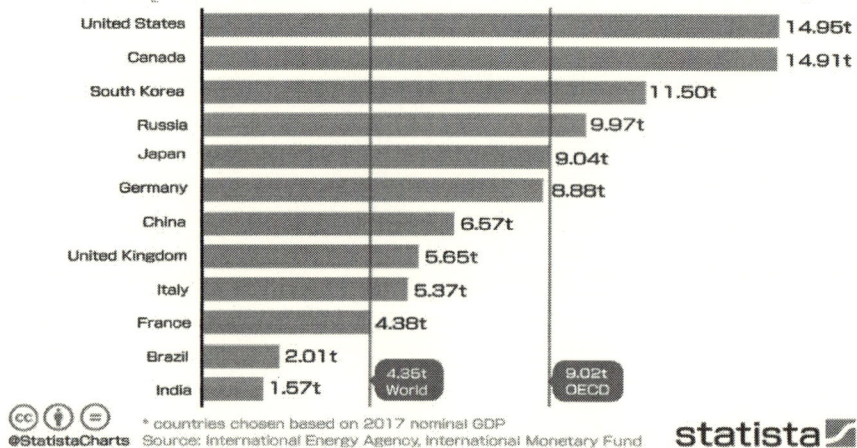

| Country | Emissions |
|---|---|
| United States | 14.95t |
| Canada | 14.91t |
| South Korea | 11.50t |
| Russia | 9.97t |
| Japan | 9.04t |
| Germany | 8.88t |
| China | 6.57t |
| United Kingdom | 5.65t |
| Italy | 5.37t |
| France | 4.38t |
| Brazil | 2.01t |
| India | 1.57t |

4.35t World        9.02t OECD

@StatistaCharts   * countries chosen based on 2017 nominal GDP
Source: International Energy Agency, International Monetary Fund

statista

## QUESTIONS

(a)    (i) Define the term *recession* indicated in bold. (Text 1)                    [2 marks]

(ii) Define the term *negative externality of production* indicated in bold. (Text 2)  [2 marks]

**(b)s** **(i) Explain the difference between GDP and GNI and suggest a reason why for China, GNI > GDP. (Table 1)** [3 marks]

**(b)h** **(i) Identify 2 gainers and 2 losers of rising inflation. (Text 1)** [3 marks]

**(ii) Draw a quota diagram to explain the effects of President Trump's decision to restrict imports of Chinese manufactures by 10 %. (Text 1)** [4 marks]

**(c)** **Draw a Demand – Supply diagram to how a carbon trading system can be used to reduce $CO_2$ emissions in China. (Text 2 – paragraph 2)** [4 marks]

**(d)** **Use a foreign exchange demand – supply diagram to explain how China's Currency board can revalue the Yuan by 7.8 % in 2019 to annual the 6.5 % devaluation in 2018 against the US$ to satisfy Mr. Trump. (Text 3)** [4 marks]

**(e)** **Draw a poverty cycle diagram to explain the poverty trap experienced by women in Tibet region. (Text 4 – paragraph 2)** [4 marks]

**(f)** **Use an AD / AS diagram to explain the effects on the Chinese economy of a major disruption in the supply chain and a lock-down of the population to combat the spread of the Corona Virus in China. (Text1)** [4 marks]

**(g)    Using the information in the texts / tables and your knowledge of economics, evaluate the consequences on economic development for China of imposing a severe 30 % carbon tax on all production of manufactures within its borders.**
**[15 marks]**

## ANSWERS:                    20.  CHINA 2.

**(a)    (i) Define the term _recession_ indicated in bold. (Text 1)                    [2 marks]**

A recession is a fall in the level production and expenditure on final goods and services.  It is measured by falls in real GDP of 2 consecutive quarters.

**(ii) Define the term _negative externality of production_ indicated in bold. (Text 2)   [2 marks]**

Negative externality of production is when MSC > MPC caused by the production process. Firms produce goods / services. The cost of making one more unit is the marginal private cost. However the cost imposed on the rest of society (external cost) is not included.

**(b)s    (i) Explain the difference between GDP and GNI and suggest a reason why for China, GNI > GDP. (Table 1)**
**        [3 marks]**

GDP is the value of final goods / services produced in a country in a given time period irrespective of citizenship.

$GNI_{China}$ = $GDP_{China}$ + [(income from China's citizens and business earned abroad) − (income remitted by foreigners in China)]

In GNI we are calculating the value of the contribution made by Chinese citizens and businesses both at home and abroad.

Data Response-Paper 2

For China GNI is significantly abroad 20 % higher than GDP implying the contribution of Chinese abroad is greater than the contribution of foreigners in China in terms of remittances. (Table 1)

**(b)h** **(i) Identify 2 gainers and 2 losers of rising inflation. (Text 1)** [3 marks]

Inflation is the rise in the general price level as measured by the rise in the CPI.

**Gainers :**

- Firms with strong pricing power can easily pass higher prices.
- Firms which can keeps costs down by say suppressing wages can keep or even raise their profit margins.
- Borrowers gain from an erosion of the value of real debt.

**Losers :**

- Workers in weak bargaining positions whose incomes do not rise as fast as prices.
- Unemployed workers find the buying power of their limited incomes is falling.
- Pensioners who have to live on fixed incomes find they can afford less and less.

**(ii) Draw a quota diagram to explain the effects of President Trump's decision to restrict imports of Chinese manufactures by 10 %. (Text 1)**
[4 marks]

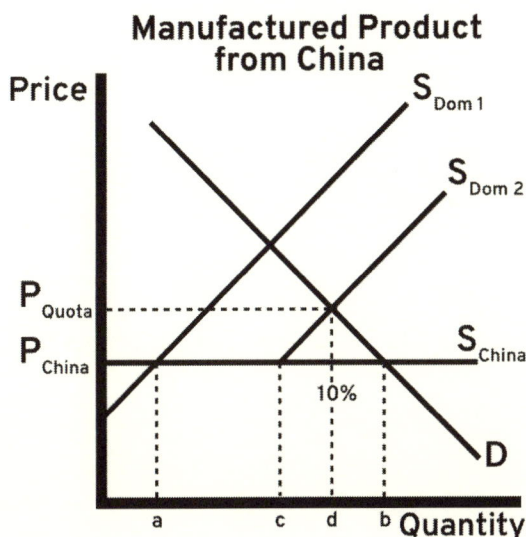

Before the 10 % restriction on Chinese imports, domestic production was (Oa), imports from China were (ab).

After the 10 % restriction, Chinese imports fall to (ac). Prices rise to $P_{QUOTA}$. Domestic producers increase output by an additional (Cd). Consumers in the U.S.

225

pay higher prices and have less choice. Retailers in the US sell less. Chinese exports to the US fall but the Chinese producers receive higher prices. There is welfare or deadweight loss.

**(c)**　　**Draw a Demand – Supply diagram to how a carbon trading system can be used to reduce $CO_2$ emissions in China. (Text 2 – paragraph 2)**　　　　　　　　　**[4 marks]**

**Market for Pollution Credits**

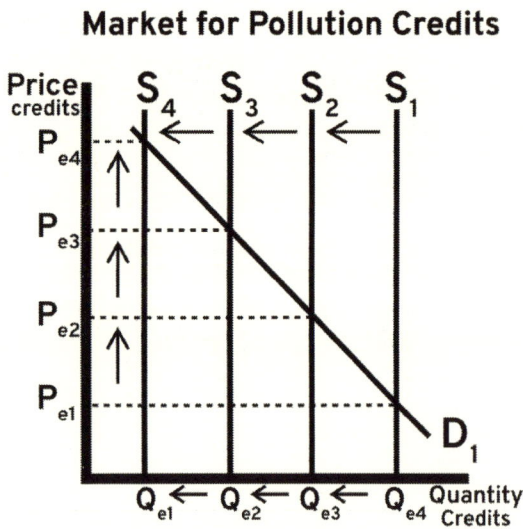

All firms might be given a certain limited starting allowance of credits acknowledging that a zero pollution from production is not possible.

However, they have to go to the market and buy credits that are available $S_1$. The equilibrium price is $Pe_1$. Over time the authorities can steadily reduce the supply of credits $S_1$ falls to $S_2$ to $S_3$ to $S_4$. The equilibrium price will rise from $Pe_1$ to $Pe_2$ to $Pe_3$ to $Pe_4$.

This means firms which are reluctant to change suffer higher costs of production and become less competitive.

Firms that change to new greener technologies gain in competitiveness especially if they take advantage of Government subsidies towards new investment financed by the revenues gathered from the sale of $CO_2$ emission credits.

**(d)** Use a foreign exchange demand – supply diagram to explain how China's Currency board can revalue the Yuan by 7.8 % in 2019 to annual the 6.5 % devaluation in 2018 against the US$ to satisfy Mr. Trump. (Text 3) **[4 marks]**

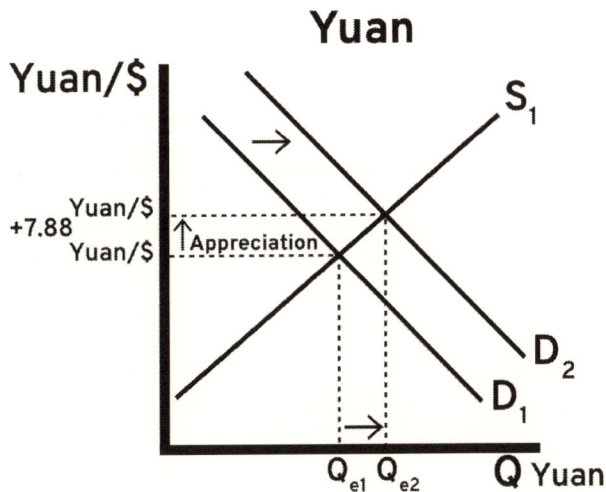

The Chinese currency board can use its vast reserves of foreign currency, particularly US $, by selling US $ and buying Yuan from foreign financial institutions holding the Yuan. The demand for Yuan rises from $D_1$ to $D_2$. Yuan appreciates/revalues by 7.8 % against the US $.

It is important to note that the Yuan is not a fully freely floating currently. China implements strict currency controls.

**(e)**    **Draw a poverty cycle diagram to explain the poverty trap experienced by women in Tibet region. (Text 4 – paragraph 2)**                                                    **[4 marks]**

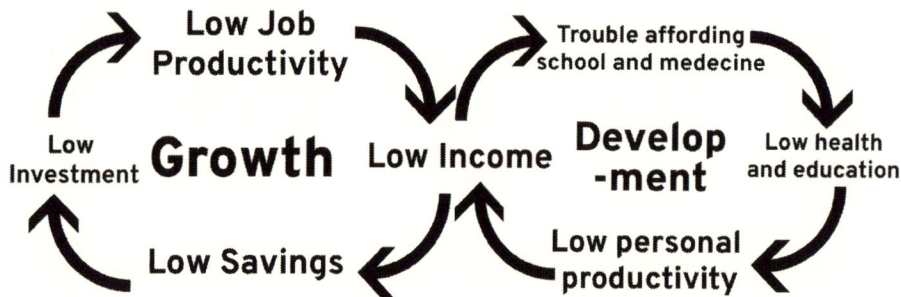

A high degree of illiteracy among Tibetan women means their occupational choices are highly limited to menial labour intensive work which is inherently low wage.

Low wages cause low savings, low investment in education and health. This results in low economic growth and fewer job opportunities. The urban areas of China progress whereas Tibetan women and the region is stuck in a poverty trap.

**(f)** **Use an AD / AS diagram to explain the effects on the Chinese economy of a major disruption in the supply chain and a lock-down of the population to combat the spread of the Corona Virus in China. (Text1)** **[4 marks]**

## AD/SRAS

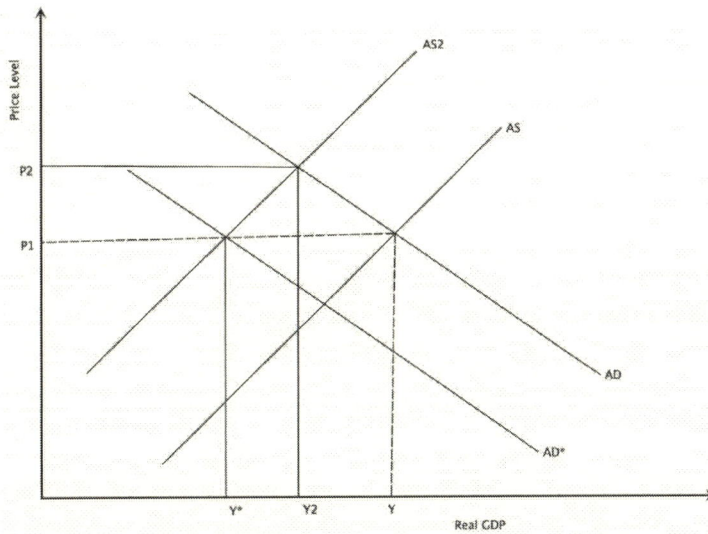

The supply chain disruption means less final goods and services are able to be produced and moved across the China and the rest of the world. SRAS1 shifts left to SRAS2 and similarly AD1 falls to AD2 as consumers being confined to their homes spend less on goods and services. The demand for Chinese exports also falls as fewer visitors travel to China. The effect on the price level is uncertain but clearly the real GDP will fall causing a major slowdown and rising unemployment as many businesses shutdown.

**(g)     Using the information in the texts / tables and your knowledge of economics, evaluate the consequences on economic development for China of imposing a severe 30 % carbon tax on all production of manufactures within its borders.                                    [15 marks]**

A 30 % carbon tax in China will increase the costs of production.

If Chinese firms respond by adapting more green production process then air pollution levels will decrease and create a healthier China, raising economic development. The green processes may well create new jobs and spur new innovation. 1.1 million Death count will fall. (Text 2)

A 30 % carbon tax may raise costs of production sufficiently as to persuade polluting producers to relocate to another more business friendly country. Here the total $CO_2$ emission in the world stays the same and China loses jobs and economic development may even fall. (Table 2)

Per capita China is less polluting than say US but as a nation is the biggest global producer. However, China is polluting on behalf of the rest of the world.

A 30 % carbon tax in China in isolation will certainly be less effective than a global policy which levels the playing field without giving any single country an advantage.

China will also have to ensure that a cut in pollution and the implements of renewable benefits the less well- off Tibetan region more than other areas if economic development is also going to reduce inequality and cut poverty.

## ABOUT THE AUTHORS

Dipak Khimji has taught Economics for 30 years on three continents. He has also worked as an IB examiner for 10 years. He is currently the Head of Economics at the International School of Geneva, Switzerland.

Barbara Macario with over 10 years of economics teaching experience is currently teaching at the International School of Geneva. She graduated with a Master's in Business Economics and Finance in 2008 from the University of Amsterdam.

Made in the USA
Las Vegas, NV
28 April 2024